Also by the Author

THE FACE ON THE CUTTING ROOM FLOOR

THE
DIAMOND
PEOPLE

Murray Schumach

THE
DIAMOND
PEOPLE

W·W·NORTON & COMPANY
NEW YORK·LONDON

Published simultaneously in Canada by George J. McLeod Limited, Toronto.
Printed in the United States of America.

First Edition

Library of Congress Cataloging in Publication Data

Schumach, Murray, 1913–
    The diamond people.

        1. Diamond industry and trade—United States.
I. Title.
HD9677.U52S38   1981   338.2′782′0973   80–14947
ISBN 0–393–01404–5

W. W. Norton & Company, Inc., 500 Fifth Avenue, New York, N.Y. 10110
W. W. Norton & Company Ltd., 25 New Street Square, London EC4A3 NT

1 2 3 4 5 6 7 8 9 0

To the many generations of Jews
responsible for the creation and preservation
of the most precious gem in the diamond business—
the code of mazel und brucha.

CONTENTS

1 The Street   13
2 Tables Are for Diamonds   27
3 Why Diamonds Are Jewish   44
4 Business Is Business   58
5 The Syndicate   78
6 Behind the Diamond Curtain   104
7 The Mechanics   125
8 The Murder   165
9 The Trial   177
10 Diamonds Versus Inflation   191
11 The Elite   212
12 Diamonds of Legend   231
13 How Long Is Forever   252

Photographs appear on pages 129 to 140.

THE
DIAMOND
PEOPLE

I

THE STREET

In the heart of Manhattan, a world persists that is very different from anything in the United States; a world that has maintained a lifestyle that is unique. It is Alice's Wonderland, with electronic calculators. Peter Pan's Never-Never Land, rewritten by Adam Smith. This is the block of West Forty-seventh Street, from Fifth Avenue to the Avenue of the Americas, which is the heart of the nation's multibillion-dollar diamond business, handling the bulk of all diamonds sold in the United States with the whimsical slogan: "There's a customer for everything."

Sometimes referred to by the media as the Street of Diamonds, it is known to its own people simply as "the Street." This strip of some six hundred feet, bounded by store windows ablaze with gems, topped by grimy offices containing an incalculable treasure of diamonds, is a shrine of individualism in a nation drifting toward corporate conglomerates. Like other businesses, it should long ago have been squeezed into cold, computerized modules manipulated by lawyers, accountants, and statisticians. But it hasn't. This tiny realm of free enterprise may be the most exciting and mysterious block in the United States. It has the glamor of Broadway, the daring of Wall Street, and the secrecy of the C.I.A. Dealers bicker over a pittance, but make handshake deals over millions. There are paneled offices with full-time cooks. There are sweatshops that are a throwback to the Lower East Side at the turn of the century. The industry thrives in a frenzy of competition, but lives in the long shadow of the omnipotent South African monopoly—the De Beers Syndicate—that long ago set the pattern for multinational cartels. It is a bizarre world that combines the crassness of the coldest commerce with the ethics of the Old Testament and the Talmud; the free-wheeling independence of a medieval marketplace with the latest technology of the twentieth century. It makes a virtue of guile, but lives by a code of honor unparalleled in American business.

The Street is introverted, but its people roam the world. They concentrate on the present, but are fully informed of any scientific or political developments that may affect their future. Most important, the Street exudes a sense of freedom, self-confidence, ambition, and limitless hope. The assurance of the men and women behind the counters of the jewel-laden showcases in diamond exchanges and stores; the aggressiveness of diamond dealers in their offices or over the green tables of the Diamond Dealers Club, where parcels of diamonds are opened and closed in endless bargaining sessions; the deft fingers of the men in workshops where diamonds are shaped and put in settings: everywhere is the feeling that hard work and resourcefulness will bring success, perhaps riches.

The spirit of optimism and daring is captured by Howard Herman, a fourth-generation diamond dealer. "I am in this business because I enjoy the tumult and the excitement," he says. "If I go to Vegas, I don't put money in the slot machines. The kind of gambling we do here is much better. Here I'm gambling on myself. All my gambling sense is in my work. I love it."

This bazaar of precious stones and negotiations in many languages has been more than a thousand years in the making. Born of centuries of persecution, pogroms, forced emigrations, and concentration camps, the diamond people are a paradox. Although their telephone calls cross the world, their behavior is suggestive of an invisible wall. The people of the Street are part of a tight community, suspicious of strangers because of their tragic history. The vast majority of the fifteen to twenty thousand people who work on this block—only a handful live there—are either children of Jewish immigrants or Jewish immigrants themselves. This block of extensive wealth is a Diamond Ghetto.

The eyes of these people are always alert and intense. The faces may break into smiles. The voices may soften. The heads may incline. But the eyes remain watchful. They may speak in English, Yiddish, Hebrew, Dutch, Flemish, Spanish, French, German, Hungarian, or Hindustani. Yet, the language of the eyes is always the same, as sharp over the counter of a noisy restaurant as over a mound of diamonds at the Diamond Dealers Club.

The reason for this vigilance is the key to the apparent chaos of Forty-seventh Street—everyone is buying and selling diamonds, or hoping to do so. Not just the diamond dealer or the diamond broker who sells on commission, or the retailer at booth or in store. Everyone. The cutter at his wheel is always on the lookout for a stone to buy from the dealers who bring him work. The woman, sorting stones with a tweezer in a dealer's office and grading them, is always alert for a chance to act as a broker on her own. The old man who runs errands, the youth who fetches coffee, the itinerant jeweler with a store in some other part of the city or suburbs—they all have diamond fever. It is a contagious dream, perhaps an illness, the sort of senseless hope that produces a mirage. Yet constantly, every day, many make a profit. Every year, some men step away from the toil of the wheel forever, to buy, sell, and pay others to grind their stones.

The normal frenzy of Forty-seventh Street came close to delirium in the early months of 1980, when the price of diamonds rose almost as quickly as the price of gold. Hordes of New Yorkers and suburbanites descended on the stores, exchanges, and gold refineries of the Street to sell jewelry. Furnaces in basements melted gold throughout the day. Diamonds were pried loose from rings, bracelets, and brooches, to be sold loose to those interested in them for investment. In wintry weather people stood in line on the Street, or pushed into packed upstairs rooms to sell jewelry at prices higher than they had paid years earlier. Some, with nothing to sell, not knowing the cause of the fever, but seeing the lines, rushed to join them, convinced that something was being given away. With its usual adaptability, Forty-seventh Street embraced—and profited by—the gold madness that had swept their industry.

Before you step into the block you see symptoms of the virus. Red neon lights, as big as those that appear on Broadway marquees a block away, proclaim: "WE BUY DIAMONDS." The windows are crammed with all sorts of precious stones set in rings, necklaces, earrings, or brooches with prices ranging from a few hundred dollars to more than twenty thousand dollars per ring. Modesty is rare on this block as store owners tack signs over bits of jewelry reading: "Biggest Bargain," "Finest Quality," "Great Value," "Work of Art," "One of a Kind," "Extra Special." It is not enough for a diamond to be pear-shaped, heart-shaped, marquise, emerald, oval, round, or brilliant. They are: "Out of Pawn Wholesale" or "Ball of Fire" or "Antique Treasures from All Over the World." There are those who proclaim "We Buy Estates" and those who offer appraisals. There are those who pierce ears, and those who give loans for diamonds "in strictest confidence." Upper floors display the signs of those who manufacture settings for gems. The strictly kosher upstairs restaurant calls itself "Yahalom," the Hebrew word for diamond. When the weather is mild, there are "pullers" at the doors of some stores, accosting those who windowshop with invitations to come in and browse. Often, in the afternoon near Fifth Avenue, merry Yiddish or Hebrew music is played from a trailer operated by the Lubavich branch of Hasidic Judaism, pleading with impatient Jews to pause and reflect on the rituals of their religion.

In the Street float snatches of conversation. "I called him. I told him to go up to fourteen. He asked me if he can go to sixteen. I told him: Go to fourteen-five even."

"I need two stones. Round and pear. Two carats. Two thousand."

A man rushes up to a counter in an exchange and blurts out, "I have to have a five twenty-two." [A diamond of five carats and twenty-two points. There are one hundred points to a carat.]

DEALER: Just sold one. Are you in a hurry?

MAN: Want to send it out today.

DEALER: I'm expecting a five thirty-four from Florida.

MAN: Lemme see it.

DEALER: I'll give you a holler.

Two men walking rapidly in opposite directions grab one another by the arm as they are about to pass.

FIRST MAN: Nu?

SECOND MAN: Ah. He says he can't go higher than thirty-two.

FIRST MAN: What do you think?

SECOND MAN: I think maybe we can get thirty-two three, maybe four.

FIRST MAN: You think we should hold out?

Pause. A quick, almost simultaneous nod from both. They continue walking in opposite directions. Obviously, the two men have gone partners in purchasing a diamond, and are already in a position to make a profit but are not sure whether they should hold out for more.

Diamond people are always going into partnership with someone on a particular deal. The next time they may be in opposition to one another. The name of the diamond dance is "the deal." It is a nonstop hoedown, with everyone changing partners. That is the dance on the sidewalk level, in the exchanges, or in the stores.

On the upper floors the dance is a bit different. There, a partnership can last a long time; the partners work as a unit in making deals. The money is often heavier and the deals often reach around the world. At times the deals are so big these partnerships form larger, but temporary, alliances. And the pace is just as fast.

In a dealer's office, the phone rings. The dealer listens for no more than a couple of seconds. Then he says, "That three-carat marquise. It's out. It will stand you forty-five [$45,000]." Brief pause. Then, rapidly: "All right. I'll mark it down and give you a call." In a small office behind a nearby panel, a woman is sorting hundreds of diamonds, her fingers moving constantly, grading them.

In the Diamond Dealers Club, a member pulls out a zippered wallet that is chained to his vest. He zips it open and removes a number of thin, white, folded papers. He unfolds them. Diamonds by the score glitter to the table. He pushes the diamonds across to another man. They are silent while the second man looks at the "goods." First with the naked eye, then through his loupe, a ten-powered magnifying glass about the size of his eye. He may buy them outright or take them on consignment, getting a commission of about 2 percent of the total sale. Rarely does money change hands here. Sometimes a memorandum will be made out by the owner, giving the number and weight of the stones and the price per carat. The memorandum is initialed by the buyer. The bargaining may deal with hundreds of stones when the purchaser is interested in only a few, or he may just want to buy one. Buyer and seller then go to a bullet-proof enclosure where an employee of the club weighs the stone(s) on an electronic scale and writes out a slip giving the weight. This is the official weight in their transaction.

An outsider to Forty-seventh Street, making an occasional purchase in a store or at a booth in an exchange, may think his or her trade is important. It isn't. Even at the booths of the exchanges, most of the business is wholesale. Many retailers say that the majority of their business is with persons they know, or who are sent by satisfied customers. The business that comes in off the street, though enormous by the standards of the average jewelry store, is very small for Forty-seventh Street as a whole. It is almost insignificant compared to the volume transacted in the offices of dealers above, secluded in the buildings where dealers tap calculators while they talk on the phone to London, Antwerp, Tel Aviv, Johannesburg, Amsterdam, Bombay, and Hong Kong. Often, in these phone conversations, the dealer switches in mid-sentence from English to Yiddish, Hebrew, French, Flemish, German, Italian, or Spanish. There are many people in the diamond business who speak five languages and some who speak ten.

Diamonds can pass with astonishing rapidity from dealer to dealer without leaving the block.

A dealer smiles as he waves a visitor to a chair. "See the man who just left?" he asks. "He brought me a stone I sold early today for forty-eight thousand dollars. A profit of maybe two thousand. That stone went from dealer to dealer today. Six dealers in one day. This man just wanted to sell it to me. He wanted seventy thousand."

Phones are rarely silent in a dealer's office for more than a minute. Conversations are brief to the point of rudeness. But no one in the business is offended. An individual negotiation may be prolonged over days with each phase of the deal a sprint of just a few minutes.

The enormous volume of transactions, often without records, is possible on Forty-seventh Street only because of the Code. In the diamond business, you never go back on your word. A deal closed with a handshake and the Yiddish words "mazel und brucha"—luck and blessing—is inviolate. It is a ritual that goes back centuries and, as we shall see, is probably ingrained in the Jewish tradition passed along by the Old Testament, the Talmud, and the teachings of Maimonides.

Nevertheless, there are the "bad apples" who give the Street a bad name, sometimes without ever violating a letter of the Code. There was the case of the broker who took a number of diamonds on consignment. One afternoon he was robbed in the elevator of one of the buildings. He claimed all his diamonds were stolen. On the Street, it was believed he lost only those he had taken in his last transaction. The suspicion was that before reporting the robbery to the police, he went to his safe deposit box in the basement vault, removed all the diamonds he had on consignment, and hid them. He claimed the loss of these stones as well. He told his creditors he could not pay for them and his word was taken. It is customary, in robberies, to forego payment. However, several months later, he was back in business and apparently quite affluent. This confirmed the suspicion of those who believed he had pocketed the bulk of the diamonds he had taken on consignment. Diamonds are easy to sell, even without a fence.

At the other extreme is the loyalty of retailers to good customers. There was the man who had bought expensive jewels for his mistress over some years. Eventually, they argued and parted. He took back a very expensive necklace he had given her. She sued, claiming he had given it to her as a gift and therefore it was hers. In court, he contended that while it was true that he had given her the necklace, he had taken it on consignment and had never paid for it. That was why he had taken it back—to return it to the man who sold it to him. The retailer testified that the man had not paid for the necklace. The court ruled that the necklace belonged to the retailer. Some months after the ruling, the retailer gave the necklace to the man. He had paid for it before he gave it to the woman. The retailer felt an obligation to an old customer.

The mazel und brucha code gives logic to the diamond business. But the ghetto tradition gives warmth to the unrelenting competition, and compassion to the endless quest for money. This tradition has shaped the block as much as the diamond. The diamond has spurred the buying, selling, trading, seeking, haggling, cutting, polishing, and setting of gems. It is the reason for the offices, workshops, exchanges, booths, arcades, stores, little factories that shape precious metals, obscure stands that sell special papers to wrap diamonds, wallets to carry them, underground vaults, and frenzied counter restaurants. But it is the ghetto tradition that has woven invisible strings that bind the highest to the lowest on the Street; that has kept alive tolerance between the old and the young; that has permitted the past to flow with understanding into the future.

The Street's beggar is a symbol of the special ghetto nature of this block. He is there every weekday, except on Jewish holidays. Old, gray, his beard disheveled, his clothes torn, he is like a character out of Sholem Aleichem's fictional shtetl, Kasrilevka. He stands in the middle of the block, on the south side, close to a building, careful never to block a display window. He rarely approaches anyone. He has his "customers" and they don't forget him. In the winter, these customers—to avoid having to unbutton coats, remove gloves, and dig into pants pockets for money—usually have the change, in some cases a bill, in an overcoat pocket. Sometimes a man, engrossed in plans for a diamond deal, will pass him, get as far as the doorway to his business, then remember, return to the beggar and give him money. When it rains and the beggar takes shelter under a building overhang, his customers seek him out for their daily *nedoveh*—donation. How much is this part of the Jewish religious tradition that stresses charity? How much is it superstitition so deep in all gamblers that luck is courted by generosity to the poor? It is impossible to know. But the interdependence of the beggar and his supporters is unmistakably a part of the social order of Forty-seventh Street.

There is also a little synagogue, two steep flights up and to the rear, over a kosher restaurant, in between two gem dealers. From the Street it can't be seen. A converted watch repair shop, with folding chairs and a maximum capacity of 125, it opens everyday for the afternoon and evening prayers. But the special meaning of this synagogue is more in its memorial plaque than in the time for prayers its congregation takes out from work. On the memorial plaque, donated by diamond dealers, are bronze strips given by family or friends that mystify strangers. These strips, in memory of the deceased, have no date of death beneath the name of the man or woman. Instead of the date are the words "Yom Kippur"—Day of Atonement. They honor those who died in the Holocaust. The survivors who donated the commemorative strips do not even know the year of their death.

A special symptom of the ghetto feeling of this block is in the pride shared by all when someone from the Street outwits the world-famous Fifth Avenue merchants—Cartier, Tiffany, Van Cleef & Arpels, and Harry Winston. For these upper-class retailers tend to look down on Forty-seventh Street. So, in 1977, when William Goldberg, of the Forty-seventh Street firm of Goldberg & Weiss, acquired, with a foreign partner, a 103-carat diamond of top quality, the Street was buzzing. First with excitement. Then with envy. But finally with pride. This fabulous diamond had come to Forty-seventh Street, not to Fifth Avenue. For months, while the diamond was in a bank vault, there was self-esteem in the gambling courage of one of their own. They knew the stone was worth millions and could have been sold for a substantial profit shortly after it was acquired. In fact, there were men in the business who said with assurance that it had been sold, and even quoted prices. But their Willie was still holding onto the diamond. Money had been borrowed, and interest rates were high. The temptation to sell and take a profit was strong. But for this kind of stone, there were not many buyers. It took courage to sit tight. He held out for more than a year before selling. The bravery reflected the whole block. It was as though, in some Russian shtetl, a Jewish boy had emerged as a world-famous violinist.

There were other coups. Glasser-Becker-Runsdorf hold the lease on a small jewelry exchange on Forty-seventh Street, where it has its own booth. This firm, facing competition not only from Fifth Avenue dealers, but also from top auction galleries, acquired a Van-derbilt estate. At this, the Street rejoiced. One of its own had invaded the realm of the goyim and had walked off with one of its prized jewelry estates. On the Street there was much speculation about how the firm had pulled off this triumph and how much it would make. No one thought it was in bad taste when, on the wall overlooking the counter, the firm displayed a large photograph of a beefy, richly gowned Vanderbilt matron. Some years later, Bobby Becker, one of the partners, brought more pride and merriment to Forty-seventh Street. At an auction in a Florida club that did not allow Jewish members, he carried off some very profitable purchases.

Another ghetto sign is the treatment of the oldsters—the veterans of many years in the business. They were handling diamonds in the early twenties, when the heart of the diamond mart was on the Bowery and Canal streets. In those years, Forty-seventh Street was mainly brownstone residential, where the milkman, in his horse-drawn wagon, delivered milk and cream, door-to-door, before sunrise. It was a quiet street, with a few bookstores, including the infant Gotham Book Mart, which has become a national literary landmark. At that time, the block had a couple of antique stores, one or two restaurants, and some upstairs lofts that turned out women's clothes. Eventually, it included a creative cell for Hattie Carnegie's fashionable hats. "It was a very quiet street in those days," recalled Frances Steloff, who founded the Gotham Book Mart and lived above it for many years. When the diamond pioneers traded on the Bowery, work had not even started on Rockefeller Center, a block north of Forty-seventh Street.

The old people who built this block have not been discarded in the responsible world of the Diamond Ghetto. They have jobs that are difficult to define, but which make them feel worthwhile. They help set up displays in windows or showcases. They fetch and deliver parcels of jewelry. They relay messages and phone calls. They listen sympathetically to wandering tourists, who may or may not be potential purchasers. To a good listener, they will sometimes tell stories of the days on the Bowery, when diamond merchants worked in shirt sleeves instead of expensive suits; when they sometimes sat on fruit crates. They tell how, when Hitler invaded the Low Countries, thousands of Jews fled the diamond centers of Amsterdam and Antwerp, joining those who had pushed up from the Bowery to Forty-seventh Street. "Hitler made Forty-seventh Street," they sometimes say. They are the oral history of the Street. Their greatest joy is to buy and sell on their own, making a profit as little as ten or twenty dollars on a ring or a pair of earrings. Sometimes they pick up a finder's fee of 10 percent for sending a customer to a merchant.

These oldsters symbolize the warmth generated in the block's ghetto climate. It is visible in the morning as men and women meet on the block on their way to work and pause to ask about one another's families; to invite one another to dinner or to talk about a Broadway show. Often there are invitations for "a quick coffee" before the start of work—and heated arguments when one tries to pay the bill. The handshakes are firm and often there are warm embraces. They know of approaching bar mitzvahs—and bas mitzvahs—

graduations, engagements, weddings, and births. And the partings on the eve of important Jewish holidays are unmistakably affectionate. Before Yom Kippur and Rosh Hashonah (New Year) the handshakes are prolonged, with a pat on the shoulder, an embrace. Before Passover and Hanukkah there is great gusto in the merry "gut yontiv"—happy holiday. As they close a deal before these celebrations, they may follow the mazel und brucha handshake by slapping one another's palms vigorously, pinching one another's cheeks, or patting one another on the face—all with a rousing "gut yontiv." On such afternoons, Forty-seventh Street is like a large family, forgetting business quarrels in good will.

Ghetto tradition, which has given the Street a protective shell, has also created an internal, subdued disagreement. As the American-born diamond merchants and the cosmopolitan Europeans have risen to power on Forty-seventh Street, they have begun to press for a new lifestyle that will preserve the best features of their heritage, yet allow them to adapt more to the behavior patterns of the rest of the nation. In arguing for this change, president of the Diamond Dealers Club, William Goldberg, says: "We have grown over the years from a relatively nondescript business into a true industry. We are honorable men and women. . . . When you give your word in this industry it is holy. We are not an industry that should behave as though it has something to hide."

The tension between old and new was sharpened by the worst crime in the history of the Street—the murder of Pinchos Jaroslawicz a diamond dealer, in 1977. The immediate reaction of the traditionalists was to withdraw more deeply into the shell. Talk to no one. Not even the police. On the other side there were those who contended that the time had come to cooperate with the authorities.

The murder—and subsequent serious crimes—brought to the diamond people a fear that was almost paranoiac. It seemed inconceivable that only a few years earlier diamond merchants were examining one another's stones on the Street, peering at them through loupes amid the usual crush of pedestrians. The secretive manner became furtive. Speech became staccato and the pace more rapid.

Men who opened stores and booths in diamond exchanges at nine in the morning were worried about being alone. Opening hours became later, until 10:00 A.M. became customary. Sometimes a man who had arrived on the block a bit early would sit over coffee at a restaurant counter, waiting for the Street to fill. The diamond people began closing earlier, too. No one wanted to be on Forty-seventh Street after sundown. No one wanted to be the last to leave an exchange or be alone in a store as the block emptied. Anxiously, they pushed jewels from trays into metal boxes, carried the boxes to underground vaults in the same building where, behind iron gates, security men watched everyone. As soon as they deposited their "goods" in the vault, they fled.

The fear became even greater in the office buildings. Diamond people skittered along the winding corridors. They avoided stairways. Closed-circuit television screens sprouted in offices, hallways, lobbies, and elevators. No door was opened without recognition from the inside, followed by a buzzer that released the lock. Diamond dealers and brokers, instead of taking all their diamonds out of the vault in the morning for their rounds, removed only the stones they planned to show early in the day. Thus, they made many trips to and from the vault, instead of just one or two.

The wariness and suspicion of Forty-seventh Street approached hysteria. One day, during lunch hour, when Forty-seventh Street is the most crowded, and presumably safe, I saw an example of how fear can make men irrational. Two young men were running along the sidewalk. Soon someone pointed at them. Then a few other figures were directed toward them. In a few seconds there were a couple of warning shouts. Then a crowd was chasing them. The young men seemed oblivious to the confusion until people began rushing at them from other directions. When they realized they were the targets, they turned into the first lobby, hoping to find sanctuary or help. The crowd pressed in after them, cutting them off before they could get into an elevator. Their fear excited the crowd. The young men were grabbed and pummeled. In a few minutes the police came running. The police took the young men away from the crowd, which, by this time, was a small mob. The young men were relieved to be taken by the police. As the police inquired from those in the crowd what the young men had done, it became apparent they had done nothing criminal. The men told the police they were running to the subway down the block because they were in a hurry. By this time, the growing crowd was boiling about a crime just committed by two young men caught in the lobby.

Ten minutes later, the men were released and walked back down to the subway. In their wake was left an uneasy sense of guilt and shame.

"This is what we have come to because of this murder," said a diamond dealer. "It is dangerous for a couple of young men to run for a subway."

2

TABLES ARE
FOR DIAMONDS

It was to have been a routine trip abroad by the wealthy diamond dealer from Forty-seventh Street. To associates on the Street who had agreed to be partners with him in diamond deals on this trip, he made phone calls from London, Amsterdam, Antwerp, Tel Aviv, and Johannesburg. Then, after he took off from South Africa, the telephone calls stopped. In the atmosphere of fear created on the block by the murder of Jaroslawicz and the disappearance of diamond dealers, there was immediate alarm. Inevitably, the dealers closest to the missing man in this venture went to an unprepossessing ten-story building at 30 West Forty-seventh Street. Over the entrance to this building, in dull metal letters, are the words "Diamond Club Building." Above these words, in the same lifeless metal, are the shapes of diamonds. In this building, the Diamond

Dealers Club occupies the top two floors. Here this small group of diamond men went to tell of the missing dealer.

Behind closed doors in the club's paneled boardroom, on the top floor, just above the clubroom for members and their carefully chosen guests, officials of the club began sounding out the fifteen other major diamond clubs of the world that, with this one, make up the World Federation of Diamond Bourses. From this international network, they learned that their missing member was in jail in an unstable African country. At the club it was assumed that he had been imprisoned on a trumped-up charge because some important official of that country wanted a fat legal ransom or because the bribe to some key official was either not forthcoming or considered insufficient.

Whereupon the club put out delicate feelers in Washington. The club learned that a partner in a prominent D.C. law firm might be helpful. This lawyer, while serving in a very important federal job during a previous administration, had assisted the African nation involved and still had powerful friends in that country. The club made inquiries at the law firm and retained it as its legal representative. After a few days, the law firm told the club that this was a touchy matter and would cost a good deal of money. The money was raised from the partners and passed, via the club, to the Washington firm. The diamond dealer was freed. No one ever asked how the money was dispensed or to whom. The club, as usual, had handled the problem without governmental intervention.

The Diamond Dealers Club, which prefers to operate in secrecy, is the most powerful organization in the nation's diamond business. The Club—as it is known to diamond dealers throughout the country—is a shadow government, in a tiny, mid-Manhattan sector, of some fifteen thousand diamond people who handle an estimated 80 percent of all diamonds that come into the United States. It is a Supreme Court for many private disputes among diamond dealers. It is an enforcer of the Street's cardinal law—a man's word must be his bond. It is, for many of its nearly eighteen hundred members, their only office. It is a gathering place for diamond dealers from all over the world. It is a major checkpoint in the international grapevine of the diamond business.

The club's officials were not guessing, for instance, when they assumed that their member was in jail as part of a legal shakedown scheme by one or more African officials. Into the vast fund of the club's unwritten archives has gone the experience of one of its most reputable members. He had been in that country seeking a permit to export diamonds. He also had a temporary partner in this operation—a European dealer who was a member of one of the European diamond clubs. The two men, while negotiating over a period of several days, noticed that an official had mentioned—a few times—that he greatly admired a certain expensive type of automobile. At the last of these meetings, he had even specified the color he wanted.

When this meeting ended and the diamond men left for their hotel, the European was quite pleased. He was surpirsed to see that the American did not share his joy. He told the American that the permit was now theirs. All they had to do was to buy for the official the car he liked in the color he preferred. The American agreed with the European's interpretation, but was reluctant to pay the bribe. He suggested that the next time either of them came here to do business, the bribe could be increased, perhaps considerably, and that failure to pay the higher price might lead to incarceration on the charge of attempted bribery. The European disagreed and finally offered to pay for the car himself. The American shrugged and agreed. The export license was obtained.

This is the kind of information that enables the club to become a veritable seismograph for the tremors vibrating in the diamond world.

A case of quite a different sort demonstrates the influence—and discretion—of the club. It involved several of its members who had been selling millions of dollars worth of diamonds in Amsterdam. In itself, there was nothing wrong, or even unusual, with dealers from Forty-seventh Street selling diamonds in Amsterdam. Many dealers from Amsterdam came to Forty-seventh Street to buy as well as sell their diamonds.

But this business was not the usual sale.

Though the diamonds were being sent by these dealers to Amsterdam and picked up there, the customers were in Spain. At that time Spain, in an effort to prevent the flight of currency, had imposed a high import duty on diamonds. But a number of very wealthy Spanish residents, as a hedge against inflation, were buying diamonds, and paying top price. The diamonds sent by Forty-seventh Street dealers to Amsterdam were being turned over to couriers who smuggled them into Spain, and delivered them to the true purchasers. Money for the diamonds was then smuggled out of the country by courier, and turned over to representatives of those dealers in Amsterdam. In Amsterdam, the money could either be deposited, used by the dealers to buy more diamonds, or to make investments other than diamonds.

In most cases, however, the money was banked in Amsterdam and transferred to banks in New York for the Forty-seventh Street dealers. Many times, the dealers here had bought the diamonds from bigger dealers on the Street, usually on credit, and so owed them large sums of money which they paid back from this account.

One day, a diamond courier was apprehended as he tried to slip across the border into Spain. The courier, during prolonged investigation, was told that unless he revealed the names of those to whom he had been delivering diamonds, he would be jailed for many years. He gave names. On the basis of this information, the authorities soon stopped another courier as he was trying to smuggle money out of the country. He, too, was persuaded to give the names of those who had been giving him money to take to Amsterdam. Then, the Spanish government froze the bank accounts of those named, pending investigation.

After several weeks, a crisis began to develop on Forty-seventh Street. Dealers who had been sending the diamonds were owed millions of dollars. They, in turn, owed large sums of money to the other dealers on the Street from whom they had obtained the diamonds on credit. If the very big dealers pressed the smaller ones for their money, there would be some bankruptcies. Even worse, word might get out about the smuggling operation and the scandal could be serious.

At this point, key figures from the Diamond Dealers Club intervened. All of the dealers involved, directly or indirectly in this operation, were members of the club. The result of the ensuing conversations was that one of the most important dealers—a man who had sold diamonds on credit to smaller dealers in this operation—let it be known that he would wait for payment. Other big dealers did the same. Eventually, the Spaniards paid the dealers who had sent the diamonds to Amsterdam. They, in turn, paid the larger dealers, and the matter was settled quietly.

Some outsiders have suggested that the club has always preferred to operate in secret because it believes that any information that goes into the ear of a government representative will somehow be passed on to the Internal Revenue Service. It is true that the people from Forty-seventh Street do not regard the IRS as friendly. This is, in part, because the IRS has long been curious about the operations of the Street, where so many transactions occur without written records. What the Street proudly calls its code of honor—agreement by handshake and the Yiddish words "mazel und brucha"—the IRS views as a possible form of tax evasion.

It is a fact that the mazel und brucha ritual and the general distrust of the government by diamond dealers predate income tax in this country by many generations. And suspicion of the police is part of Forty-seventh Street's heritage of Jewish persecution.

Nevertheless, in 1978, the Diamond Dealers Club began an unprecedented drive to change some of the strongest traditions of its own organization, and of Forty-seventh Street. These steps it took quietly, as it did everything else. The results may be of enormous significance for the entire diamond business of the United States.

Murder and fears spurred the resultant changes.

On March 7, 1978, some eighteen months after the murder of Pinchos Jaroslawicz, and only six months after the conviction of his killers, Forty-seventh Street was again shaken by terror. This time another highly esteemed diamond dealer, Martin Peretzky, vanished with about $500,000 in diamonds. Two days later, the block was rocked once more when Narian Gupta, a gem dealer from Forty-seventh Street, was reported missing with about $250,000 in precious stones. He was found slain in an isolated section of Pennsylvania. The jewels were gone. On May 27, the seventy-one-year-old body of Peretzky was found floating in the Hudson River, off lower Manhattan. He had been strangled and robbed of the diamonds some three months before the body was thrown into the river.

During the months of dread on the block, there evolved in the Diamond Dealers Club a strategy to fight murder in the business. The new approach was a challenge to one of the strongest traditions of Forty-seventh Street—distrust of the police. The Diamond Dealers Club became the undercover intelligence arm of the police in diamond murders, and the unofficial data bank and dragnet for witnesses for the district attorney's office. There were no press conferences to announce this change. It was also done quietly.

"We are passing along to the cops all information about any guys who could be preying on people in the diamond business," an officer of the club told me after the disappearance of Peretzky. "We are steering the cops. And I have to hand it to the cops," he added grudgingly, "they are checking out everything."

About the same time, again without any fanfare, the club ended its ban against female members. It became the first diamond club in the world to admit women as equals.

Finally, it began fomenting discussion among its members of a proposal to put the entire diamond business under one roof—a massive skyscraper.

Basically, the Diamond Dealers Club, under a new regime, headed by Brooklyn-born William Goldberg, was trying to ease some of the constricting traditions that made Forty-seventh Street an object of suspicion and kept it a Diamond Ghetto.

The need for change is demonstrated most forcibly by the clubroom itself. It is as strange as a ten-carat diamond, set in a ring of brass. The clubroom is no hushed atmosphere of thick rugs, leather armchairs, oaken tables, and fine cuisine. It is a bleak chamber the size of a ballroom in a rundown hotel. It has a linoleum floor that gets so slippery on rainy or snowy days that handwritten notices are taped on the floor-to-ceiling pillars in the room, warning the members to be careful.

But the atmosphere is breathtaking and eye-dazzling. All the excitement and competition of Forty-seventh Street are intensified when confined within these drab walls. The unusual energy of the diamond business becomes bedlam. And, always on view, are hundreds and thousands of diamonds, being picked over and studied with bare eye and loupe.

The tension that leads to the fever of the clubroom begins building in the packed elevator that goes nonstop from the shabby street lobby to the ninth floor, with its tiny, crowded anteroom.

Guarding the entry to the clubroom are two sets of bullet-proof glass doors, the first of which is transparent and the second opaque. These doors open only to buzzers pressed by a club employee after recognition of the visitor.

Once inside, the visitor has to be fast on his or her feet. People charge back and forth between tables, telephone booths, and a bullet-proof enclosure where club employees weigh diamonds on electronic scales. They then write down the weight on slips of paper handed to members who brought them the diamonds as part of a business transaction.

The public-address system is loud and almost incessant, summoning members to pick up an incoming phone call or to meet someone waiting in the outside foyer. Conversation has to be loud, and a member, seeing someone with whom he wants to do business, may have to shout to get his attention. The dominant languages are English, Yiddish, and Hebrew. But no matter what the language, it is always quick. The surest way to halt conversation is to drift within eavesdrop range. In spite of this secrecy, one can often hear numbers being uttered. But they reveal little. The numbers may represent a price per carat, the weight of a diamond, or the number of diamonds. As dramatic as the rapid speech of the bargaining is, the pauses as men study "the goods" are equally so. Sometimes the diamonds are in heaps—dozens of small stones in each mound. Or a loupe might be turned on a single glittering stone of considerable size. The fingers of the dealers are deft as they wrap and unwrap "parcels" of the special double-sheeted paper used to wrap diamonds. The inner sheet, usually a shade of pale blue or gray is a thin, strong tissue. The outer sheet is white and strong, a sort of wax paper.

The diamonds are scrutinized by men facing one another or beside one another at long, cheap, wooden tables. The choice seats are beside the transparent windows with the northern light. This is the side of the room used by dealers with polished diamonds. Those with rough stones—usually a small minority on any day—study and bargain over their wares near the translucent windows with the southern light. In addition, the room has the usual flourescent ceiling lights, and some table lamps.

Pacing back and forth among the members, sitting down with one, getting up, then sitting with another, are men with plastic name cards on their lapels. They are visiting dealers. On their cards are the names of those who vouch for them. Copies of their cards are also on one of the bulletin boards in the room. These visiting dealers, like the members, will sometimes conclude negotiations with the handshake and "mazel und brucha" that mean a deal has been made. They may or may not exchange a memorandum on the transaction. It is not likely that cash will change hands. In many of the deals between members at the club, diamonds only change hands temporarily—with one member taking them on consignment to sell for a 2 percent commission.

The bulletin boards of the club are interesting. They contain notices of diamonds lost and of diamonds found. One day a diamond was found at the club, and a note was put on the bulletin board. The required six months passed without a claimant. So the stone was turned over to the finder. Honesty was particularly profitable in this case. During the months this stone was in the custody of the club, the value of diamonds had appreciated so rapidly that this diamond, originally worth about fifteen thousand dollars when it was found, had increased in value by a few thousand dollars by the time it was given to the finder.

That diamonds can be lost so easily at the club is, quite possibly, indicative of the sense of security the members feel there.

A better sign of the trust among the members is the story about a curious epilogue to a diamond deal. Two men had been discussing a diamond at a table near one of the north windows. One of the men left. Less than a minute later, the other man rushed over to Albert Lubin, counsel to the club.

"Al, tell me," he said, "did you see the man I just sold a diamond to?"

"I saw you sitting with a man," said Mr. Lubin, "but I can't swear that I saw you sell him a diamond." Then, with a grin, he told the seller the name of the buyer. He needn't have, because the next day the buyer called on the seller to give him a check and discuss another deal.

One of the strictest rules of the club concerns food. If members want to eat, they have to sit at the counter where it is sold. No food may be brought to the tables. God forbid a diamond should be lost in an egg salad sandwich and be swallowed. The tables are for diamonds.

The small room set aside for prayer in the club also has the special excitement of the diamond business. In this little room men go rapidly through their afternoon prayers. They usually know them by heart. Occasionally, emerging from their mumbling will be an Amen. But within seconds before they start praying, and seconds after, they may be discussing diamond business with another member who has also just finished his prayers.

For an organization as secretive as the Diamond Dealers Club to become an ally of the police—who are, if anything, even more secretive much of the time—was obviously very difficult. The police, for instance, were convinced that the club was enormously wealthy. One detective told me that the club got a percentage of all transactions on the premises. When I asked him how the club kept track of those thousands of deals every year, so many of which had no records, he looked sage and said, "They have ways of knowing such things at the club." In point of fact, the club gets no money from these transactions, according to officers. Its income is derived from the $2,500 initiation fee for new members, the $210 annual dues and occasional assessments. If any profit accrues to the club at the end of a year, it is given to recognized charities.

With this sort of misunderstanding between the club and the police, it required a shock as powerful as murder to compel the club to take a new attitude toward them. The Jaroslawicz murder forced the reappraisal. Yet even when officials of the club decided to help the police and the district attorney, there was no public announcement to members.

"We just let it be known to members," an officer of the club told me, "that this should be done. Sometimes members did not believe that we wanted them to talk to the police and to the district attorney. They came to officers of the club to make sure this was what we wanted. We told them they should talk. That was the first time the club ever took such a position."

The decision to cooperate with the police was, for all its problems, easier in some ways than allowing women to become members. For not only was the world-wide diamond tradition against such a revolutionary change, but the club's constitution forbade it. The constitution limited membership to males twenty-one years of age or more, and the exceptions in favor of women, provided for in the constitution, were, in essence, even more demeaning than outright exclusion. A woman, before the constitution was altered, was permitted membership privileges—not membership—if her husband had died a member in good standing. This privilege was forfeited if she remarried. The other exception was if a woman's husband, a member in good standing, became incapacitated. Here again the privilege was revoked when he recovered. By "privilege" was meant that a woman, under these exceptional conditions, was admitted to the clubroom and could conduct business there.

A very delicate problem the club had to face in deciding to

admit women was the concern that this would offend the scores of Hasidic members of the club. Hasidim are not supposed to touch a woman that is not a wife, and they prefer not to talk to strange women. And there were non-Hasidic members who felt that admission of women would somehow make life more difficult at the club, and diminish its prestige.

The first woman to be admitted was Ethel Blintz. Her presence did not cause much of a furor. For one thing, she was descended from a family of diamond dealers. Second, she had a Hasidic partner. Finally, since no more new members were being admitted due to lack of space, it was unlikely that her admission would start a flood of applicants. About the same time that she was admitted, twelve other women, who had the privilege accorded to widows, were given full membership.

Even under the best conditions, membership is preceded by careful screening. Every applicant must have been in the wholesale end of the business for at least two years, be endorsed by four members, submit two letters of reference, and a statement of financial status from a bank. Then the aspirant goes before a nine-person membership committee that inquires much more deeply into his or her financial background, getting detailed records. If the committee approves, the applicant's name and picture go up on the bulletin board. If, within ten days, any member of the club objects, the card is removed and the application is reconsidered. If the applicant is sustained, the picture goes back up on the bulletin board for thirty days. Then the applicant becomes a member.

Theoretically, rejected applicants can apply to the club across the street, at 15 West-Forty-seventh Street, which is called the Diamond Trade Association of America. But this club, which has about seven hundred members, is regarded on the Street as mainly for dealers in stones other than diamonds, such as emeralds, rubies, and sapphires. It is also for those who specialize in rough diamonds. This smaller club was started during World War II by refugees from Germany who were in the gem business in the Low Countries. For a time, after the war, there were efforts to merge it with the Diamond Dealers Club. The merger failed because of a dispute about who should be the officers of the new club.

An important source of power for the Diamond Dealers Club is its influence in settling disputes among its members. Considering the argumentative nature and the sharp bargaining among many diamond dealers, it is astonishing that these disagreements do not wind up in court. That is taboo for members of the club and is very rare for anyone on the block.

The club has its own arbitration and conciliation procedures that are far more effective, faster, and cheaper than the use of lawyers and courts. Each year the club gets about 150 cases, about half of which are settled by conciliation. The rest go to arbitration. The arbitration panels are made up of three members, one of whom is chairman. The panelists are chosen by lot from a board of thirty-two panelists who are elected for two years at no salary. The chairmen are also chosen by lot from a board of eleven chairmen, who are elected for two-year terms, and serve without pay. Each year half the terms of panelists and chairman expire.

The adjudication by arbitration is known in this and in allied diamond clubs all over the world as *bestuur*—a Dutch word meaning, roughly, a governing council or managing group. In these proceedings the loser can be fined a considerable sum, in addition to being ordered to pay even more to the winner. The fines do not go to the club. They go to established charities.

Among the most painful disputes are those when partners dissolve their business. Usually, they have been partners for many years. One of the points of dispute in such cases is the ownership of the diamonds in the firm. Over the years, the arbitration panels have developed what is called the "knockout" system. All the diamonds are spilled onto a large table in the boardroom, where arbitration is held. The partners bid against each other on every stone. High bidder gets the diamond.

Bankruptcy cases are ugly on Forty-seventh Street. There is

always the suspicion that the bankruptcy was contrived. With so much of the diamond business on credit, it is relatively simple for a man or woman to acquire many diamonds without payment, and then declare bankruptcy, paying off about fifteen or twenty cents on the dollar. The self-styled bankrupt can claim to have sustained heavy gambling losses or to have lost diamonds. It is almost impossible to disprove these claims.

If a club member declares himself or herself bankrupt, the creditors go before an arbitration panel. An agreement is reached on the percentage to be paid by the bankrupt to his creditors. But there is another condition, if he wishes to remain a member of the club. He is obligated to continue paying creditors until they have been paid in full. This can take many years. The alternative is to face expulsion. When this happens, the expelled person's name goes up on the bulletin board of this and every other diamond club in the world.

Most arbitration cases seem to stem from what might be called either misunderstandings or sharp bargaining. For example, during prolonged negotiations, one man might think the other was making an offer of $10,000 a carat. But the other man may insist that his bona fide offer was $9,500 a carat, with the possibility that he might go as high as $10,000. With a ten-carat diamond this could mean a difference of $5,000.

One dealer may have told another, in offering a diamond for sale, that he had paid $50,000 for the stone. And he may have mentioned, in passing, information that enabled the second dealer to know from whom he had bought it. After the second man bought the diamond for, say $55,000, he could have started making the rounds to dealers to sell it. He may come to one dealer who tells him he has no intention of buying this diamond for $60,000 since he had sold it for $40,000. The man who currently owns the stone, brings the man who sold it to him to arbitration proceedings on the grounds that he had lied in saying he had paid $50,000 for the diamond. The arbitration panel could rule, as it did in one such case, that if the man who had bought the diamond for $55,000 on the basis of false information, could sell it for more than $60,000, the two men could share equally in everything over $60,000. But if he sold it for less than he paid for it, the two men would share equally in the loss.

One of the most unusual cases to go before arbitration involved a somewhat absent-minded or fatigued diamond dealer. He had a ten-carat diamond worth about $18,000 a carat. Somehow, during a bargaining session, which involved a number of stones, he said he would sell this stone for $8,000 a carat. The other man agreed quickly. The mazel und brucha, the handshake, and the buyer was off with the stone. No cash, no records. Not too long afterward the seller realized his mistake. He asked the buyer for the diamond. The buyer refused. The case went to arbitration. The arbitrators ruled this was an "honest mistake" and ordered the buyer to return the stone. The buyer contended he had done a good deal of work seeking a buyer for this stone and had found a customer willing to pay him a good profit. The board therefore ruled that the buyer was entitled to a broker's fee of 2 percent. The seller appealed and won revocation of the fee. The appeals board ruled that while the seller had been care-less, the purchaser knew this and it was an "honest mistake." How-ever, the seller was ordered to pay $600 to charity.

When word got around on Forty-seventh Street about this rul-ing, it caused discussion. Experienced diamond dealers from other parts of the world cited this case as proof that the diamond business in Antwerp and Tel Aviv was much tougher than in New York. In Tel Aviv and Antwerp, they contended, the seller would have lost the case without question, and the buyer would have been permitted to keep the diamond.

One of the most heinous offenses on Forty-seventh Street—or anywhere in the diamond business—is to impugn the financial in-tegrity of someone else.

There was the case of one member of the Diamond Dealers Club who, during negotiations with another member, handed him a stone worth more than $50,000. He was then paged to answer a phone call. The next day he could not find the diamond. He phoned the man he had been talking to when he walked off to take the call.

The man said he had looked at the diamond but had returned it. The owner of the stone did not believe him. He went to an officer of the club, preparatory to asking for arbitration. The club officer, who had known both men for many years, found the story unbelievable. He called the accused man, who offered to take an oath that he had not kept the diamond. Since he was an Orthodox Jew, it was unusual for him to offer to take such an oath. The club officer suggested that both men, before getting involved in arbitration, agree on a rabbi to hear them. They picked a rabbi. He set a date for a hearing. The night before the meeting with the rabbi the complainant recalled he had shown the diamond to another man the day he was at the club. He telephoned the other man. The man told him he had taken the diamond on consignment.

Now the question was: What punishment was to be meted out to the member who had maligned another member without cause? It was true he had told no one his complaint except the club officer. Nevertheless, this slander had caused the other member mental anguish. The aggrieved man was asked what punishment he considered fair. He told the officer of the club that he did not want any money. He suggested the offending man make a sizable donation to charity. This was done. Eventually, the club officer brought the two men together and they shook hands.

Probably the most painful case ever to go into arbitration did not involve a sale. One day there was an argument between two members at the club about who had preempted a seat at a table near a window with the northern light. Tempers flared, voices rose, and suddenly one man bellowed: "Hitler didn't kill enough Jews." For once the noisy room became silent. Among the club members are a number of men whose families were killed in concentration camps. Some men at the club have the numbers from the camps still tattooed on their arms. The fact that the anti-Semitic slur was made by a Jew was no excuse. The arbitration panel fined him $25,000. The check was made out to a Jewish charity.

Before the Diamond Dealers Club was founded in 1931, diamond dealers in New York used to congregate on the sidewalk at the corner of Nassau and Fulton streets, in the city's financial district. They cluttered up the sidewalk, haggling and examining one another's diamonds. Occasionally, irate pedestrians would shove them onto the street. The first office was one room, about twenty by forty, on the top floor of a three-story walkup at Nassau and Fulton. The annual dues were twenty-five dollars. Three years later, the club moved to a somewhat larger office a short distance away on Nassau Street. Diamond exchanges in those days were mainly on the Bowery, in the vicinity of Canal Street.

Prosperity and Hitler forced a subsequent change of location. As some dealers became more affluent they set up offices in mid-Manhattan, as close as they could get to the luxury stores of Fifth Avenue. The block of Forty-seventh Street, between Fifth Avenue and the Avenue of the Americas, was ideal. It was central, and rents were reasonable.

When the Nazis overran Belgium and the Netherlands, the Jewish diamond dealers of Antwerp and Amsterdam fled. Many eventually arrived in New York. By this time, more diamond dealers from downtown Manhattan had moved uptown. The Diamond Dealers Club was ready for its next move. In 1941, it took over the ninth floor of a building at 36 West Forty-seventh Street, forcing out Hattie Carnegie's little factory of fashionable hats, which moved up one flight. When a ten-story building was erected at 30 West Forty-seventh Street, the club took over the top two floors.

By the 1970s, with the diamond business booming, the Diamond Dealers Club became so overcrowded and the backlog of applicants so large that a movement was started to relocate into a towering skyscraper at Forty-second Street and Fifth Avenue that was being completely renovated. The idea was that if the club moved there, so would the rest of the business. In this, the diamond men would be following the example of Israel, which first had its diamond people in one skyscraper and then built a second to form a complex. A strong argument in favor of the move was the greater security, as demonstrated in Israel. The matter was hotly debated at the club, but voted down. Thereafter, there were discussions among leaders of the Diamond Dealers Club and important New York real estate men who proposed tearing down old buildings in the vicinity of the block and erecting a huge structure for the city's diamond business, as well as the club.

3

WHY DIAMONDS
ARE JEWISH

"That which has gone out of thy lips thou shalt keep and perform."
—DEUTERONOMY XXIII: 23

When David Schamroth, a diamond broker, died, on October 21, 1974, the media did not consider the event interesting. He was not a rich man. There was nothing suspicious. No violence. Not even robbery. He died of a heart attack, at the age of seventy-seven. Yet the life and death of David Schamroth serve as a parable for the diamond business, particularly on Forty-seventh Street. In his story we can see why the diamond business became Jewish and remained Jewish; why the mazel und brucha code and arbitration of disputes became so indigenous to the only industry that has been Jewish-dominated for centuries—and to no other business. The trials and triumphs of this diamond broker and his wife were those of a race that learned, many years ago, the basic requirements for survival in the diamond world—how to cope with insecurity, the courage to take gambles as a matter of course, and the joy of bargaining.

Five years after Mr. Schamroth's death, one of his two daughters, Mrs. Annette Lachmann, perceived in it the ultimate proof of his strongest principle.

"Honor meant everything to him," she said, after recalling the circumstances surrounding his death, behavior patterns that would seem strange to anyone unfamiliar with the diamond business of Forty-seventh Street. "He raised us never to break a promise," she recalled. "I remember when I was a girl if, when I wanted comic books, I said to him: 'You promised me five comic books, you promised,' and I got them right away. He was so proud that he kept a promise. He was so proud that everyone in the diamond business trusted him."

And yet, like so many thousands of Jews in the business, he had never intended to enter this field. He was driven into it by persecution. Equally important, he understood its moral code before he knew anything about the work of buying and selling the goods.

Long before he became interested in diamonds, Mr. Schamroth built up a prosperous fur business in Antwerp, after fleeing the pogroms of Kraków, Poland, where he was born. Then, in 1938, he became convinced that Hitler and his anti-Semitism would spread across Europe. He left Belgium, promising his wife he would send for her and their two young daughters as soon as possible. In New York, two of his cousins, Isadore and Leonard Schamroth, were diamond dealers. So, with their help, he went to Forty-seventh Street as a diamond broker. He knew nothing about diamonds. But the cardinal rule of the diamond trade—that a man must keep his word—he accepted as ritual.

Barely a year after he arrived in New York, though his earnings were meager, he sent for his wife, Rose, and their two girls, Annette and Malvina. But before Mrs. Schamroth could get the visas, the Nazis invaded Belgium. Mrs. Schamroth and the girls fled to France. They were concealed by peasants on a farm near Dunkirk.

When British troops were evacuating France for England, they offered to take the Jewish refugees with them. Mrs. Schamroth declined. She was convinced that somehow, from France, they would have a better chance to reach New York.

She was mistaken. Nazi troops found them and sent them back to Belgium. Mrs. Schamroth did not give up. By selling almost all her possessions, she raised enough money to bribe Italian fascists in Belgium to get aboard an Italian bus going to Portugal. In Lisbon, she bought passage for herself and the children on the *Quansa*, bound for Mexico. Almost all the passengers were refugees from the Nazis. When the *Quansa* sailed, she shook off her fears of the Nazis. Prematurely, it turned out.

When the ship reached Mexico, the authorities there refused to allow the refugees to debark. The vessel was ordered to leave, presumably back to Europe. The captain stopped the vessel in Norfolk, Virginia, for fuel. There it became the subject of controversy, with the press taking up the cause of the refugees. To gain time, the skipper went to jail in Norfolk. Congress passed a special bill to give the refugees political asylum in the United States.

There is a widespread belief that everyone in the diamond business, if not affluent, makes a comfortable living. Many earn marginal livelihoods. Mr. Schamroth, when his wife and children finally arrived in New York, was earning so little that Mrs. Schamroth went to work on Forty-seventh Street as a diamond polisher. When her energetic, convivial husband became more successful, she quit work to spend her time with home and children. Mr. Schamroth's reputation as a man of his word became so widely known that he was named to the arbitration board of the smaller diamond club on Forty-seventh Street, the one founded mainly by refugees from Antwerp. The club became his office and his social center. He ate lunch there. He played cards there. He bought and sold diamonds there. On Forty-seventh Street, though he was not nearly as prosperous as his two cousins, he became almost as well known and equally respected. His credit was good anywhere on the block.

Early in October of 1974, he was laughing over lunch at the club, when he collapsed. His cousin, Leonard, phoned Annette because Mrs. Schamroth was in poor health. In the emergency ward of Saint Clare's Hospital, her ashen father brushed aside her anxious questions. He had something more urgent to say and he feared he might not have the time to tell her.

Huskily, he told her that the next morning, before the vault opened on Forty-seventh Street, in which he had a safe deposit box, she must be there with her mother. Mrs. Schamroth, as co-signer for the vault with her husband, had access to the box. In it, Mr. Schamroth told his daughter, were many diamonds. They were not his. He had them on consignment from a dealer. The diamonds had to be returned to the dealer first thing in the morning. He gave her the name and address of the dealer.

The next morning, Annette, her mother, and sister were at the vault waiting for it to open at nine o'clock. After being checked out by the security man, they removed the diamonds and delivered them to the dealer. Only then did they rush to the hospital. Mr. Schamroth's first question was whether the diamonds had been returned to the dealer.

Mr. Schamroth's condition improved. Before he was released from the hospital, the doctor warned him to rest for several weeks before going back to work. But on October 21, less than a week after he had left the hospital, Mr. Schamroth, scoffing at the protests of his wife and daughters, hurried back to the tumult of Forty-seventh Street.

Early that afternoon, Annette was telephoned. It was her uncle, Isadore Schamroth. He told her that her father had collapsed in an office on Forty-seventh Street and been taken to a hospital. He thought it was Saint Clare's. Annette phoned Saint Clare's to ask if her father was there.

"Who are you?" she was asked.

"I'm his daughter."

"Are you calm?"

"Yes."

"Better take a taxi."

When she reached the hospital, her father was dead.

The notice of the death of David Schamroth was posted in both diamond clubs on Forty-seventh Street. The funeral chapel was jammed.

As vividly as Annette remembers the seven days of mourning, in the Orthodox tradition, with the family—clothes slashed, sitting on boxes in the apartment with mirrors covered—she recalls two other incidents. One day, a diamond dealer who had come to pay his respects, told Annette that he owed her father money. He said her father had sold diamonds for him, but had not collected his 2 percent commission. He told her the amount and said that when she had a chance, if she would make out a bill, he would send her a check. The next day another diamond dealer told her the same thing. The checks were for several hundred dollars.

"These two men did not have to tell me or anyone else about the money they owed my father," she said years later. "There were no records. These transactions were conducted like almost everything else in which my father was involved on Forty-seventh Street—on the word. This was the way my father was. This was the way they were. The word was sacred to my father and it was sacred to them."

Did Mr. Schamroth adhere so strictly to the industry's code of honor because he was a devout Jew? Mr. Schamroth, like so many Jews on Forty-seventh Street, was not very religious. Annette says he went to synagogue only on the holiest of Jewish holidays—Rosh Hashonah and Yom Kippur. The only other Jewish holiday he observed was Passover, at which time Jews celebrate the flight of their ancestors from the slavery of Egypt. For Mr. Schamroth, this was not so much a religious observance as it was a joyous family reunion, a gathering of particular poignance for Jewish refugees from Hitler.

Nevertheless, it was mainly the force of Jewish tradition, with its origin in the teachings of the religion, that impelled Mr. Schamroth to order his daughter, with what might have been his last breath, to return the diamonds in his safe deposit box to their rightful owner. The same tradition prompted the two dealers to tell her they owed her father money.

Whether the diamond people of Forty-seventh Street—or of Tel Aviv, Antwerp, London, Amsterdam, Paris, Rome, Johannesburg—are as devout as the Hasidim or as anti-religious as a number of Israelis, the belief that the Word must be kept was drilled into them as children before they ever listened to rabbis. Only a small percentage of the Jews on Forty-seventh Street can quote the portions from the Old Testament, the Talmud, or the teachings of Maimonides that shaped their business ethics. Yet this inherited morality is as much a part of them as their awareness that whether they go to synagogue or not, they are Jews. For Jews in the diamond business to break their word is not merely unethical. It is sacrilegious. This is why they accept as just the excommunication from the industry of those who go back on their word.

The roots of the ethics on Forty-seventh Street must, therefore, be sought in the millennia covered by the writings of the Old Testament, the Talmud, and Maimonides. Here are the orders to keep one's word; the urging to settle arguments by arbitration; the mandates to pay debts and avoid purchases of stolen goods; the condemnation of those who malign the character of others and of talebearers who create mischief.

The constitutions of the world's diamond clubs are clearly, though probably not consciously, derived from these writings.

The Talmud, for instance, which details in millions of words how a Jew should behave toward man and God, promises that the wrath of God will descend upon one who breaks his word. It is written there:

"He that exacted punishment from the generation of the Flood and the generation of the Dispersion (Tower of Babel) will exact punishment from him that does not abide by the spoken word."

Professor David Weiss, of the Jewish Theological Seminary, one of the most illustrious of modern Talmudic scholars, says it is impossible to underestimate the seriousness of the punishment in this section.

"No stronger image could have been used," he says. "Here you have a curse that goes back thousands of years. The threat of such a curse would make people terrified to break their word."

Another section of the Talmud supports this interpretation. It says: "He will exact vengeance of him who does not stand by his word."

Maimonides, in Book XII of his Code, reinforces the warnings of the Old Testament and Talmud to adhere to one's pledge. The rabbi-physician-philosopher—he was also, for a time, in partnership with his brother, a gem dealer—writes that a Jew who breaks his word has "committed an act not befitting an Israelite and must submit to the curse expressed by the formula, 'He who is punished.' " The Hebrew for "he who is punished," is "mee shepora." This term became so ingrained in Jewish life that they made it part of their business terminology and carried it into their work with diamonds.

The impact of this belief remained so pervasive among Jews that, in the nineteenth century, it became the theme of one of the most famous Yiddish plays, *The Dybbuk*, a drama by S. Ansky (pen name for Shloyme Zanzl Rappoport) that has become part of international theater. The moral of this tragedy is that even if a Jew breaks his word unknowingly, he must be severely punished.

The story of *The Dybbuk*, though steeped in the supernatural, is significant because it reinforced among many thousands of Jews—well into the 1920s—in deeply dramatic terms, the credo of Old Testament, Talmud, and Maimonides. In *The Dybbuk*—a dybbuk is the spirit of a dead person that enters the body of a living one and rules it—a solemn pledge is made by two young men in a Russian *shtetl* (Yiddish word for a small Jewish community). The men, named Sender and Nissin, had gone to yeshivah together and had married in the same week. They vow to one another, after the marriages, that if one fathers a daughter and the other a son, that the son and daughter will marry. Shortly after the marriages, Nissin and his wife move to a distant town and the men lose touch.

Sender fathers a daughter and becomes wealthy. When she matures, Sender seeks a wealthy husband for her. Meanwhile, a poor young man with a passion for the Talmud turns up in this town, and Sender takes him, for a time, into his own home. Sender finds a rich groom for his daughter. As the marriage nears, the impoverished Talmudic scholar begins talking strangely and dies. Then Sender's daughter becomes mysteriously ill. When medical help fails, the rabbi is called upon. As the rabbi is questioning the ailing young woman, the voice of the Talmudic scholar says, from within her, "I am her predestined groom." In trying to exorcise the dybbuk, the rabbi learns of the pledge made between Sender and Nissin. Sender says there was such a pledge but that he did not know that Nissin had a son. The rabbi rebukes him for failing to inquire and accuses him of seeking only a rich son-in-law. Sender admits his error and agrees, in atonement, to give half his fortune to the poor. The dybbuk still refuses to be exorcised, but finally agrees when the rabbi threatens him with excommunication. As soon as the dybbuk is exorcised the young woman rises from her spell. But then she falls into a faint and dies. Her spirit and that of the young man go off together.

Thus the code of mee shepora has been enforced and a word has been kept, even after death.

The diamond industry's commitment to arbitration clearly stems from the Old Testament and the Talmud. One Talmudic section says:

"Settlement by arbitration is a meritorious act, for it is written: 'Execute the judgment of truth and peace in your gates.' (Zechariah VIII: 16). Surely where there is strict justice there is no peace, and where there is peace there is no strict justice. But what is that kind of justice with which peace abides? We must say: Arbitration. So it was in the case of David, as we read: 'And David executed justice and righteousness towards all his people.' (Samuel VIII:15). Surely where there is strict justice there is no charity and where there is charity there is no justice. But what is the kind of justice with which abides charity? We must say: Arbitration."

The Talmud delves deeply to consider, as it often does, human frailties during arbitration and spells out proper behavior for an arbitrator.

Thus, to those who might be fearful of offending a powerful litigant, the Talmud says: "Ye shall not hold back your words because of anyone."

The Talmud also considers the delicate, but often important point that one of the litigants may be a person of such power that the arbitrator may fear to rule against him and yet not want to hand down a decision that is contrary to his own judgment of the facts. It is written:

"When two come before you for judgment, before you have heard their case, or even afterwards, if you have not made up your mind whither judgment is inclining, you may suggest to them that they should go and settle the dispute among themselves. But if you have already heard their case and made up your mind in whose favor the verdict inclines, you are not at liberty to suggest a settlement."

In short, as an arbitrator, once you have reached a decision, you may no longer tell them to settle the grievance among themselves. You have to deliver the verdict.

Professor Weiss observes that even the idea of a guilty party in diamond clubs paying a fine to charity rather than to the club is traceable to the Talmud. Inherent in Talmudic writings is the concept that charity lessens the shame of a misdeed. Thus, the Talmud notes that a person who has stolen can atone somewhat by doing something for the community, such as drilling a well for public use.

We have seen in the chapter on the Diamond Club of Forty-seventh Street, how seriously the diamond people consider the act of impugning another's integrity and character. This attitude is an outgrowth of the Old Testament and Talmud as well.

One section of the Talmud says: "He who bears tales against his fellow violates a prohibitive commandment, saying: 'Thou shalt not go up and down as a talebearer among thy people.' (Leviticus XIX: 16)."

Another section says: "Who is a sycophant? One who loads himself up with matters, and goes from this one to that one, saying to each, such did that man say, thus and such have I heard concerning that man even though it be true, behold him, he destroys the universe. There is yet an extremely grosser iniquity, which too is included in this prohibitive commandment, and that is, the evil tongue, one who spreads scandal among his fellow."

Another section says: "The wise men said: 'There are three transgressions which call forth retribution from the man who perpetrates in this world, and disinherit him from a share in the world to come. They are idolatry, adultery and bloodshed; but the evil tongue outweighs them all. . . . The evil tongue kills three persons, the one who speaks it, the one of whom it is spoken and the one who receives it.' "

Still, the teachings of the Old Testament, the Talmud, and Maimonides, for all their righteousness, logic, and influence on non-Jewish peoples, would have had little effect on the diamond business—along Forty-seventh Street or anywhere else—were it not for the curious developments in history that made the diamond business Jewish, centuries ago, and kept it that way. For more than five hundred years, the trade in diamonds has flourished only in nations where Jews were welcome and has withered when they were expelled.

The Jews served a long apprenticeship before they became famous as the fine artisans, judges, and dealers in diamonds. Long before the birth of Christ, they were acquiring skills in working with precious metals and stones—not diamonds. In their temples of Biblical times they used the richest metals and most expensive gems to decorate the walls and ornament their Torahs. In shaping wine goblets and basins for sacraments they enhanced their reputation as craftmen hundreds of years before the Renaissance.

Professor Salo W. Baron, an expert on Jewish history and particularly on Jewish life during the Middle Ages, says there is overwhelming evidence that by the Middle Ages the fame of Jews as artisans with gold, silver, and gems had already become established in Europe. For example, he says, European rulers, despite anti-Semitic tendencies, were using them then to work on the minting of coins because of their skill. There are, he says, Polish coins of the tenth and eleventh centuries that have Hebrew inscriptions because the

Jews who minted them did not know Polish. Jews were entrusted in this period with the minting of coins even though they were excluded in Europe from most guilds, such as textiles and housebuilding.

It was inevitable then, that Jews, with their expert knowledge of precious metals and gems should move successfully into the area of money-lending to non-Jews whose main collateral was jewelry and other objects of easily negotiable metals and gems. Some rulers— Theodoric the Great in Italy, or Charlemagne, in France and Germany—partly out of tolerance, but more out of a desire to increase the wealth of their kingdoms, encouraged Jews to practice their jewelers' skills. The Church, by excluding Jews from the life of other European peoples, forced the Jews to broaden their international outlook. The waves of Crusades made the Jews expert in learning how to conceal or transport wealth before their homes and villages were pillaged.

Thus, the forces of history as well as religious teachings, compelled Jews to learn to trust one another to the point of carrying out international negotiations without written records lest the documents fall into non-Jewish—hostile—hands. To abide strictly by one's word became essential to the business as well as obedience to their common religion.

The role of the rabbis in Jewish life was also important in maintaining an ethical business code that crossed national boundaries. For instance, non-Jews engaged in international business could do little to enforce an agreement. If a Frenchman reneged on a debt to a Hungarian or vice versa, there was very little that could be done to collect. But if a Jew living in France failed to pay a business debt to a Jew living in Hungary, the Hungarian Jew could complain to his rabbi, who would write to the rabbi in France, who would then instruct the French Jew to honor his obligation as a matter of religion.

The Renaissance, with its increased tolerance of Jewish enterprise, particularly in Italy, and later in Germany and the Low Countries, enabled Jews to entrench themselves in those countries as important artisans and merchants in jewelry. How much the Jews worked with diamonds is difficult to say. Some writers say the Jews were using diamonds before the birth of Christ, and there are references by Hebrews before Christ to the precious gem called "shamir" as being able to cut the hardest stone. This could have meant that the ancient Hebrews were using what are now called industrial diamonds to work with other stones, rather than alone for their own beauty.

Certainly, Alexander the Great, in his invasion of India, more than three hundred years before Christ, learned about gem diamonds and probably brought some back. The very word diamond stems from the Greek *adamas*, meaning "unconquerable."

By the time Benvenuto Cellini was born (1500) the Jews had already learned to facet diamonds and were among the most expert in Europe at this technique that enormously increased the beauty of these gems.

That the Jews should have quickly learned this technique before non-Jews was partly the result of another creation of anti-Semitism—the ghetto. These usually walled enclosures for Jews were imposed upon them in the fourteenth, fifteenth, and sixteenth centuries, ostensibly to prevent them from contaminating the religions of non-Jews. But these isolated "cities" made the rapid exchange of private information unavoidable. In addition, the Jewelers Guild was one of the few organizations that was not barred to Jews. It was hardly necessary for Jews to be taught in their ghetto synagogue-schools to be wary when dealing with non-Jews. The suspicion and secrecy that exist on Forty-seventh Street today descend from the ghetto psychology that created them.

Ironically, one of the most vicious anti-Semitic movements—the Inquisition—did a great deal to enhance Jewish influence in the diamond trade. The expulsion of scores of thousands of Jews from Spain and Portugal in the fifteenth and sixteenth centuries brought many of them to the Low Countries. In Spain and Portugal a number of Jews had become successful, and some quite important. In Lisbon they had become among the world's most highly skilled artisans in jewelry. The Jews expelled from these two countries, particularly from Lisbon, made Amsterdam the great diamond center until Hitler invaded the Netherlands.

From Amsterdam, with early Dutch settlers in New York, came the Jews who paved the way for Forty-seventh Street. The Jews of early New York were so much in control of jewelry, in general, that one Jew, Meyer Myers, in pre-Revolutionary New York, was president of the Jewelers Guild in the city.

Nevertheless, it was not until early in the twentieth century that the diamond business began to boom in the United States. This was due to the coincidence of the growth of vast fortunes—and no income taxes—in the United States, and the discovery of diamond mines in South Africa. The combination created a demand that was, at first, supplied by Europe. But by the end of the first decade, Jewish diamond merchants, generally from Europe, had made New York City—not yet Forty-seventh Street—the diamond center of the nation. The control of the diamond market by New York Jews provoked considerable curiosity. W. R. Cattelle, in his 1911 book *The Diamond*, noted that nearly all of the Jews in this business in New York were of foreign birth and that a number had drifted into it from the jewelry trade. "The European connections of these Jews," he wrote, "gave them an advantage over competitors."

"But there are other reasons," he wrote. "The trade is one that appeals to the Jew. There is an element of uncertainty in it. Every transaction must be fought out individually for profit, and the profit is an unknown quantity until the deal is closed. For centuries, in most countries, many avenues of life into which the struggle for supremacy among men tempts the adventurous, have been closed to him, and he has been obliged to try his mettle in the more peaceful contests afforded by trade. Into the sale of a diamond he puts the soul of a duellist. It is not alone for the money in it he seeks to get a good price, but to win in the battle of wits. . . . Another reason for the success of the Jew in this field is willingness to pay well a subordinate who is efficient. Practically, the Jews are the most democratic of all people. They gauge a man by what he can do. Name, birth, breeding, learning even, count but little in their estimation." To this he added the Jewish "unbounded capacity for work and an almost instinctive understanding of the principles of finance."

Only one more step was needed for the development of Forty-seventh Street. Hitler supplied it, as we have seen, by driving Jews out of Amsterdam and Antwerp. At the same time, he revived in them the ghetto psychology that had been lying dormant in the freedom of the Netherlands and Belgium, though the teachings of Judaism and the ghetto history had already created the code by which the Jews of the diamond business lived.

Today, the mazel und brucha code is so much a part of Forty-seventh Street that it has become an ornament in the Street's self-mocking humor. Sooner or later, nearly everyone in the business hears the "mazel und brucha story."

The tale is that once there was a diamond dealer on Forty-seventh Street who, no matter how much money he made, never stopped complaining. His gripe was always the same—his wife. She was a nag. She was a spendthrift. She had no understanding of how hard he worked. She could always find a woman friend whose husband was making more money than he was.

One day, as he was whining in the Diamond Club about his wife to another dealer, the listener, who had heard these complaints many times, finally interrupted and said, "I don't know. It seems to me you have a very good wife. She's intelligent. She's attractive. She dresses with taste. I don't know why you're always moaning about her."

The husband was astounded at this defense. "Would you take her?" he demanded.

The other man remained silent.

The husband pressed him. "If you think she's so wonderful," he said, "how much would you give for her."

The friend pondered for a while. Then he said, "Nothing."

The husband grasped his friend's hand, shook it and shouted, "Mazel und brucha! It's a deal."

4

BUSINESS
IS BUSINESS

Talmud or no Talmud, the mazel und brucha code is strictly wholesale in the diamond business, and has little currency on the retail
level of the Street. The customer, stepping from a crowded sidewalk
into an even more congested diamond exchange, is just an outsider
and not entitled to the special protections and provisos set up for
those who are part of the Diamond Ghetto. The world of the diamond exchanges—and the retail stores—is the only part of the world
of Forty-seventh Street known to retail customers. This is based on a
very hard-nosed credo. It is: Business is business. To appreciate the
distinction between this concept and the mazel und brucha approach, you should know the story of the train accident, another of
those parables that are part of the special wisdom of the diamond industry and derivative of the centuries in which ghetto Jews learned to
express their thoughts and yet evade persecution.

The story is that one night there was an accident at a grade crossing. When the parable was first being told, it was probably a train running into a horse-drawn wagon. Today the accident is a collision between a train and an automobile. At this crossing, there was supposed to be a switchman swinging a lighted lantern. During the investigation, a witness said he saw a person who may have been a watchman, but not a lantern. The switchman swore he was on the spot, swinging the lantern long before the train reached the crossing, but that the driver ignored him. The first assumption by the investigators was that one of the men was lying. But then it occurred to someone that both could be telling the truth. The explanation could be that the switchman was swinging the lantern, but it was unseen because it was not lit.

This tale, usually told with a chuckle, sums up a favorite axiom of life among those who sell retail on Forty-seventh Street. It is: "You don't lie. But sometimes you don't tell the whole truth."

Thus, when the man behind the counter tells a customer, "To my own brother I couldn't sell for less," it may mean that the seller does not like his brother. Or it may mean what the retail trade considers a permissible white lie.

Example: For quite a while I was puzzled by the fact that some of the men who rent booths in the diamond exchanges on Forty-seventh Street seem to do very little business. They will sit in a chair in the tiny booth, not moving for half an hour or more, or merely lean on the little showcase counter. Sometimes, particularly on Fridays, they don't bother to come in at all. Yet they have no trouble paying the rent. They dress well. They send their children to college. The booth always has a telephone, often two—one solely for outgoing calls. One day I asked a veteran of Forty-seventh Street how these apparently marginal operators survived. He thought for a few moments, then said, "They manage. They do a little business now and then. They have a bit of luck once in a while. And that carries them along."

Several weeks later, I asked the same question of a diamond dealer. He grinned. He told me the story of the train accident. Then he told me about a diamond he had purchased for $20,000 from a man who had a booth in one of the diamond exchanges.

"How come, you could ask me," said the dealer, "that this man in a little booth in the diamond exchange, a man who does not seem to do much business, how come he has this diamond. I'll tell you. It is because these days the prices of diamonds are so high. So there was this widow and she was reading all these advertisements about good prices for diamonds, and seeing the commercials on television and hearing them on radio. So she decides to take a look at the jewelry her husband gave her over the years. She sees this diamond ring her husband gave her maybe forty years ago. She says to herself: 'Who knows. Maybe these advertisements are true. Maybe this is the time to sell.' So where should she go? Forty-seventh Street. She goes in and out of the exchanges and maybe the stores too. She comes finally to this booth. She looks at the man. He is elderly. He seems honest. She shows him the ring. He can tell by the ring that it goes back a long time. But the stone looks like good quality. He can't tell the weight for sure, but he figures it for more than a carat. Of course, sometimes when you take a diamond out of a ring you find a flaw you didn't see before. Still, in this business you have to be a gambler. While he's louping the ring, he's thinking how to handle her. He's thinking it will be a mistake to ask her how much it cost. First of all, she will lie and second, she will get suspicious right away. Better not to ask. Better just to make an offer that is probably better than she got so far, an offer that will seem like a lot compared to what her husband paid. So he says to her: 'This ring. It's old-fashioned. That we both know. But the diamond it is not bad. Your husband was a man of taste. He was not a piker. One price. Five thousand dollars.'

"The old lady, she's so happy, she says yes right away. For her it's a wonderful deal. A $4,500 profit on a $500 ring."

The story is finished. The diamond dealer smiles.

"That man who told you how these people in the booth make a living, he didn't lie to you. He just didn't tell the whole truth. I know people in these little booths who manage so good they have salesmen on the road, buying and selling for them in Los Angeles, Chicago, Miami."

What the diamond dealer didn't say was how much of his own transaction with the man from the booth was in cash; how it would be recorded in his books, if at all. Will the tale of this ring, from beginning to end—from the old lady to the booth to the diamond dealer—be all in cash and never declared in their tax returns? Very possibly.

The exchanges of Forty-seventh Street are quintessential ghetto business. Noisy, crowded, energetic, intense, disputatious, and secretive. They are an important reason that Forty-seventh Street has the nickname "rue de la Payess." The Jewish word "payess" means sideburns. The Hasidim, so vividly conspicuous as they jostle through the exchanges, have long side curls. Sometimes, also because of the atmosphere of the exchanges, the block is referred to as the "casbah." The exchanges seem better suited to an old-fashioned public market. If the showcases were on wheels, like pushcarts, they would not seem unsuited to the emotional barter. It is hard to say whether the workers or the customers are more uncomfortable. Yet no one seems to mind the crush.

An exchange is made up of hip-high showcases that stand end to end. The booths formed by these showcases, while they vary in size, are usually not much more than twenty-five feet square. Considering that two persons usually work a booth—husband and wife, two brothers, or unrelated partners—this makes life cramped. The booth may also contain two chairs on each side of a tiny table on top of which may be diamond scales, a ledger containing the prices at which the merchandise was purchased, and a small metal box containing memoranda signed by the persons who took diamonds on consignment. Somewhere a couple of phones have been plugged into the wall, an electronic calculator and a gauge to measure the diameter and depth of the diamonds have been placed, along with a book that gives a rough approximation of the carat-weight of a diamond with those dimensions.

Some booths—the big ones— have small, concealed enclosures off to the side. Their major function seems to be for the quick—and sometimes costly—games of gin rummy addicts. They play in pairs. There's no room in these phone booth–sized human coops for more than two persons, particularly when they are handling the cards, sometimes slapping them down on a tiny table.

The rents for these booths vary by size and position. The closer to the front window, the higher the rent. In one exchange, in 1979, the rents ranged from $2,500 a month for a window booth to $150 for a crushed enclosure at the rear. In 1978 and 1979, with diamond prices rising so steadily, the demand for booths was so insistent that, as leases expired, some landlords doubled the rent. As a rule, the landlord for an exchange rents it from the owner of the building. In some cases, the owner of the exchange also owns the building. One of the reasons that, in 1979, building owners began pushing exchanges through an entire block—from Forty-seventh to Forty-sixth streets, or from Forty-seventh to Forty-eighth—was to eliminate a "rear" to the exchange. Top prices could be charged at either side for window space.

The value of every inch of rented space in the Forty-seventh Street exchanges is shown in the case of a booth tenant who figured out that some unused space just off his booth could be made into a private toilet. The landlord studied the situation. He turned it down. Instead, he installed still another booth that would bring in much more money than the tenant would have paid for the toilet. When booth occupants have to go to the toilet, they use the key to a toilet elsewhere in the building.

For the customers, there are the aisles, rarely more than three feet wide. If some customers are looking at merchandise in one booth, while other customers are examining gems in booths across the aisle, both leaning over the counters, their rears protruding, they can be almost certain that passing customers—sometimes two abreast since they are engaged in intense conversation—will jostle them. Occasionally, there will be a high stool on which a customer can sit. But these are rare. People who are jostled do not complain.

Hang straps from the ceilings and the customers could feel as though they were in the subway.

Except for the merchandise, the glass showcases are plain. Velvet lining for the boxes is not unusual. The glitter of gems and precious metals magnetizes the thousands who pass through the exchanges every day, often just to behold what is one of the great floor shows of New York City—complete with lights and dialogue. The brilliant lights of lampstands on counters flash on and off as buyers and sellers study gems. And the dialogue is as unique as Runyon's.

A young man edges up to a booth. He waits until a customer finishes—not so much out of courtesy, but secrecy. When the customer leaves, the following conversation takes place.

BROKER: You get any good white ones hold for me. For a few hours. A day.

BOOTH MAN: I get some, I'll try.

BROKER (*insistently*): These people I'm seeing, they don't play. They buy.

BOOTH MAN (*casually*): That's the general idea.

BROKER (*passionately*): Big ones.

BOOTH MAN (*still calmly*): What do you mean, big.

BROKER: Seven and up [meaning more than seven carats].

BOOTH MAN (*nods*): If I get I buy.

BROKER: Remember.

BOOTH MAN: I'll remember.

In another exchange, a booth man is shuffling worriedly through papers on a shelf. His booth is too small for a table. The man in the neighboring booth reassures him, telling him it will turn up. The man keeps turning over old trade journals, envelopes, flipping through the pages of a ledger. Suddenly he comes upon an envelope. He hands it to his neighbor. "Somebody left it for you this morning. He didn't say anything. Just asked me to hold it for you." The neighbor opens the envelope. It contains a terse handwritten note and $7,000 in cash.

At another booth, a broker asks the tenant if he has any two-

carat diamonds. Booth man shows him a few. Broker selects one.
"How much?" he asks. The booth man consults his inventory book.
He doesn't have to. He knows what he paid. He tells the broker,
"Fifty-three," meaning $5,300 per carat. This may or may not be the
truth. The broker takes it on consignment. He knows the booth man
wants $11,000 for the diamond. If the broker can sell it for more,
that's his business. The booth man knows him well enough not to
ask him to sign a memorandum.

When he leaves, another broker comes to the booth with a
diamond. They talk price. "You gotta get 47, right?" This may mean
a total price of $4,700 or $47,000 or perhaps $4,700 per carat. The
booth man loupes the diamond. He takes it on consignment. Makes
a notation in his inventory book. If he can't sell it soon, he will buy it
for his own stock.

Another broker comes by and hands the booth man a diamond
he had taken from him on consignment. He goes through his
stack of memos, picks out this one and destroys it. The broker does
not ask to see the memo to make sure it's not blank or someone
else's.

A booth man, having just finished bargaining with two customers almost simultaneously, reaches back toward the wall, grabs a
phone, dials it, and pulls the wire toward the counter so he won't
miss anything in the aisles.

"What gives with the bracelet," he barks into the phone. . . .
"Come on. Why so long . . . What kind of *tsimmes* is this. All it
needs is you shorten it a little. The ankle is eight inches. So you take
out a little from the chain and you make it eight and a quarter . . .
Sure I'll pay you . . . Don't hock me a *chynik* [Don't beat my tea
kettle]. Look. I have to have this. It's for the guy who fixes my car.
No bracelet, I don't have the car. No car, I can't come to work. And
no business for you. Okay. I'll send someone over for it in a couple
of hours. Yeah. He'll have the money."

Another booth. The phone rings. The booth man snatches it
up. All he says is: "Okay, thanks." Then to his friend he says, very

quietly, "Our friend down the street is in trouble." What he means is that the man on the phone from another exchange informed him that a broker's check has bounced. This means that he and his partner will be wary of extending credit to this man until they know the check has cleared.

The sayings of the exchanges are pithy. One is: "You can make a lot of money with your mouth." Another is: "You can walk from here to Chicago and not find five dollars. So if you can make a few dollars, make it." This means that sometimes it's better to make a quick sale for a small profit than to hold out in hopes of a larger one.

This is the language endemic to a world that lives by "Business is business." How do these men and women of the exchanges and stores justify their departure from the mazel and brucha code that binds them in wholesale trade? All the holy teachings of Judaism— Bible, Talmud, Maimonides—forbid lying. The Talmud even speaks against misleading a person, "thievery by words." And yet the Talmud makes allowances that could be cited by the people of the Street. First it says that it is permissible to break a vow made during business negotiations—certain kinds of vows. For instance, if two men are bargaining, one says he cannot possibly pay more than a certain amount and the other says he cannot conceivably accept less. Yet they make a deal that is somewhere in between. Both men have violated a vow. This, says the Talmud, is permitted.

The Talmud makes another important distinction—between necessities and luxuries. Explicitly the Talmud condemns excessive profit in necessities such as food and clothing. But allowances are made for luxuries. Without knowing that the Talmud is on their side, the diamond people of Forty-seventh Street consider this in their dealings with the public. They may say, during the heat of bargaining across a counter, "You are taking the bread out of my mouth." But they know that gems are not food.

Fairly characteristic of the ethical tone of the exchange is the case of the man who offered a ring at a booth for $10,000. The booth man shook his head. "Not for me."

"How much."

"The booth man took up his loupe and examined the ring slowly. "Maybe four," he said.

"You gotta be kidding."

The man in the booth offers the loupe and ring to the seller. "See for yourself," he says. "The quality is not the best. It has a spot. The cut is old-fashioned. The ring has to be repaired. For eight no chance of a profit."

The seller does not look through the loupe, thereby confirming the suspicion of the booth man that he does not know much about diamonds.

The seller says, "You know you can sell this stone for ten an hour after I leave."

"Then you sell it."

The man with the diamond picks it up, starts wrapping it as though he was getting ready to leave. "Okay," he says. "Make it seven."

The booth man asks to see the diamond again through the loupe. "Best I can do," he says, "is fifty-five."

The sale, after another ten minutes, is made at $6,000.

The next day the booth man sells it for $19,000.

Still it is a mistake to assume that the diamond people are heartless. If anything, since they are their own bosses, they will, out of whim, goodness of heart, or feelings of guilt about earlier transactions, indulge in spontaneous kindness that is inconceivable in the computer-ruled corporate world.

There was the case of the attractive, smartly dressed woman in her upper thirties or low forties. She was with a woman who could have been her mother. The two walked casually along Forty-seventh Street about noon. They could have been two suburbanites who had come into midtown this Wednesday for a matinee, and had decided to windowshop among the gems. They went up one side of the Street and back on the other, looking at the merchandise and particularly at the prices on rings and bracelets. At one of the exchanges, they turned in. They stopped at a counter near the door. Behind the counter was a middle-aged woman with a broad-boned face and expressionless eyes. The younger of the two women told her she wanted to sell some jewelry. The woman behind the counter nodded. The younger woman took a diamond ring and two bracelets from her handbag, and put them on the counter. The woman behind the counter looked at the three pieces, then at the two women.

"How much you want for the ring?"

"Five thousand."

The woman behind the counter looked at the two women again. The younger woman seemed uneasy. The older one tense.

She showed the ring to the man working with her. He louped it. She told him how much had been asked. His first reaction would have been to offer much less and bargain. As he looked at the two women, he changed. Instead, he said, very courteously, "This is a nice ring. Your evaluation is not unreasonable. But it's more than I want to pay." He handed back the ring. The younger woman was very uncomfortable. He added, gently, "Try others in the Street. But if they are offering less than $4,000 come back here and I'll buy it." He walked away.

The young woman started to put the ring and bracelets back into her handbag. The hard-faced woman behind the counter asked, "Were there any children?"

"No."

"That's a little better, maybe."

As the two started to walk away, she said, "If you can't get $4,000, come back here." She paused, then said, "When you go into the next place, don't tell them how much you want. Let them make the offer."

When they had left I asked her why she had been so solicitous. She looked out at the crowded street after them, shrugged, then said, "I could see she got a beating in a divorce. Really hurting. The ring used to mean so much to her. She comes here because she wants to forget. You see them day after day. This time I guess it got to me." The eyes were still expressionless.

The exchange is the limbo of Forty-seventh Street's diamond

business. The dealers are wholesale. The stores are retail. The booths do both, though some booths bargain more heavily with dealers while other booths do the bulk of their business with retail customers. Coming to their counters are the indefatigable Hasidim who work as brokers and dealers, buying and selling, side by side, with naïfs looking for a ring, watch, necklace, cuff links, pin, or brooch. To the same counters come thieves—men who have filched jewels from wives to get money for horse-playing, or wives selling jewels for money to play cards. At these counters anyone can find anonymity. Those who work the booths never know what to expect. That they seem distrustful is natural. What is surprising is that they trust anyone at all.

There was the hard-jawed man in the leather jacket. He came to a counter with three diamond pins. He wanted $4,500 for each. The counter man looked at them through a loupe. He said he did not want them. The customer tried to negotiate. The booth man declined. After the customer left, the booth man said the stones in the pins were zirconium. "I could see through the loupe that where the facets meet that the line was not as fine as it is with diamonds. There was almost a bevel." Then he appraised the customer. "He asked for $4,500 each. If he asked for much less you become suspicious right away because that's what diamonds would be worth if they're any good. So this is a man who knows something about the business. He's all larceny. And so is anyone in the Street who buys the stuff. The person who buys those pins will figure that guy either stole them or doesn't know anything about diamonds. Yet I guarantee this guy will sell the phony stones right in this block. Maybe he'll take thirty-five or twenty-five, or even less. The guy who buys the pins will think he's making a nice killing. Then he'll try to sell. Maybe he'll sell to someone in the trade who knows him and would never think he's handling phony stones. Those stones could go through four or five hands until someone discovers they're phony. If all the buyers after the first one are in the business they will all get their money back until the pins wind up again at the booth. What will he do with them? Probably wait for a sucker who is not in the business and sell the pins for what he paid for them. Or less. Glad to get rid of them. Toward an outsider he will feel no obligation."

A different kind of case that helps build distrust among booth people is the following:

A man and young woman from out of town came into an exchange and he bought a diamond wedding ring for her. A few years later, this man's brother went to the same booth to get a diamond wedding ring as well. A third brother also bought a diamond wedding ring at the same booth. When, a few years later, the fourth and youngest brother came to the same booth for a diamond wedding ring, the booth man explained to him that diamonds had risen considerably in the past few years, and he would have to pay much more for the same kind of stone. He suggested that the young man either settle for a smaller stone or one of lower quality. The young man said no. The booth man then recommended a practice that is not uncommon—that he purchase a modest ring for the wedding and some years later, when he is more prosperous, buy a better ring. The young man said he'd discuss it with his fiancée. He phoned and said the woman had decided to look elsewhere.

A few days later he phoned the booth. He was jubilant and a bit derisive. He said his fiancée had found just the ring they wanted and at the right price. She had bought it, he said, right on Forty-seventh Street and she was coming over to pick up the ring. The booth man said that if the stone was what the young man said and of the right quality, he would buy it from him and give him a profit of $500. Later in the day, the young man brought the ring to the booth. The booth man louped the stone and quickly detected a black spot. He handed the loupe to the young man and told him where to look. The bridegroom saw it. The booth man did not tell him that the store at which the ring was purchased is notorious on Forty-seventh Street for selling shoddy diamonds. Yet that store is one of the most successful on the block.

No group in the business is more exposed to con artists than the booth people. One day a young man offered a booth tenant a diamond ring. The booth man louped the stone. It seemed of fair qual-

ity. It was set in a solid gold ring. The seller was poorly dressed,
seemed furtive and eager to sell. The booth man cut the original
price to a third before buying. Later, when he removed the stone
from the ring, he saw that it was badly flawed. He had bought the
ring because he was convinced the seller was a thief or a petty fence.
The young man had done a good con job.

The bane of the booth people are the women who want to return jewelry their husbands have bought for them. One of these was
a woman from the Midwest whose husband had bought her diamonds earrings more than a year earlier. The next time she was in
New York, she went to the booth and complained. The booth man,
foreseeing a spell during which she would spend a long time picking
over his stock to find something she wanted instead of the diamond
earrings, offered to buy back the earrings at once at the price her husband had paid. She became suspicious and, after looking at a few
other pairs of earrings, left.

Occasionally, an outsider will try to pose as someone in the
trade to try to get a discount. Also, the outsider may have heard
that on Forty-seventh Street booth people will not cheat those in the
business. The outsider will claim to be from another city, and know
the names of some dealers in that location. One quick method used
by veteran booth men to detect such poseurs is to suddenly hand him
a diamond and loupe, and ask his opinion of the stone. Non-profes-
sionals give themselves away by the way they loupe the stone. They
either hold the stone too close or too far from the loupe. They also
lack the sure deftness in handling the diamond while they loupe it.

Does it pay for someone buying retail to have a "friend in the
business"? Usually. But it is almost certain that the "friend" will
want a commission from the seller. The commission, or "finder's
fee," is usually 10 percent. The commission will be included in the
overall price, though the customer will not know it. One booth man
insists that the "friend" tell the customer that the commission is included in the price.

It is generally easy to recognize the true friend at work. The following is an example.

First the friend and the booth man discuss their own business. He offers a few stones. They discuss prices. When their own business is concluded, the friend says, "I have to get an engagement ring for Helen's nephew. But the most he can spend is fifteen [$1,500]." They discuss size and quality of the stone. Both realize they can't get much of either at that price. "If you see something," says the friend, "let me know." About this time a cutter comes to the counter. He knows the booth man. They have been partners on diamonds from time to time. "I know where there's a nice stone," says the cutter. He may own it or know another cutter who will sell it to him for $1,700. "Can this young fellow go to $2,000?" The friend replies, "For this guy a $500-jump is a lot of money. Fifty dollars. A hundred. Yes. But 500. Too much for this kid." The cutter says he will look for it. Nobody makes notes. They will all remember. If the booth man or cutter finds the right ring, he will take a profit. But less than if the customer didn't have a friend.

Diamond people tend to be wary of "friendship" deals. They can be burned if there is no clear understanding beforehand.

This happened to one booth man who was told by a friend that he had a relative who wanted to sell some personal jewelry. The jewelry was of good quality, he said. The booth man told his friend to send the relative, and he would give her as good a price as he could. The relative delivered the jewelry. Ordinarily, after tough haggling, the booth man would not have paid her more than $25,000 for the jewelry. At most, $30,000. But because he had promised his friend to give the relative a good price, he paid the woman $36,000. A few days later the booth man's friend phoned to ask for his finder's fee of $3,600. The booth man could not refuse. He wound up selling the jewelry for a total profit of $2,000. Thus, the man who had sent the woman got more than he did.

What is a reasonable profit for retailers on Forty-seventh Street? Some say they are willing to settle for 15 or 20 percent. There is no doubt that others make a profit of better than 100 percent. Moreover, many do not pay sales tax or they take cash payments that are not declared on their income tax returns. Certainly, the customer who does not have to pay sales tax does not object. For that matter, how many business men, doctors, lawyers, dentists, handymen—all of whom may have cash income—are likely to declare this income in full—or at all. As we shall see, one of the reasons that the price of diamonds rose so sharply in the late 1970s was that persons who had cash they wanted to conceal bought diamonds with it.

At the other extreme are retail booth men and women who, though they look for tax loopholes, are very proud of their reputations. Usually they have been on the Street for more than twenty years; some were in the business in Holland and Belgium until they fled Nazism.

A husband and wife in an exchange booth who sell only retail are reluctant to sell to persons who come in off the street. Most of their business is with people they have served for years or with those recommended by them. If asked by a customer he does not know to allow an independent appraisal of the gem by an outside expert, the man will break off the sale and ask the customer to leave. There are many men in the Street and in the jewelry sections of department stores who appraise diamonds for a fee.

"I don't want to sell to such people," he says. "The truth is if a total stranger comes in I hardly waste any time on such business." This couple is highly respected on Forty-seventh Street.

This booth man's anger, when an appraisal is suggested, is more than resentment at the implication that he is dishonest. He shares the general feeling of the block that the appraisers know much less about diamonds than those who sell them. Diamond merchants on Forty-seventh Street say that the best of the appraisers are most likely to be found in department stores. And even there, the only competent ones are those who have been in the work for a long time. Senior appraisers at department stores, though honest, are not as knowledgeable as experienced diamond people. According to booth people, collusion between appraisers on the Street and retailers— whether in booths or in stores—is not uncommon.

Some booth people say that, from time to time, they will send the same stone for appraisal to different department stores but the evaluations are so far apart they are ludicrous. One booth man tells the story of a young woman who used to sell dresses in a department store. As business boomed in the jewelry department, she was transferred to that section. She seemed to be a good saleswoman with a feeling for jewelry. A short time later she was made an appraiser.

One of the cardinal rules of life in a diamond exchange, when a booth man is buying, is that he has to consider two profits. If he is going to resell retail, he will charge a higher price and that ends his concern. But if he has to resell to a broker or dealer, he must calculate the broker or dealer's profit when making the purchase, in addition to his own. Booth people must not let themselves be hurried when buying diamonds.

Example: A man rushed up to an exchange booth.

"Give you first look," he blurted "I want fast action. I want seventy-five." He meant $7,500 a carat.

"How many carats?" asked the booth man.

"Five and a half."

The booth man took it between thumb and forefinger, looked at it for a few moments. "It's a light five, I figure," he said. This means he thought it was a shade under five carats. Then, louping the diamond, he said, "It's off color."

The owner of the diamond argued what should have been the usual prelude to bargaining. The booth man showed little interest. The owner left. Later the booth man explained: "There was no sense bargaining. We were too far apart. I could not possibly give more than six. A stone that size I have to figure I will have to resell to a dealer. It's not for retail. Not from a booth in an exchange. Maybe from Van Cleef & Arpels. Not here. So if I have to sell to a dealer I know I want to make a profit. And I know that any dealer who buys from me, he has to see a profit too. For me it was easier not to buy in the first place. Of course, with some stones I'll buy for my inventory. Some stones, you know you just put them away and the price will go up. But the quality of that stone was not good enough for inventory."

Some booth people, though sharp competitors, have entente cordiales in limited areas. These apply to dealers they suspect of trying to play booth people off one another in bidding for their stones. If a dealer the booth man suspects of such tactics comes to him with a stone and a price seems close, but no deal is closed, the booth man, as soon as the dealer leaves, will phone the man with whom he has the entente. He will tell them what the price was. The other booth man will go no higher. With such ententes the understanding is: if the other makes the deal at that price, the two booth men are partners in the deal.

Among the booth people who sell mainly or entirely to the retail trade, there is a vast range of integrity. Some are motivated solely by greed. One booth man is so unprincipled that the owner of the exchange has decided not to renew his lease when it expires. He says this booth tenant could give the whole exchange a bad name. There is one small exchange on the block that, whether deservedly or not, is known to the trade as the "den of thieves."

Among those who have retail stores on Forty-seventh Street, there is just as wide a range in principle as among booth men. The owner of one store is most proud of the fact that he is now selling to a third generation of customers in the same families. He virtually ignores any customer who is not known to him or is not recommended by old customers or dealers he trusts. The business he may miss by his indifference to the street trade, he says, means less than the headaches. To him, the growing shame of Forty-seventh Street is that more and more stores are now using "pullers." These are people who will step out of a store if they see a possible customer looking in the window, strike up a conversation with the shopper, and try to induce the person to enter the store and "look around." One diamond store that uses "pullers" has the worst reputation on the block. The term "puller," incidentally, dates back to the early decades of the twentieth century, when immigrants, looking for clothes on the Lower East Side, were literally pulled into cheap clothing stores when they paused outside windows and high-pressured into buying inferior merchandise.

It was at that time and area, and not much later, that the diamond exchanges developed their colorful history. The exchanges became established in the Bowery, in the vicinity of Canal Street in the 1920s. Some still remain. According to the late Bobby Becker, with the firm of Glasser-Becker-Runsdorf, which leases an exchange on Forty-seventh Street, and has a booth about five times the usual size, the first exchange in the Bowery was opened in the late twenties by his father, Morris Becker, with a partner named George Harris. It was on the street level of a six-story building at 80–82 The Bowery. The dingy booths of this exchange were so primitive, the booth merchants sat on orange crates. When the elevated train roared overhead the merchants and their customers either had to shout or be quiet. In the summer, the men not only removed jackets and ties; they rolled up their trousers as well. When the depression came, the booths were renting for as little as ten dollars a week.

Howard Herman, whose father had a window booth in another Bowery exchange, says no one made use of the sidewalk windows. Sometimes they put their hats in them. One day, when a shabby panhandler drifted into the door of the exchange, a friend of Mr. Herman's sold him Mr. Herman's new hat for a pittance—just a joke among the high-spirited diamond people of the Bowery exchanges.

A good deal of the zest persists among the exchange people on Forty-seventh Street, particularly among those who have descended from the booth people of the Bowery. It was saddened by the influx of Jews who fled Hitler. But the underlying competition has, if anything, become even sharper.

This is shown as much in the acquisition of diamonds by the retailers, as in the sale. In addition to the three major sources of diamonds for retailers—dealers, brokers, and street trade—there is a fourth. Estates. Some booths and stores post signs prominently saying they buy estates. Since banks often sell off jewelry as part of certain estates, it is important for the booth people and store owners of Forty-seventh Street to get a favored position with the banks.

"Friendship at a bank," says a booth man, "is something you get with a gift. In return, the guy from the bank gives you a quiet call ahead of time about some estate that's coming up. There are these sales with sealed bids. But sometimes these sealed bids are not kept sealed until all the bids are in. If you have made a friend at a bank, he calls you when the bids are opened. Then you put in a quick bid that is higher than the others. So you get the goods."

The gifts to bank informants can take the form of cash, jewelry, or the sale of jewelry to the bank helper at a price so ridiculously low he could sell it easily for a considerable profit.

One day, while I was chatting with a booth man, another booth man came by and told him quickly, "The guy came through. I can't swing it alone." What this meant was that the informant at a bank had tipped him off about an imminent sale of jewelry from an estate, but that he did not have enough money to swing it alone. The two booth men went partners. They would split the profits.

At least twice, since the diamond exchanges moved up to Forty-seventh Street, the booth men considered improving their image. Each time, they formed an association, hired a publicity agent, and held a few gatherings, usually disputatious. The sense of individuality in the business was just too strong. The image-making endeavors failed.

In the seventies, when the fear of crime spread along Forty-seventh Street, the exchanges profited. While crime increased in the offices of the grimy buildings, there had never been a serious crime in an exchange—probably because they are so densely populated and visible from the street. Exchange crimes are normally by pickpockets, purse-snatchers, or an occasional snatch of a jewel from a counter top when the booth man's attention is diverted.

The growing popularity of the exchanges brought about a variant in 1979 that came to be known as the Fort Knox of Forty-seventh Street. It was an arcade that ran from Forty-seventh to Forty-eighth streets in the middle of the block. It had stores on each side of the arcade. In a subbasement, beneath the arcade, were offices that featured very tight security, where diamond merchants could examine wares without fear.

As these new diamond exchanges were built, two contrary schools of exchange decors developed on the Street. One group felt that the more booths squeezed into an exchange, the better because the busier an exchange looks, the more customers it attracts. The other group argued that if an exchange was too crowded, booth occupants would find it easier to eavesdrop on competitors and steal business. Also, this second group contended, suburbanites, already being drawn to the suburban malls for jewelry, might find the congestion of Forty-seventh Street too uncomfortable.

But no matter how many structural changes are made in the exchanges, and regardless of talk of image-changing, the fundamentals of the business remain unchanged.

"In this business," says a booth man, "you have to wheel and deal."

5

THE SYNDICATE

In the disputatious diamond business, there is one point on which everyone agrees: the Syndicate is the supreme power of the diamond industry. It is omniscient as well as omnipotent. Its vast funds make it a separate government. It long ago set the pattern for multinational corporations and the oil cartel. The richest of multimillionaire diamond dealers is just another fief in the realm of the Syndicate. This corporate deity has no temple where diamond merchants can pay their respects, but every diamond bought, sold, or traded on Forty-seventh Street—or anywhere else, for that matter—pays monetary homage to the might of the Syndicate.

The heart and soul of the Syndicate is De Beers Consolidated Mines, Ltd. As a publicly owned business based primarily on its possession of diamond mines in Africa, De Beers issues annual statements to stockholders, in which it tells, year after year, of its growing resources, its technological advances, its rising profits, dividends, and cheerful plans for the future. It is in these reports that De Beers masters the art of commingling aesthetics and accountancy: the attractive, multicolored reports with pictures of diamonds scattered among the stolid columns of nine- and ten-digit figures; the impressive photographs of huge machines in operation at the mines; and charts that show a soaring profit line.

This literature, so dear to De Beers stockholders, is not what makes the corporation so feared. The true strength of De Beers lies in its amorphous creation known as the Central Selling Organization. This subsidiary of De Beers determines the price of rough diamonds, which in turn determines the price of cut diamonds, at a ritual held ten times a year known as the "sights." Only the elite of the world's diamond dealers and manufacturers are invited by the Syndicate to the sights, where they receive an allocation of rough diamonds at prices set by the Syndicate. Technically, the sights are operated by the Diamond Trading Company, an arm of De Beers, similar to the Central Selling Organization. Emily Hahn, in a series of articles for the *New Yorker* magazine in 1956—for which she was permitted to witness one of the sights—called the Diamond Trading Company "perhaps the lowest-pressure selling outfit in the world." Because 80 to 85 percent of the world's rough diamonds are sold at sights (the U.S. Bureau of Mines estimated world production of diamonds in 1979 at 39.6 million carats, of which 10.6 million carats were of gem quality and the remainder industrial) there is little need for a hard-sell by this fully controlled operation of the Syndicate.

A vivid demonstration of Syndicate power came in an almost casual act in the late 1970s as a new building was being completed in London for the sights. It conveyed a polite message to the leading diamond dealers in the United States and the world.

It was suggested to them by London diamond operatives, who clearly were authorized to speak for De Beers, that the diamond princelings would like to pay homage with gifts to beautify the interior of the new building that they would be visiting from time to time—on invitation. However, an uncontrolled stream of presents might lead to duplication or clash with the overall artistic decors that had already been planned. It might be better, therefore, if the diamond dealers just gave cash. At the same time the donors would enjoy the knowledge that they had helped create this elegance. To avoid the unnecessary agony of deciding how much to give, the hint was dropped that contributions more than $10,000 would be considered in poor taste. This was interpreted by the privileged donors to mean that the donation should certainly be in four digits, within easy distance of $10,000, but clearly not less than $5,000.

Such a contribution was not a great amount to pay for the leaders of the diamond business in the United States—some sixty or seventy persons. In fact, there were a number of rising diamond merchants on Forty-seventh Street who would have paid for the privilege of being solicited for this donation. It was a mark of preference by the Syndicate.

One man who was asked to contribute to the new Syndicate building in London found the request offensive. But it was not the money that bothered him. Like all others in this group, his wealth was in the millions. It was their approach that he resented. He saw it for what it was—a shakedown—so he instructed his top executives to make no contribution. His subordinates were alarmed. To antagonize the Syndicate was very risky, they argued. But he contended that their "request" was no different from a demand by a gangster to pay "protection" money as insurance against property damage. His subordinates pleaded with him to make the donation. Finally, with considerable anger, he told them that if the company wanted to make a contribution, it could. But he did not want to hear about it. Not ever. The contribution was made.

One of those subordinates with whom I discussed this episode afterwards said: "I was ashamed that we gave in. I knew my boss was right. I respected him for his courage. But we had to do it. We did not dare offend the Syndicate. No matter how powerful you are in the diamond business, you kowtow to the Syndicate."

In its quest for power and profit, the Syndicate will, if it can, ignore the laws of other nations, even of a country as powerful as the

United States. It flouted our anti-trust laws in setting up a network that fixed and raised prices of diamond grit in the United States, and by establishing sales territories. These industrial diamonds, while very cheap, are vital to our technology. How important these non-gem diamonds are to us was explained in criminal and civil indictments by the anti-trust division of the Department of Justice when it cracked down on De Beers in 1974.

The indictments accused a Syndicate subsidiary—De Beers Industrial Diamond Division, Ltd. of Johannesburg—of using two New York companies—Anco Diamond Abrasives Corporation and Diamond Abrasives Corporation—to "fix, stabilize, and raise the retail prices of diamond grit; to allocate territorial markets in the sale of diamond grit; and to allocate customers in the sale of diamond grit."

These illegal practices, the indictment revealed, had been carried out over a five-year period.

The power implicit in control of the supply, price, and allocation of diamond grit in the United States was made clear in another section of the indictments that said:

"Diamond grit has experienced great adaptability and rapid growth in industry because of its unique mechanical properties, including its superb resistance to high temperatures, abrasion, and acids, its extremely high thermal conductivity, and the fact that diamond is the hardest of all known substances. Because of these unique properties, diamond grit is considered indispensable to the communications, electrical, constructions, electronics, mining, metalworking, automotive, aircraft, and other industries which have ultrahard materials, close tolerances, fine finishes, interchangeability, speed, and precision. In 1972, there were approximately 16.1 million carats of diamond grit consumed in the United States.

"There are no facilities in the United States for the commercial mining of natural diamond grit. Therefore, virtually all of the natural diamond grit (excluding reclaimed) consumed in the United States is imported from abroad. By far the principal supplier of natural diamond grit is the defendant De Beers. A substantial amount of

synthetic diamond grit consumed in the United States is also imported from abroad."

The Syndicate, through other subsidiaries, produces synthetic
diamond grit abroad.

So overpowering was the case built up by the anti-trust division
that the Syndicate decided it would be better to admit guilt than to
have its crimes detailed in court. It pleaded nolo contendere to the
criminal charges and signed a consent decree to the civil ones. The
fine was $40,000, a minute sum for the Syndicate, probably a small
fraction of what it had earned by price-fixing diamond grit in the
United States. However, Joel Davidow, who handled the case,
pointed out, in 1980, that the maximum fine at that time was
$50,000.

The forces involved in the creation of the Syndicate in the early
1930s, and the rebuilding of it after collapses, reveal a corporate
struggle so massive that it drew the Rothschilds and the House of
Morgan into the fray. The wealth that has given the Syndicate its
present form kept it alive despite wars, recessions, and depressions. It
established its own secret police that crossed national boundaries to
track down smugglers, and gathered information about diamond
merchants who were involved in operations considered improper by
De Beers.

The Syndicate is and has always been ruthless. But, for all its
power, it is basically a benevolent despot. Even those who fear it
concede that without it the diamond industry might become chaotic,
and certainly less profitable. And when they mutter despairingly of
its power, they also tell tales of how the Syndicate tries to be just,
showing generosity to compensate for unintentional unfairness, but
never admitting to its earlier fault.

Of particular significance—contrary to the expectations of those
who think capitalistic power is incorrigibly evil—the Syndicate has
been insistent in trying to improve the working and living conditions
for blacks in South Africa. It has been far ahead of the South African
government in attempting to end apartheid. In its business operations there, the Syndicate has been a virtual pioneer in paying equal

wages to blacks and whites for the same work. Often in the face of strong government opposition, it has created better housing for blacks. But some cynics argue that the Syndicate is merely being a shrewd business organization, protecting itself against possible uprisings by blacks that have occurred in other African countries; currying good will with those who may be the future rulers of South Africa. The fact is that the Syndicate was progressive in its attitude toward blacks *before* revolutions occurred in other African nations. Here again, skeptics contend that this was not so much altruism as it was a realization that the blacks represented a huge labor pool with a better potential for efficiency than bigoted government officials were willing to admit.

Quite possibly, much of the Syndicate's liberal attitude was shaped by its heritage. The Syndicate, though first conceived by the bigoted Rhodes, was made possible by Jews whose character and outlook were shaped—directly or indirectly—by ghetto life in Germany and England. Many people on Forty-seventh Street came from backgrounds not too different from those who were instrumental in showing Rhodes how to make the first Syndicate function, and recreate it when it weakened. Like the men of Forty-seventh Street, they were Jewish immigrants who were drawn to the diamond industry by a tradition that had made diamonds a Jewish business in Europe long before diamond mines were found in Africa.

The liberalism of the central power within the diamond industry was demonstrated in 1977, during the course of an episode that also showed the Syndicate's aloofness from the drudgery that has made Forty-seventh Street the heart of the Syndicate's biggest customer—the United States.

On October 14, 1977, Harry F. Oppenheimer, chairman of the board of De Beers, boss of the Syndicate, and sometimes referred to as the King of Diamonds, was making a brief visit to New York City. He had not come, as might have been expected, to do some diamond business. He had come to make a speech under the auspices of the Foreign Policy Association at a luncheon at the Pierre Hotel on Fifth Avenue, a short walk from Forty-seventh Street. On the program, Mr. Oppenheimer was listed as chairman of the Anglo-American Corporation, which, like De Beers, is based in Johannesburg. Anglo-American has holdings in gold that are even more valuable than the diamond wealth of De Beers. Through a private holding company, E. Oppenheimer & Son, the family controls both De Beers and Anglo-American—an investment in the vicinity of $10 billion. In an article in 1979, Forbes magazine ranked De Beers alone as fifty-eighth among its top five hundred in stock value, and in profits about thirteenth, ahead of Shell Oil, and only slightly behind Texaco.

Mr. Oppenheimer's speech was "Prospects for Change in Southern Africa." Short, somewhat portly, the sixty-eight-year-old tycoon spoke with spare gestures. Occasionally, he buttoned and unbuttoned the jacket of his gray suit or put his hands in his pockets. He seemed relaxed, very much like a professor discussing a complicated subject with graduate students. His manner was benign, but firm. The voice was clear and unemotional. The ideas, however, were strong. So much so, in fact, that he identified them as his own opinions which did not reflect the attitude of his corporate entities, a distinction that is as difficult to make as separating the power of a man's wealth from the man.

Mr. Oppenheimer condemned his government's policy of apartheid. He called attention to the upheavals in other African countries that had produced states run by blacks. He did not minimize the impact of black unemployment, black poverty, and their lack of educational opportunity as factors in South African unrest.

"The measures of repression which the government have felt necessary in order to maintain law and order under these deteriorating conditions are the cause of widespread anxiety and indeed revulsion. You will see, therefore, why I say the government's policies are in ruins."

Then, just as frankly, he discussed the reaction of his country to efforts by the United States to change his government's attitude.

"I hope you will not think it offensive if I tell you the disagreeable truth, that practically no one in South Africa believes that

American policy is primarily inspired by idealistic interest in the welfare of South Africans, black or white. . . . The American attitude towards Southern Africa begins to appear to be based neither on the defense of human rights nor of majority rule, but on a policy of supporting blacks against whites and armed blacks against unarmed blacks. . . . Now I would not like you to think that I share this way of looking at things. Quite the reverse is the case. . . . But you will not be able to bring about peaceful change unless the Afrikans-speaking whites who dominate the government can feel confident that their identity as a people—in South Africa 'Die Volk' is an emotive term—with the maintenance of their language and particular outlook, will be safe and they will not be swamped and lost in an alien environment. . . . After all, it has not proved so easy to preserve human rights and freedoms in other parts of Africa, that we South Africans should be too severely condemned for doubts as to whether the sort of arrangements accepted when most of the new African countries obtain independence would work satisfactorily with the much more complicated racial distribution of our society and much of our highly developed economy."

It was about an hour after this speech when I interviewed him in his attractive, but hardly lavish hotel suite. He seemed genuinely surprised when I asked him if, during his visit to New York, he had been to Forty-seventh Street. He replied that he had never been to Forty-seventh Street, though he was well aware of its important function in the diamond industry.

"When I come to this city," he said, "it is to get a feel for world economy at this financial capital. I'm not here to buy a company or sell some shares."

He said he had read about the murders in the diamond district that had received such intense attention from the media.

"I simply know nothing about it," he said. "I feel very sorry for those who have been killed or hurt. But I don't think the crimes will have the slightest impact on the industry."

He had the usual answer for my question as to whether De Beers was a monopoly.

"It is not a monopoly in production," he said. "We have no means of controlling the quantity of diamonds that are produced. The organization is big enough to hold stocks of diamonds in bad times. All we're able to do is to even out extremes of prices."

How did the Soviet Union coexist with his cartel's curious marketing operations? There was a time, he said, when the Soviet Union, after discovering huge diamond mines in Siberia, had broken with the De Beers marketing operations and had been selling on its own. That Soviet policy, he said, had changed.

"They don't act in such a way as to disturb the market." He smiled. His way of saying the Russians have found it more profitable to sell rough diamonds through the Syndicate.

Mr. Oppenheimer, incidentally, was not wearing diamonds. His only jewelry were a simple wedding band, an unadorned wrist watch, and cuff links. He said he did not recall ever wearing or owning a diamond and that his father, the founder of the Syndicate, had selected the diamond engagement ring he gave to his wife.

"I belong to a generation in which men did not wear jewelry." He added quickly: "Things have changed. I'm not against that change." He smiled.

That Mr. Oppenheimer did not bother to visit Forty-seventh Street that day—or any other time while he was in New York— shows how vast the gap is between the Syndicate and the greatest diamond market in the world. He had not rejected the idea of visiting Forty-seventh Street. It did not even occur to him as being interesting.

"What we do," Mr. Oppenheimer told me that day, with dry humor, "is have a large office in London to sell diamonds."

This London office and the sacred rites of the diamond business known as "the sights," is the key to the power of the Syndicate. It is impossible to understand the relationship between De Beers and Forty-seventh Street without some comprehension of how the Central Selling Organization conducts the sights.

Ten times a year—every fifth Monday—the sights are held. They run for a week. Though they are held in Lucerne and Kimberley as well as London, it is the London gatherings that are, by far, the largest and most important. To be on the list of those invited to the sights is the culminating ambition of any diamond manufacturer or dealer. The difference between the two is that the manufacturer sells mainly to retailers and the dealer sells mostly to other dealers or brokers. The worst professional calamity for a manufacturer or dealer is to be stricken from the list, which only the Syndicate has the power to do. It is the sole preparer of the list. Generally, once you make the list, you can stay on as long as you wish—as long as you do not offend the Syndicate. To be on the list means not only the utmost in status, but also a virtually guaranteed profit. In 1978 over $2.5 billion in rough diamonds, more than 20 percent from De Beers mines, were sold at the sights.

The sight is the occasion upon which the chosen few, among more than three hundred manufacturers and dealers in the whole world, are allocated diamonds by the Syndicate. For the sightholders, as they are called, this is their major source of rough diamonds. Any other rough diamonds they may buy will probably cost them more.

About three weeks before the sight, the invitees are notified by London to put in a request for an allocation of rough diamonds. The request is in dollars. The tendency among sightholders, particularly in a period of steadily rising diamond profits, is to ask for more than was received the last time. Having submitted the request, the sightholder waits. On the Wednesday or Thursday before the sight, the sightholder is told what the Syndicate has decided to give him.

On the day of the sight, the sightholders go to the Syndicate building on 17 Charterhouse Street—it was 2 Charterhouse Street until the end of 1979—where they are handed a small brown cardboard box. It might be the size and shape of a shoebox. The Syndicate functions on the principle that if you really have it, you don't have to flaunt it. There is something calculated about being given the small brown box—like tossing a bone to a dog.

The sightholder, with his precious brown box, is then escorted to a viewing room and left to study the diamonds. Inside the box are paper parcels of diamonds. The parcels are the same folded paper to be found on Forty-seventh Street, or any other diamond center. On the paper is printed the size of the enclosed diamond and the price. The sightholder studies the diamonds and the prices. Why he does this is not quite clear. He has no choice. He takes what he gets and at the price that the Syndicate has set. The diamonds will range in quality. This enables the Syndicate to sell diamonds that are not of the best quality as well as those that are.

The last man to spurn a box at a sight—and he may have been the only one in history—was the late Harry Winston, thereby proving that even in the diamond world, where chutzpah is like money in the bank, Winston's courage was remarkable. What happened then has become one of the murmured legends of the diamond business, though some details will probably never be ascertained. Winston is dead and the Syndicate is mute.

What is known is that Winston was not invited to the very next sight. He foresaw the possibility that despite his importance he might have to wait a long time doing penance before he could get rough diamonds at a sight. So he decided that somehow he had to gain access to a supply of rough diamonds beyond Syndicate control. In Angola, a Portuguese colony at that time, were some productive diamond mines owned jointly by a company and the Portuguese government. The company had a contract to sell its output through the Syndicate. But the contract was running out and Winston learned that the company was unhappy. He negotiated a tentative deal, whereby, when the contract ran out, the mine would sell its diamonds through him.

According to Richard Winston, a nephew of Harry, a British cabinet member phoned top officials of the Portuguese government and said that the British government would regard a deal between the mine company and Winston as an unfriendly act. The Portuguese officials relayed this information to Winston, who called upon the United States Department of State to get the British off his back. The State Department told him it could not interfere.

The deal fell through. But Winston was restored to the sight list, with a high rating for diamond allocations. The Syndicate had made its point. No one is so important that he is beyond the discipline of the Syndicate. Winston never again refused a box.

There is little doubt that the Syndicate cracked down on a number of Israeli dealers who, contrary to the wishes of De Beers, were involved in considerable speculation and hoarding of diamonds during 1977 and 1978. Some of these Israelis learned, suddenly, that banks were not eager to extend them credit. A few went bankrupt. A number—there is no way of learning how many—lost their sightholds. The Syndicate professes to have no knowledge about these matters. But it is obvious that the fate of the Israeli speculators was a lesson that was learned at once by the entire diamond industry.

Generally, the Syndicate shows its favor or displeasure in a much milder fashion at the sights. The most common favor is to remedy an unintentional slight at a previous sight. An example is the story told to me by a dealer about his experience. As he was going through his box of diamonds one year, he found one that he thought was very much overpriced, considering the quality. He called it to the attention of one of the employees of the Syndicate. There is nothing gangsterish about Syndicate men at a sight. They are often from Oxford and Cambridge and almost invariably polite, sometimes rather coldly so. In this case, the employee listened attentively. Then he took the diamond, hefted it, studied it. He pronounced it worth the price. The dealer had no intention of refusing a box because of the one stone. And it is against the rules to refuse a stone. So he ended his protest quickly, took his box and departed. At the next sight his allotment was more than he had any right to expect. He was convinced that the Syndicate had chosen this way to rectify the previous sight's injustice.

There was another dealer who was at his first sight and very excited. Like a number of sightholders, he was the second generation on the list. He took the box, studied every diamond very carefully. The veterans look at the big ones and then sample the rest. He was displeased with a number of the stones. He insisted on seeing one of the executives. He was led into an office. A small man rose from a desk, greeted him, shook his hand, asked about his father, and the young man was led from the room.

Five weeks later he was again at the sight. This time he made no complaint about the quantity or quality of his allocation. As he was about to leave, he was accosted by one of the employees who escorted him to the office he had visited in his protest at the previous sight. The man asked him what he thought of his allocation. He responded that he was pleased. The executive patted him on the shoulder and as the young dealer was about to leave, the executive took from a jacket pocket a large diamond of good quality and gave it to him. The diamond would have to be paid for, of course. But it was a good buy. The Syndicate was teaching the young man a lesson. He never complained again.

It is very probable that in the vast majority of cases in which a dealer finds diamonds that are greatly overpriced, or feels that the general level of the quality in his box is lower than it should be, there was no malice intended. De Beers people point out that in sorting its diamonds for the boxes there are five grades, covering more than two thousand classifications. Every effort, they say, is made to distribute fairly. There are other instances where dealers feel their allocation has been held down unjustly and it may turn out that a number of allocations were held down at this sight because the Syndicate decided it wanted to curtail the supply in the market.

In some cases, however, there is no doubt that the reduced allocation is deliberate. This can happen if the sightholder has violated the cardinal rule of De Beers to sell diamonds into the retail market for jewelry rather than for speculation. The sightholder may have been selling too much of his supply to other dealers as a means of making a higher profit. That the Syndicate should know this presupposes an incredible espionage system. But on Forty-seventh Street—and in other diamond marts—there is no doubt that the Syndicate has ways of learning everything.

To begin with, the Syndicate makes a very thorough investigation of anyone who applies for admission to the inner circle of sightholders. Many are turned down for years before being finally accepted. The investigation of the applicant requires him to show, for instance, in addition to years in the business, a strong financial responsibility. For this, the Syndicate talks to others who have dealt with him. With diamond clubs at all major diamond centers—outside the United States, they are called bourses—this access is not too difficult. De Beers also has close connections with the banks that extend credit to dealers.

One of the most serious offenses for a sightholder is to sell "in the dark." In the middle and late seventies, as the value of diamonds rose so sharply, some sightholders barely glanced at the contents of their boxes. When they received the boxes, they sold them unopened to another dealer, making a 25 percent profit. Any sightholder known to have done this was almost certain to lose his invitation to sights. There are also those who pay scant attention to their boxes at the sights because they feel there is little they can do about it. One dealer told me that "for all the good I do I could send an errand boy."

There are, however, three important reasons to go to the sights. First, is the possible bonus. No one knows when his box will contain a large diamond—more than 14.8 carats—and of good quality. The sightholder has the right to decline this stone without prejudice. Refusal is rare in days of soaring prices for quality diamonds. A second reason for not passing up sights is that dealers from all over the world are in London about the same time and get a chance to do business.

But even if the sightholder does nothing but pick up his box and pay for it, it is wise not to pass up sights.

"It is good to be seen," a dealer told me. "If you are not seen it could count against you in future allocations. You can't be too careful about giving offense."

The road that led to this most efficient cartel began in anarchy, a colorful and boisterous diamond rush that acquired the term "Diggers Democracy." For sheer vigor, independence, wild competition—and larceny—the early years of the diamond rush rivaled anything seen in the gold rushes of California or the Yukon. For in gold rushes, a nugget, even a large one, was not enough to make a fortune. A lode was needed. A rich strike. But in the diamond fields, one large diamond, something a man could hold in his hand easily, a piece of carbon weighing less than a quarter of a pound, could mean a life of affluence. There were many instances, in the early years of the diamond rush in South Africa during the late 1860s and 1870s, of diamonds found lying in the open. No tedious digging and panning required. These were alluvial diamonds.

The first great diamond strike set the tone for limitless optimism. In 1866, on a farm in South Africa, along the bank of the Orange River, Daniel Jacobz's young son, Erasmus, was playing, as he often did, with the shiny stones. He found a particularly pretty one and brought it into the house to his mother. She kept it there and one day she showed it to a visiting neighbor, Schalk van Niekerk, whose hobby was collecting unusual stones. He passed it along to a trader, John O'Reilly, who was going to Grahamstown. He showed it to a geologist, Dr. W. G. Atherstone. It was identified as a diamond weighing 21.25 carats. Eventually, it became known as the Eureka.

Several other diamonds, much smaller and less valuable, were found. But the resultant outburst of prospecting was unsuccessful and the first finds were dismissed as pure luck. In 1869, another unusual stone, bigger than the first one, was offered to van Niekerk by an African witch doctor. He had no way of knowing whether this rough, but glistening stone was a diamond or was even of any great value. But he took a chance. He bought it for everything he possessed: five hundred sheep, ten oxen, and a horse. It proved to be a diamond of 83.25 carats, which, when cut and polished, was a 47.70-carat jewel that was given the name "Star of South Africa." Schalk van Niekerk was a rich man and the diamond rush began. From all over the world the daring men came. It is believed that in 1870, some 50,000 persons pushed into this arid African area as rich diamond mines were discovered. Claims were staked so closely that streets collapsed. An account of life in the diamond fields in the New York World spoke of a dance on graveled floor in a topless tent, attended by 140 men and 16 women. Male attire ranged from swallowtail to work clothes, and music was supplied by accordion, flute, violin, and drum. During this period, according to *The Story of De Beers*, by Hedley A. Chilvers, even the president of Pretoria worked a claim.

One of those in Africa at that time was an eighteen-year-old Englishman named Cecil Rhodes, who had come to live with his brother because of ill health. His response to diamond fever was lukewarm. He thought cotton farming had a better future. The son of a vicar, he considered diamond mining a vocation for gamblers and similar types. His older brother, Herbert, was more venturesome, and Cecil Rhodes, who was not doing well as a farmer in Natal, joined him on an ox wagon, into which he piled many books, including a Greek lexicon, for the trek to New Rush, the raffish mining town that eventually became Kimberley. According to John Flint's biography, *Cecil Rhodes*, the future empire builder's main reason for making money was so he could afford to attend Oxford. With some 10,000 pounds he went to the University. Poor health forced him back to Africa, but he later returned to Oxford and, in 1881, after a student career that was not very distinguished, he received a pass degree.

His stay at Oxford was particularly important because it was there he listened to a lecture by John Ruskin extolling British imperialism, a conviction that was to grow into a veritable religion and make him almost unique among the diamond pioneers. His main desire for wealth was not to enjoy luxury, but to use it to create an Anglo-Saxon empire that would rule the world. It was this dream, steeped in snobbery and bigotry, that drove Rhodes to prepare the way for the first diamond cartel, the predecessor of the present Syndicate.

Rhodes's "Confession of Faith," printed in its entirety as an appendix to Mr. Flint's book, says, in part:

"Why should we not form a secret society with but one object, the furtherance of the British Empire and the bringing of the whole uncivilized world under British rule for the recovery of the United States, for the making of the Anglo-Saxon race but one empire. What a dream, but yet it is probable, it is possible. . . . Africa is still lying ready for us. It is our duty to take it. It is our duty to seize every opportunity of acquiring more territory and we should keep this one idea steadily before our eyes that more territory simply means more of the Anglo-Saxon race, more of the best of the most human, most honorable race the world possesses."

This was written in 1877, when Rhodes was twenty-four. It became a basic motive for his subsequent establishment of the Rhodes scholarships that bring to Oxford gifted Americans. Since Rhodes knew his health was poor, he was in a hurry to amass wealth through the formation of a diamond cartel that would enable him to help spread the gospel of world domination by Anglo-Saxons.

The road to monopoly was opened as the alluvial deposits became played out. The choice was to give up scrabbling in the yellow soil or take a chance on digging into the "blue ground" far below, an operation that would require a great deal of capital for equipment. Many gave up. Others combined claims and worked them jointly. But even these groups lacked the money and machinery to get hundreds of feet underground. Two men had built up the funds for such an enterprise. One was Rhodes. The other was an aggressive Jew from a London slum who had survived in Kimberley by street-peddling, trading, buying and selling claims. This was Barnet Isaacs, who had changed his name to Barney Barnato, a merry, flamboyant type, ideally suited to the rough-and-tumble atmosphere of the diamond town. Though uneducated, he prided himself on his ability to recite the Hamlet soliloquy—standing on his hands. Unlike Rhodes, who was cool, unsociable, not much interested in women, Barnato was popular, congenial, a man who enjoyed spending as well as making money. Barnato was not interested in empire-building. Yet this was the man Rhodes had to defeat or win over to create the first diamond cartel. But he could not beat Barnato, who by 1880 had formed the Kimberley Central Mining Company, the biggest in Kimberley. By 1885 Barnato was richer than Rhodes.

Rhodes would probably never have created his cartel except for another Jew, Alfred Beit, a cultured, subdued, sensitive man, who was imbued with the tradition of keeping one's word. Originally

from a middle-class Hamburg family, Beit had served an apprenticeship in diamond work in Amsterdam, then the major diamond
center in the world. He probably knew more about diamonds than
anyone in Africa when he arrived there in 1875, to work for his
cousin, who had a diamond-buying firm. In the showdown between
the De Beers Company controlled by Rhodes and Barnato's Kimberley Central, Beit made Rhodes's victory possible.

The fight broke out into the open in 1887, when Rhodes started
to buy stock in Barnato's company. A large bloc was owned by two
other companies, the second of which was French. Rhodes lost out
in his dealings with the first company because the holder of those
stocks considered him dishonorable. To buy the French company
required about 1.5 million pounds. Rhodes did not have this
amount of money because he had spent a great deal buying shares in
Kimberley Central in a vain effort to get control of the Barnato company. Beit, who had financial connections in Europe, advised
Rhodes to seek the support of Lord Rothschild in England. Rothschild extended a loan. But even this was not enough. Once more
Beit rescued Rhodes. Beit persuaded other European financiers to
help Rhodes, convincing them that there was enormous profit in a
diamond cartel. In 1888, after a heated contest between Rhodes and
Barnato for Kimberley shares that sent the price from fourteen to
forty-nine pounds a share in weeks, Rhodes acquired control. But
Rhodes still needed help from Barnato to give the new company a
charter that would extend its power far beyond the diamond business— to railroads, land, and anything else required to build an empire. Here Rhodes found a method that had nothing to do with
money. He realized that Barnato, the Whitechapel Jew, deeply resented being barred from the Kimberley Club, an exclusive organization that did not allow Jews, so Rhodes invited him there. Despite
the anger of the other members, he nominated him for memberhip
and won. Barnato wanted more. He wanted to be named, along with
Rhodes and Beit, a lifetime governor of the new company. Rhodes
acceded. Finally, after a night-long meeting, Barnato gave in and on
March 13, 1888, the new De Beers Consolidated Mines was regis-

tered, with almost unlimited powers and a subsequent promise by
Rhodes to the stockholders of the old company that the new one
would be "the richest, the greatest and the most powerful company
the world has ever seen." It was a long leap from the 16,000-acre
farm that the De Beers brothers had bought in 1860 for fifty pounds
and then, because they hated the disorder and squalor of nearby
diamond miners, the Boers (the word derived from the Dutch "boor"
meaning farmer) sold it in 1871 for 6,000 guineas. It has been estimated that the value of diamonds taken from the De Beers farm
since it became a mine has been over two billion dollars.

It was for De Beers Consolidated Mines that Rhodes dissolved
the Kimberley Central, selling its assets to the new company. In
1890 the diamond cartel was formed to control the supply of diamonds in the world and the prices as well. The credit went to Rhodes, but it was Beit who did the organizing. In *Cecil Rhodes: The Co-
lossus of Southern Africa*, the authors, J. G. Lockhart and C. M.
Wodehouse, in appraising the role of Beit, say: "The world was un-
aware of his [Beit's] true character and, while he lived, did him a
great deal less than justice."

Thereafter, Rhodes became increasingly concerned with using
De Beers to build his empire. He became deeply involved in politics
and, in the process, increased the tensions between the Boers and the
British. In 1880 he became prime minister and a virtual dictator of
Cape Colony. In this capacity he became a key conspirator in an
aborted effort to seize the Boer-dominated Transvaal for Great Britain. This failure became so embarrassing for England that he was
forced to resign as prime minister in 1896, and the next year he was
sharply criticized by a committee of the House of Commons. Thereafter, he spent most of his time developing the new nation of Rhode-
sia that had been named in his honor. In the Boer War, which broke
out in 1899, he was, for a time, in command of some troops and was
besieged in Kimberley. He was considered a nuisance by the British
military and eased out. He died in 1902, at the age of forty-nine, a
few months before the war ended. The wealth he had accumulated
he used to set up the Rhodes scholarships and public services.

A few months after Rhodes died, there arrived in South Africa a young man who was to remake the Rhodes cartel for the twentieth century, giving it the basic form it has today. The newcomer, unlike Rhodes, knew a great deal about diamonds and was interested in diamonds as a business. He was more concerned in building a corporate empire than a political one. Ernest—eventually Sir Ernest— Oppenheimer came to the heart of the diamond world at a time when the Rhodes concept of cartel was already becoming inadequate and was headed for almost certain disaster because of its lack of vision. It took Ernest Oppenheimer more than a quarter of a century to build the diamond cartel he wanted. In the process, he first built his own diamond company, expanded on a large scale into gold, joined—and broke away from—the De Beers–operated cartel and, eventually, won control of De Beers and built the Syndicate and business his son now controls.

Ernest Oppenheimer, like Beit and Barnato, would have been at ease on Forty-seventh Street. A German Jew, one of ten children of a cigar merchant, he was born in 1880, in Friedburg. He followed two older brothers, Bernhard and Louis, to England to work for a diamond firm called Dunkelsbuhler and Company, founded by Anton Dunkelsbuhler, who had been in the South African diamond fields in the 1870s. When Ernest joined the company in 1896, at the age of sixteen, he learned about diamonds in the traditional fashion, by sorting them. He had what Forty-seventh Street calls "the feel" or "the eye" for diamonds. He also, it developed, had what Forty-seventh Street calls "a nose" for business. For six years he learned about diamonds. Then, in 1902, the year after he became a naturalized English citizen, and shortly after the Boer War ended, his company sent him to South Africa as its representative. By this time the cartel was not only functioning, but had come under criticism in England from those who attacked "monopoly capitalism" in Africa. Gold had been discovered in Africa in the Witwatersrand and, by 1902, gold production was valued at more than seven million pounds, compared to the diamond output valued at slightly less than five million pounds. The firm that young Oppenheimer represented had become sufficiently important to rate a 12 percent quota in the Syndicate's diamond allocations.

The year after Oppenheimer came to Africa, he realized that De Beers was not as smart as it should be. It was then headed by an Anglo-Saxon type that Rhodes adored, Francis Oats. The first of Oats's colossal blunders was to disparage the value of the Premier mine discovered at Elandsfontein, near Pretoria. He said it was "salted" and declined to take it into the cartel, despite pleas by Beit that it had enormous potential. The Premier became one of the most productive mines in the world and set up its own selling organization.

The next mistake by Oats came at the worst possible time. In 1907 a serious depression hit the United States, which was buying some 70 percent of Africa's diamond production. The ensuing slump, as it spread around the world, hit the diamond business particularly hard. On the heels of the falling diamond prices came the discovery of alluvial diamond fields in South West Africa. Oats called these deposits "superficial." But they were greater than those of South Africa. Several firms withdrew from the cartel. A German-based company, the Diamond Regie, was set up to handle diamond sales from South West Africa.

Though business improved by the end of 1909, ending the worst of the diamond crisis, it was clear that the cartel was shaky. Several of the companies in the cartel had lost money. Some mines had closed. For the first time since the cartel was formed there was a lack of confidence in world financial capitals in the future of the diamond industry. New leadership was needed.

During these years the reputation of Oppenheimer grew. He had been quick to realize the value of the alluvial deposits in South West Africa and scoffed at the De Beers appraisal of it as a "transient competitor." Finally, in 1914, French interests who had substantial stock in De Beers, sent him to South West Africa. His purpose was to discuss the possibility of cooperation between the cartel and Regie. He had just finished three years as mayor of Kimberley in which he had displayed a talent for working with divergent factions. Oppenheimer seemed to be making progress in winning over Regie when World War I began and it became impossible to continue negotiating in the German colony with a German company.

Convinced that De Beers was too sluggish, he quietly began to form a company that would rival De Beers and open a path for him to win control of De Beers and establish a far more efficient cartel. He needed capital. One source was J. P. Morgan. Another was the Rothschilds. By 1917 he was corresponding with Herbert Hoover, suggesting the formation of a new company and seeking American capital. He knew that Hoover was connected with Morgan interests. Through Hoover, he wrote to others close to Morgan. On September 25, 1917, he formed the Anglo American Corporation, with J. P. Morgan and Company among the large shareholders and capitalization of one million pounds.

This company had a gimmick far ahead of its time—tax advantage. Its profits could be taxed only by South Africa and that government could tax only what was earned in South Africa. Any business it engaged in elsewhere would not be taxed.

As soon as World War I ended, in 1918, Anglo American Corp. began moving strongly into South West Africa to gain the acquisition of gold interests in other parts of Africa. In 1920 a company formed by Oppenheimer, called Consolidated Diamond Mines of South-West Africa, Ltd., took over the German producers in that country. As part of this takeover, Oppenheimer agreed to sell the South African diamonds through the De Beers cartel. By 1921 he was in a position to write to American associates that, in addition to increasing gold holdings, he planned to create "step by step, a leading position in the diamond world, thus concentrating by degrees in the corporation's hands the position which the pioneers of the diamond industry formerly occupied. . . . It is quite evident to my mind that eventually an amalgamation of the big four diamond producers [De Beers, Premier, Jagersfontein, and Consolidated Diamonds] will be brought about and I see no reason, if we continue our diamond policy, why we should not play a leading role in such an operation."

Nevertheless, Oppenheimer's company was not in the cartel.

He knew that of two companies with power in the cartel—Barnato Brothers and Breitmeyer and Company—the latter was opposed to him. But in 1924 he joined the cartel anyway. Unfortunately, the friction was too great and he was expelled. In 1925 he was still strongly in favor of a cartel, but one that worked according to plan. At the annual meeting of Anglo American, he said: "We are now, and always will be, prepared to assist in bringing about the restoration of the practice of effecting sales through one channel."

The Oppenheimer strategy was to woo Barnato Brothers into joining him in the formation of a new syndicate. Barney Barnato was long dead—he committed suicide by jumping off a ship—but his family still held the company. With Barnato Brothers on his side, Oppenheimer, representing both companies, offered to buy the entire production of De Beers. After hard bargaining, De Beers yielded. Now Oppenheimer was stronger than the cartel that had expelled him. His next step was to take over the old syndicate. He did this on October 22, 1925. But he was still not a member of the board of De Beers, the company he had long wanted to dominate. The year after he formed the new syndicate he was named to the board of De Beers and three years later, shortly after the stock market crash of 1929, he was named chairman of the board.

Now he was ready to shape a syndicate that would be able to stabilize the diamond industry enough to withstand even serious slumps. The Great Depression of the 1930s was the perfect test. Not only did the depression drive down diamond prices, but the industry was also shaken by the discovery of new large sources of alluvial diamonds in the Lichtenburg area of western Transvaal in the coastal areas of Namaqualand.

This was his time to prove a statement he had made in 1927 to stockholders of Anglo American, telling them they need not fear new diamond sources. "The danger to the security of the diamond industry," he said, "is not the discovery of a new and rich diamond field, but the irrational exploitation of it."

With the courage and support of the Morgan and Rothschild interests, Oppenheimer had worked out, early in 1929, plans for a new syndicate to be called the Diamond Trading Company, to include directors chosen by Morgan and the Rothschilds. When the crash and depression hit and the future seemed dismal, Oppenheimer was ready. To him the only way to avert disaster for the diamond industry, with producers dumping diamonds on the market and the Soviet Union choosing this time to unload large amounts of crown jewels, was to buy and hold.

During 1930 and 1931, despite the deepest pessimism, Oppenheimer directed purchases of diamonds by his new syndicate and curtailed production. Looking back on this critical period in 1953, he said that in those years he bought some thirteen million pounds worth of diamonds at depression prices. When conditions improved and the diamonds were sold at the higher rates "we reaped a golden harvest." The Syndicate's cash resources were increased by some forty million pounds.

To guard against the recurrence of a price collapse in diamonds, the Diamond Producers' Association was formed in 1933, this time to include important diamond producers and arrange for the sale of its members' output through the Diamond Trading Company, Ltd., which took the yield of alluvial fields.

"The Diamond Trading Company," he said several years later, "therefore handles approximately 95 percent of the total world production of diamonds, and it will be appreciated that, although the ideal of 100 percent has not yet been achieved, we are nearer to it now than at any time in the past, and what I may call the 'uncontrolled' diamond production is really a negligible part of the trade."

When, in 1957, Sir Ernest died, he had made his syndicate fully operative, had expanded enormously the wealth and power of both De Beers and Anglo American, and, perhaps most important, had given his son some twenty years of instruction and experience to rule. Harry Frederick Oppenheimer, born 1908 in Kimberley, went to school in Johannesburg until he was thirteen, and then was sent to England, returning in 1931, after graduating from Oxford. He had the unique advantage of being able to watch his father lead the empire through the depression that destroyed so many huge businesses.

He left his father's side only to volunteer at the outbreak of World War II, serving as an intelligence officer in front-line reconnaissance with a South African armored-car regiment of the British Eighth Army in the Libyan desert. One of the lessons that stayed with him as he saw his father forced to sell properties to save others in the depression, was to have substantial cash or very liquid assets on hand at all times. Another point that was driven home from the years with his father was that no matter how carefully a leader plans, he must be flexible enough to adapt to the unexpected.

He demonstrated his leadership—that extraordinary combination of patience and pressure, of hard thrusts and devious persuasion—in working out an arrangement with the Soviet Union and in halting the speculative orgy in Israel. He displayed statesmanship in courting the favor of important African blacks before they were national leaders and in walking the tightrope between bigoted whites and radical blacks. He has taken precautions for the future by expanding some Syndicate operations into nations outside Africa. Synthetic diamonds are made in Sweden and Ireland. The enterprise he heads now is in oil, gas, and chemicals in Canada. It has also moved into computer service and insurance.

In explaining why Anglo American was investing in countries outside Africa, he once said: "You have got to assess the risk and obviously if you are getting into places where the risk looks high, you must be sure that the profit potential is also high. The trouble in so many countries today is that the political risk is increasing and the potentiality for profit is diminishing at the same time."

He took his fling at politics, serving in the seat in the South African Parliament that his father had held, often attacking the government's racist attitudes.

Considering the changes in the huge organization he heads, he has said: "I think our real problem, being now at the 'respectable' state, is to remain pioneering and retain the speed of decision."

In his personal life, for all his admiration for his father, his lifestyle is somewhat different. Though he and his wife, the former Bridget McCall, live in the spacious house built by his father that overlooks the rolling country near Johannesburg, the dark paneling has been altered to white walls. He raises and races horses, but is not a big bettor. He has some Impressionist paintings, some first editions, but could hardly be considered a serious collector in either field.

One day, in 1975, musing about power as an offshoot of big business, he told an interviewer from *Optima*, a Johannesburg magazine: "I don't think that business has much power anywhere today. Personally, I'm not keen on power in the abstract sense, and I'm not in the least interested in controlling something just for the sake of controlling it. But I do want the power to do big, difficult things."

6

BEHIND THE DIAMOND CURTAIN

What the home-run hitter is to baseball and the singing star is to the Broadway musical, the big dealer and manufacturer are to the diamond business. The Syndicate sets the basic rules. But the major dealers and manufacturers, almost obsessive in their work habits, set the tempo, fuel the excitement, and bring mystery to the diamond world. When a million-dollar diamond starts New York's diamond quarter humming like a diamond saw, it is one of these men who has bought it. When one of them walks into a bank, exuding self-confidence in his expensive, well-tailored suit, he gets an effusive greeting and quick action. He doesn't wait in line. When he goes to the Diamond Dealers Club, his visit to the crowded, noisy, main floor is often perfunctory before he goes upstairs to gather with his peers in the comfort of the boardroom.

In the diamond enclave of New York—and other major diamond marts—these are the men of status, money, and permanence who give to the frantic business a core of stability. The smaller dealers, the brokers, the men and women of the jewelry exchanges, the coveys of small traders who live by wits and energy are largely dependent upon them for the basic supply of diamonds that keep them in action. On Forty-seventh Street and the spillovers of diamond business on Forty-eighth and Forty-sixth streets, and along the few blocks of nearby Fifth Avenue, they know—and watch—one another. When they meet, they are courteous, even beaming. But in private they are often inclined to be qualified in appraising each other.

They will say: "He's a good man. But not the man his father was." Or: "I remember when he used to come to me to buy a few stones to stay alive." Or: "He does a lot of business. But he talks big."

In the trade, a fuss is sometimes made about the distinction between dealer and manufacturer. On this top level, however, the differences can be hazy because all the important dealers usually do some manufacturing and the manufacturers generally do a considerable amount of dealing. The distinction is really one of degree. A firm that cuts most of its rough stones at its own factories to sell mainly to retailers is a manufacturer. A company that may have some of its own cutters, sell some of its cut diamonds to retailers, but uses mainly freelance cutters and sells most of its stones to other dealers, is a dealer. But when the manufacturer and the dealer both sell to other dealers—and buy from them as well—and almost certainly sell to diamond investment firms, if not directly to investors, the distinctions tend to blur. What is important is that in the major markets they are in competition for the "goods" and this, as much as the barbed humor of the business, may account for their almost instinctive putdowns of one another that always remind me of the exchange I heard one morning in a Forty-seventh Street restaurant. The place was crowded for the breakfast crush, with diamond people pressed side by side on stools, shouting orders, competing even here.

One of the customers, as he snatched up his check, snapped at the harried counterman: "Why are the French fries cut in such large slices?"

The counterman retorted before the customer was off the stool. "Because everyone here has such a big mouth."

The big dealers and manufacturers are not shy. They would not last long in the business if they were. But they could give the C.I.A. lessons in secrecy.

For instance, after the murder of Jaroslawicz in 1977, the police were particularly concerned with the possibility that organized crime had moved into the diamond industry. They found nothing to substantiate these wild media rumors. Yet a few years earlier, in a case that did not involve violence but millions of dollars, there were strong indications that organized crime, or a powerful gang, had muscled into the diamond business of New York. The police were never told, and there has been no recurrence.

A well-known diamond firm with a good reputation began increasing its purchases of diamonds. This, in itself, was not a matter of concern in the diamond district. Quite often a company will take this sort of gamble, even when prices are very stable. The purchases are made on credit, primarily from big dealers and manufacturers. So it did not arouse suspicion in the world of mazel und brucha and the handshake. After a while, however, as purchases continued without payment, some of the sellers began to press for partial payment. The diamond buyer was apologetic, but promised payments soon. The creditors agreed to wait a bit longer. But eventually some of the dealers and manufacturers began to compare notes and realized that this company had bought millions of dollars worth of diamonds and, so far as they could see, had paid for nothing. Several of them descended on the head of the firm. He finally admitted the truth. He could not pay them. He had tried, before going on the buying spree, to get a loan from several banks without success, whereupon he approached usurers, who are invariably mob-controlled. Their interest rate, surprisingly, was not as high as he had expected. This should have warned him. He borrowed from them, and bought diamonds. But instead of letting him pay off the debt as he sold some of the diamonds, they insisted he keep buying more diamonds. How much he bought no one knows. It ran into the millions, perhaps as high as ten million.

The dealers and manufacturers, when he told them this story, insisted he start paying them at once. He then told them the business was no longer his. He was just a front for the men who had loaned him the money. He pleaded with them for more time to persuade his backers to pay for some of the diamonds. Within a week, tough-looking men visited some of the more aggressive creditors and told them it was better to be unpaid than dead. The firm that had borrowed the money went bankrupt. A few of the creditors thought of taking the matter before the Diamond Dealers Club. There are rumors that officers of the club were threatened. There was no hearing at the club. The bankrupt diamond men did not return to the business. No one went to the police or the district attorney.

After this bankruptcy, the creditors began to wonder about others—much smaller ones—in other parts of the country. Quietly they made thorough inquiries. They found no evidence of mob activity in these failures.

Nevertheless, they decided to form a watchdog committee of important dealers and manufacturers to guard against future mob incursions. This group met periodically and discussed diamond firms that had been making large purchases. Were they paying back? In full? In part? Did their credit seem good? Were they selling what they had bought or just building inventory? The idea was good but there was one serious flaw. A tradition, a lifetime of guile and competition, made it difficult for all of them to be entirely honest. Thus, one man, when asked if some diamond merchant should be given more credit, would reply that he was having trouble with this purchaser when, in fact, he was doing well with the man. But he knew that what he said would discourage others from extending credit, thus allowing him to do more business with the purchaser at a better price since he was the major supplier. On the other hand, one of the group might give good marks to the credit of a man he thought was wobbly. By doing this, he would be assuming that the others would then give this man credit and the man would be able to repay him more quickly. Some heated arguments eventually broke out. The group disbanded. The diamond dealers and manufacturers became more secretive than ever.

Another deep secret in the business involves one of the top diamond dealers.

Following a million-dollar diamond robbery at Kennedy Airport, the police drifted into the diamond area, looking for clues. Within a few weeks, agents from the F.B.I. began questioning important dealers and manufacturers. In particular, they were interested in the whereabouts of a specific diamond dealer. He was not one of the big ones, but well-known and active. The diamond men told the F.B.I. they had not seen him in the area for a couple of weeks. This was true. Some of the men who were questioned knew that this dealer had left the country within a couple of weeks of the robbery. They were quite sure he was living in Israel. Of this they said nothing. They did not think he had committed the crime or had had anything to do with planning it. But some of them thought that this dealer may have fenced the diamonds. One estimate was that he had paid $150,000 for diamonds worth about a million dollars. They assumed he had gone abroad with the gems and would dispose of them at his leisure—at a considerable profit. This, too, they did not tell the F.B.I., though it was clear to them that the F.B.I. was thinking along the same lines. About eighteen months later, gossip drifted into the diamond district that a very wealthy relative of the absent dealer had died leaving him a fortune. The rumor was that he was planning to return to New York. The word was that he was doing business in Antwerp for cash. Several months later, the dealer was back in New York. He rented a sizable office and furnished it well. He had no trouble paying for the diamonds he bought. He allowed credit to others. His own credit rose. He became one of the best-known dealers in the diamond center. He is highly respected except by the few who were questioned about him by the F.B.I. And they, too, do business with him since his credit is good.

The major diamond dealers and manufacturers knew about the missing dealer's renewed activity in Antwerp because they are always in touch with all the important diamond centers in existence, not just by Telex to the Antwerp office, but by frequent trips abroad. These are the men who give international reach to the sliver of mid-Manhattan that makes New York City the major diamond market in the world. Jet lag is as much a part of their lives as the loupe. A simple way to discover the global range of these nabobs of the diamond industry is to try to meet with them on short notice. In at least half the cases you will be told they are "out of town." When will they be back? Hard to tell. A week. Maybe two. Perhaps even a month. You will get the same answer from the receptionist behind bullet-proof glass. You are not getting a runaround. He is really away and nobody knows when he will be back. Not even his wife, who has had to learn to live with uncertainty and fear for his safety.

The main reason there is so much uncertainty about the duration of a trip is that it is often a matter of improvisation. To these men, "out of town" is not Miami, Chicago, or Los Angeles. It is London, Antwerp, Tel Aviv, Johannesburg, Moscow, Bombay, or Hong Kong. It can mean side trips to Paris or Monrovia, to Geneva or an obscure village in India. It can be Amsterdam, Tokyo, Rome, Cannes. Or the Central African Republic, Sierra Leone, Namibia, Angola. Food can range from rancid mouthfuls to gourmet banquets. All they can be sure of when they go "out of town" is that the tension will be constant. It is fairly normal for these diamond leaders to spend millions of dollars buying and selling diamonds on a single trip.

Publicity is to be shunned for reasons other than security when they are on the move. There are, inherent in the legitimate business of buying and selling diamonds, such intangibles as smuggling, bribery, tax evasion, any of which may be decisive in making a deal. Diamond men accept this as a part of the business. New York diamond dealers have a colorful way of saying someone was engaged in smuggling diamonds. They will say: "He submarined the goods." In Antwerp, one of the crossroads of the world for smugglers—where the smuggling of diamonds has been estimated at millions of dollars per day—the diamond people around the Pelikanstraat say that the definition of a liar is "a diamond dealer who swears he never had a mistress and never sold in the black market." The antics of the habitués of Israel's diamond center at Ramat Gan were described by the pun-loving William Farrell, when he was covering Israel for the *New York Times* as "the carat and the shtik."

The start of these trips is usually routine. Very expensive, but routine. It begins with the plane hop to London for the Syndicate sights we have discussed. For some of them the London trip, though they have good accomodations and few problems, is a bit irritating. There is, some of them think, a discernible attitude of condescension among some of the Oxford-and Cambridge-educated Syndicate employees. Far more annoying to a number of American dealers is the presence of the so-called London broker they would just as soon not have. To them the fees they pay the London brokers are, at the very least, an expensive imposition.

Every dealer with a sighthold must have a London broker whose job it is to be the liaison between the Syndicate and the sightholder. The sightholder pays the London broker one percent of the value of his allotments. Since a sightholder's allotments of diamonds for the ten sights each year can run to $10 million, this means that the London broker can earn a fee of up to $100,000. But the broker can represent more than one sightholder. American dealers say these brokers have to be approved by the Syndicate.

What do the brokers do for these fat fees? There was a time, say the dealers, when the brokers earned their keep. They would argue in behalf of a dealer to have a dealer's allotment increased. They would plead with the Syndicate to lower the price of a dealer's sight box or increase the quality of some of the stones. Sometimes the broker would win for the dealer a reduction in the overall price for the allotment or get a larger allotment for a subsequent sight. Unfortunately, the sightholder can no longer bargain with the Syndicate.

So far as disgruntled dealers and manufacturers are concerned, the London broker is little more than a glorified clerk. He sends word to the sightholder of the date of the next sight and asks him to submit, in dollars, his allocation request. The sightholder does so. Then, several days before the sight, the London broker is told by the Syndicate what the dealer's allotment is and he forwards this information to the sightholder. The sightholder cables the money to a London bank. At the end of each year, the sightholder sends to his London broker a synopsis of his previous year's business. Presumably, the London broker uses the synopsis to try to win an increase in the sightholder's future allotments. But American sightholders feel the institution of the London broker could easily be abolished. It is true that the sightholders pass along these fees in the sale of their diamonds. They just resent what they think is a racket, particularly when they know that in London there is a tendency to circulate gossip about the uncouth behavior of American sightholders.

Antwerp is the next stop for at least 90 percent of the Americans who go to the London sights, and it is much more interesting. Here, along the narrow streets near the railroad station, where new buildings stand beside the old, and narrow streets wind near wide thoroughfares, the whole diamond world meets: Arabs, Zambians, Zairans, Russians, South Africans, Israelis, Americans, Dutch, French, Italians, Indians, Japanese, and Chinese. From wherever there are diamond mines or a substantial diamond business, representatives turn up in Antwerp. At first glance everything is serene and sedate. Security is tight, with the plainclothes police, uniformed guards, and the most sophisticated alarms. Holdups and violence are very rare. For those who come from New York, with its pervasive fear of crime, Antwerp streets are a relief. It is a pleasure to do business here. The diamond clubs are spacious and comfortable. The diamond people are thoroughly professional. For some, it is a return to home with visits to some of the diamond merchants who live in the quarter. Of Antwerp's 200,000 only 13,000 are Jewish. Before Hitler there were more than 50,000 Jews. After World War II, the Belgian government sent emissaries to London and New York to persuade Jewish diamond dealers to return to Antwerp. In some cases they did so, for the Belgians, as much as they could, resisted Nazi anti-Semitism, hiding Jews, or helping others to flee when they could no longer save them.

In Antwerp, American dealers and manufacturers get their first strong sampling of Russian diamond dealing. For the Soviet Union, while it sells its rough stones through the Syndicate as we have seen, uses Antwerp as its major outlet for cut stones. Americans seem agreed that the Russians are very tough bargainers, perhaps too inflexible, when the buyer in Antwerp can do considerable comparison shopping. These alternatives are what add so much spice to Antwerp's diamond business. Apart from the substantial local trade in the writing of phony invoices for those who want to beat taxes, there is the flood of smuggled goods.

First, there is a large volume of rough diamonds smuggled into Antwerp from Africa, and delivered to the local offices of diamond firms that have their headquarters in India. The stones may be cut in Antwerp. But it is much more likely that they will be smuggled into India by passengers or crew on commercial planes. Since India specializes in cutting the small stones known as "melees," an industry in diamonds that is truly cottage has grown up in the town of Surat, a few hours drive, mostly on dirt roads from Bombay, or less than an hour by light plane. The cutters of Surat work as independent contractors. Their numbers run into the thousands. After the stones are cut, they are returned to Bombay and smuggled out again, if possible, on commercial airlines to Antwerp.

Less complicated, and in even greater volume, is the smuggling of diamonds from Antwerp to the west. Most of the important Antwerp diamond firms have accounts in banks in Amsterdam. People from these companies quite frequently take parcels of diamonds, get into a car, and drive across the border into the Netherlands. The extensive smuggling conceals assets for tax purposes. There are no import or export duties in Belgium or the Netherlands on diamonds, and the customs men at the border are not eager to look for them. An American familiar with this operation tells me: "It is a lot easier to smuggle diamonds across the border into Holland than [it is to smuggle] cheese. Their main concern is dairy products." Once in

Holland, the motorists take the diamonds to their bank and the bank arranges to mail the diamonds to the foreign purchaser, usually in New York. There is still one more wrinkle in the Antwerp diamond business. A number of firms—mostly the larger ones—have accounts with banks in Liechtenstein, the lovely tax haven. Diamonds can be secreted there or sold without problems. It would be naive to suppose that American dealers do not take advantage of the money-saving operations to be found in Antwerp. Finally, it is generally assumed that Israelis, who have a reputation for resourcefulness, are deeply engaged in diamond-smuggling in and out of Antwerp.

In Antwerp I found one of the so-called London brokers willing to reply to the accusations by American dealers. This broker—his headquarters is Antwerp—admitted that some of his colleagues might not work hard for their clients, but claimed he earned his fees by getting sightholds for his clients and advising them in other ways. "We are moral partners in their business," he said. "We want our clients to grow and be responsible." It was true, he conceded, that he could not have become such a broker without approval by the Syndicate, specifically, the Central Selling Organization. But he insisted that there was no conflict of interests when, as a dependent of the CSO, he was asked by a client to present a grievance to the CSO. "The CSO," he said, "is the God of the diamond industry. It is true that the CSO deliberately promotes a love-hate relationship with its sightholders. How else could they instill the fear that is necessary so their customers will be concerned with more than just making money; with helping the future of the diamond industry?"

The atmosphere of the diamond clubs in Antwerp is special. Here, there is little of the hubbub and tension of Ramat Gan and Forty-seventh Street. These clubs are calm and diamonds are not displayed here often. In Antwerp, the clubs are where the diamond people meet, talk, have leisurely lunches, and go through exploratory preliminaries to business deals for millions of dollars that will take place later in attractive offices on upper floors, generally over numerous cups of strong coffee. Sometimes, during negotiations, the word "cavallo" may be dropped. A cavallo—Italian for horseman—is one of the most intriguing occupations in the secretive diamond industry. He is usually Italian and works on his own. For a fee that varies with the risk, he will guarantee to smuggle millions of dollars in diamonds from a seller to a buyer, often leaving with the seller large amounts of cash as security until he collects upon delivery. Raoul Delveaux, head of Antwerp's Diamond High Council, when asked about the role of the cavallo, just smiled and shrugged. "We Flemish," he explained, "have been occupied by so many nations, we had to learn to cope with onerous regulations. And so the cavallo has become a part of the business."

It is with mixed feelings that diamond dealers and manufacturers from New York arrive in Israel. As affluent Jews, they have contributed large amounts of money to help Israel. They are proud of Israel's achievements. But as competitors in the international diamond trade, they have reservations. They are reluctant to compete as mercilessly with the Israelis as they would with other nationals—or with one another. At the same time, they are convinced—from observation—that the Israelis will be not just ruthless, but dishonest, at times, in trading.

Still, when the Americans take the road out of the heart of Tel Aviv and see, miles in the distance, the twin skyscrapers of Ramat Gan, the nation's diamond exchange, they are unrestrained in their praise. These two twenty-eight-story buildings are the outgrowth of a few handfuls of Nazi refugees from the Low Countries who came to crowded Petah Tiqva in 1937, when the land was still Palestine. In 1980, when the second of the two buildings went into operation, Israel's diamond industry had surpassed citrus fruits, bringing in more than a billion dollars a year. Fortunately, diamonds are not subject to weather, not perishable, and are sold only for hard currency, or other diamonds.

In the spacious diamond club at Ramat Gan, with its lofty ceiling, tall windows, long library tables, they can't help making comparisons with the dingy Diamond Dealers Club of Forty-seventh Street. Here there is laughter among the men with loupes. There are also many more Japanese and Chinese—a rarity on Forty-seventh

Street. In this club they see men examining diamonds so small that they pick them up by pressing a moist finger to them. New York does not bother cutting such small stones. But a veteran recalls that there was a time when, in Antwerp, there were craftsmen so skillful they could cut perfect stones that were five hundred to the carat. In these buildings, the American traders can roam through the clean offices and corridors, ride high-speed elevators, make phone calls, buy food from carts, josh with people they barely know—all without the slightest sense of fear that is found in New York's diamond section. Their only uneasiness comes as they are about to enter. Here security is very strict—even for Israel, where it is customary to check people when they enter a concert hall, theater, and, sometimes, a supermarket. Bags have to be opened, they pass double doors, electric eyes, TV monitors. But once inside they know they can walk about with pockets full of diamonds, and show them to one another anywhere in the building. Before they leave, they can have diamonds placed in the vaults.

A short distance away are the squat cutting factories, so much cleaner than those in New York. Here is the core of Israel's prodigious cutting industry that is, in a way, as much a triumph as the nation's kibbutzim. But while growing, with constant government support, the industry has been marked by scandals that have made well-informed Americans a bit wary of Israeli diamond deals.

To get the diamond industry started, the government set up an agency that bought rough diamonds in the Central African Republic, which does not market its stones through the Syndicate. Eventually, Israel had offices in Bangi and Monrovia, Liberia—a major market for African smugglers and assorted connivers. The rough diamonds that Israel bought in the Central African Republic were offered to diamond manufacturers who could not get a Syndicate sight, and lacked the credit to get stones from large dealers and manufacturers. There was one condition, however: the purchaser had to set up a cutting factory in Israel and use Israeli workers. For this, he would get the diamonds at a reasonable price and on good credit terms.

For example, a manufacturer might be charged $25,000 for the roughs he bought from the government. He would spend another $5,000 on labor. He would sell the cut stones for $35,000. From this he would pay back the government the $25,000 for the rough stones and the small amount of interest. He would then have a profit of $5,000 on a $25,000 purchase. For Israel, this was good because it brought in American dollars and helped build a diamond industry.

This worked well as long as the manufacturer knew his business. But some manufacturers were incompetent, wasting too much diamond in the cutting. When it came time to sell the diamonds, they might only receive $20,000 instead of the $35,000 paid to a competent manufacturer. They would have to explain to the government why they could not pay back the full amount of the purchase price, let alone the interest. The government, bearing in mind its long-range objective of developing an industry, would assume that he would do better in the future as he and his cutters became more experienced. To keep these manufacturers in business, the government told them to give back the cut diamonds. In return, they would give the manufacturer more rough diamonds. The idea was good. Unfortunately, it did not work either because there were too many incompetent manufacturers, or they did not learn quickly enough. Soon the government had on its hands a large number of cut diamonds.

To sell these diamonds, the government opened an office in New York, sent the diamonds there, telling its operatives the price it wanted for the stones.

Here is where the scandal began, reaching from the New York office into the Israeli government. The government might send to its New York office a parcel of stones and say it wanted $200 a carat. Employees in the New York office knew the stones were worth that amount, and that they could probably get it by hard bargaining. Instead, corrupt employees would send word back to Israel that the best they could do was $180. In this there was connivance with Israeli officials, who returned instructions to accept the $180 a carat. Then, employees in the New York office would offer the diamonds to New

York dealers for $190 a carat, on condition that the check be made out at the rate of $180 a carat, and that they be given $10 a carat in cash. New York dealers would know the diamonds were worth more than $190 a carat, so they would agree. The $10 on each carat would be shared between the corrupt workers in New York and their superiors in Israel. The operation became known, and was abolished.

Nevertheless, it can be argued that even with this dishonesty, the time it bought to build the Israeli diamond industry was important.

Another scandal involved large purchases made by some banks in Japan. Apparently, the Israelis did not check on the credentials of the banks or realize that the banks were not too carefully regulated in some respects. The banks went bankrupt and kept the diamonds. A third scandal surfaced in Tel Aviv in 1978, when the diamond exchange warned members that bank drafts on such institutions as Chase Manhattan and the First National City Bank in New York were being forged in Israel. Millions of dollars worth of diamonds were bought by some Israelis with these forged drafts. Members of the exchange were told to clear suspicious checks before releasing the diamonds.

The reaction of American dealers and manufacturers to such Israeli tactics was summed up for me by a very large American buyer of diamonds.

"We know this thievery and cheating is done only by a very small minority in Israel," he said. "And we have our own bad apples too. We know that Israel is trying to build and how much Israel is dependent on money it gets from diamonds. We contribute heavily in fund drives for Israel and we tell ourselves: 'There but for the grace of God.' Our sympathy for Israel is very strong. We feel a responsibility toward Israel. But we think they should feel some sort of obligation toward us and not cheat."

Since the diamonds that feed the smuggling enterprises of Antwerp and the subterfuges of Israel are from diamond operations in Africa that bypass the Syndicate, American dealers and manufacturers are drawn to African places not on normal tourist runs—Sierra

Leone, Zaire, Angola, Ghana, Guinea, Tanzania, South West Africa-Namibia, the Central African Empire, and Liberia. The flow of smuggled diamonds in Africa is so enormous that, for decades, De Beers has had a large, private police force roaming the continent, not only to root out smugglers, but also to learn which sightholders have been buying from them. The assumption is that sightholders who deal with smugglers will find their allocations cut and may even be dropped from the sights. Consequently, when large American diamond operators venture into Africa, they are especially careful. That they continue to deal with smugglers at all is evidence that competition and the gambling spirit in the diamond industry are more compelling than fear in these nations where bribery and corruption are taken for granted.

The scope of African smuggling operations is indicated by a former member of the De Beers police, known as the International Diamond Security Organization, or IDSO. In his book, *Diamonds Are Dangerous*, J. H. Plessis says that smuggled gem diamonds involve so much money that they helped to finance uprisings in Syria and Algeria. In fact, the huge amounts of smuggled industrial diamonds enabled the Soviet Union to expedite the manufacture of precision tools and instruments to build its H-bomb and other sophisticated weaponry. According to Plessis, in 1956 his superior told him that in trying to track down smugglers he could not count on police cooperation. In his investigations, he wrote, he dealt with bookmakers, tribal chiefs, and respected business men, all of whom were part of smuggling operations. The smuggled diamonds were carried in false heels, body apertures, horse hooves, the grease of auto chassis, infants' feeding bottles, smoking pipes, crutches, and violins. He said he was part of "a whole army" working for De Beers.

A statistical indication of the diamond smuggling in Africa was part of a report that appeared in *Jewelers' Circular-Keystone* in 1979, which observed that while the government of Guinea claims to produce between 600,000 and 700,000 carats a year, the official exports from that country are only 80,000 carats, the assumption being that the rest went to smugglers. The story said that smuggling was so great it "threatened De Beers's control of production."

One of the casualties of the civil strife in Lebanon was the loss of the most delightful of smuggling markets, Beirut—lovely climate, good restaurants, beautiful beaches, excellent living accomodations, efficient banks, and cosmopolitan culture. It has since been supplanted by Monrovia, where its Intercontinental Hotel is a sort of smugglers headquarters.

A major American operator describes purchases there as being quite simple. After the diamonds are bought, the purchaser has to have them "koshered" for export. Bribery is the key. Officials not only give the dealer his "kosher" export license, but even allow him to value the goods at considerably less than they are worth to avoid paying the full export duty.

Moscow is a very different story. The nineteenth floor of Prospekt Kalinina 29 is either the only incorruptible diamond center in the world, or the scene of the best-kept secret in the diamond business. That Moscow is immune to bribery, smuggling, or other illegal operations is even more astonishing because the center is operated by the government. It is no secret that the Soviet Union has had trouble coping with traditional "favoritism" of bureaucracy and with black markets in other areas.

Only the most important American dealers and manufacturers can do diamond business in Moscow, and by invitation only. The Moscow diamond center is extraordinary in another respect which may explain, in part, its high ethical standards. Here the Russians sell. They do not buy. And they sell only cut diamonds, not rough. American money must be in the Russian bank before the diamonds are released for export.

The visiting American, when he reaches the diamond floor, is assigned an office. There, he sits and studies every diamond. He must buy all or nothing. He cannot say he does not want one of the parcels of diamonds, or even a single diamond in a parcel. He has to buy big. Thus far—except for the fact that he is buying cut instead of rough diamonds—it seems very much like a Syndicate sight. Now comes the big difference. In Moscow, the buyer can bargain. The feeling some Americans get is that the Russians are not as expert as the people in Antwerp, Ramat Gan, or New York. The Russians are told the bottom line for the sale by their superiors and have to get more than that. Consequently, they start the bargaining as high as possible above this bottom line. "If you do not know what you are doing," an American operator told me, "you can take a beating."

The bargaining can go on for many hours. It begins in the office. Then, in the evening, comes dinner—sumptuous meals with no apparent limit to the liquor. Each meal is like two meals. The appetizer is a big plate piled with smoked sturgeon, caviar—red and black—and lox. The lox is salty, not the Nova Scotia variety. Large pats of butter come with this dish. The Russians smear the butter heavily on slabs of bread. There is a suspicion among Americans that this is not only their taste; it also enables them to line their stomachs in order to prepare themselves for the heavy drinking ahead, which they hope will give them an edge over the Americans. They try, with great joviality, to persuade the Americans to match them in drinking "bottoms up" style. After the "appetizer" comes the main course, and more liquor.

Americans I know who have been to Moscow say they have never met a Jew among the Russians and are convinced there are none involved in this enterprise. They say they do not know why this is, but it may explain why the Russians are not as knowledgeable about diamonds as experts in other parts of the world. They suspect that the Russians feel they have reason to distrust their Jewish population when it comes to dealing with Jews from the United States. They fear that their Jewish ties might overcome Soviet patriotism. Therefore, Soviet Jews have been excluded from the business altogether. The Russians might also fear that Russian Jews would make private deals with the American Jews that would enable them to set up foreign balances in anticipation of leaving the country. Some Americans suspect that the offices in which they examine the diamonds and the hotel rooms are bugged. One American, if he is with a partner on such a trip, while looking over diamond parcels in the office, will tell the partner he thinks the diamonds are worth, say, $500,000. But on a pad he will write 550, meaning $550,000. This technique is used throughout their "private" discussions.

The smaller dealer who goes abroad works even harder than the big operator. He does not have a branch office in Antwerp, for instance. So when he is there, he has to make plans with a local dealer to use his office and guidance as he makes the rounds of diamond clubs and dealers. For this, the paperwork, and the handling of export arrangements, the local dealer charges a two percent fee.

In Africa, the smaller dealer does not have the leverage of a large one when buying from smugglers since he cannot buy in huge amounts. Because his bribes are not as hefty as those of more important competitors, he does not get as favorable a discount on the diamonds when having them "koshered." In Ramat Gan, he is also at a disadvantage since he is dealing mainly with operators like himself who are very hungry and have little compunction about employing unfair practices. Finally, the money he is spending is probably borrowed at a higher interest rate than the larger operators are able to secure. These handicaps are reasons which impel the smaller dealers to indulge in tactics the bigger ones disdain or, more likely, have outgrown.

On one occasion, for instance, a small dealer in New York learned that a diamond bracelet that belonged to a foreign celebrity might be available for sale. He flew to the foreign country and made the purchase. When he returned, he removed all the diamonds, using each stone for a diamond ring. He then advertised the diamonds as coming from this famous bracelet. However, what he did not say was that, in addition to the diamonds from the bracelet, he bought twice as many similar diamonds in New York, which he used for mounting in the diamond rings as well. The diamonds for these rings were also sold as being from the famous bracelet.

Whether the dealer is big or small, the trip abroad, while it may be challenging and exciting is almost always exhausting. If the big operator is lucky, he may, upon his return to New York, be able to take a short rest, generally not much more than a weekend. More likely, he will want to check in at the office as soon as possible to find out what's been happening in his absence. A Telex to Antwerp and long-distance calls from abroad are hardly sufficient. So for a week or so after he returns from the trip he will be under greater pressure to catch up, handling the present and trying to cope with the future in a world that has become particularly complex with inflation and roller-coaster gold prices.

How much of the diamond stock should be held for inventory and which ones should be selected? How much should be sold to dealers, to retailers, to investment firms, or even loose to investors? He has to meet with other dealers and talk to important retailers. He has to supervise the cutting, whether by his own or freelance men. He has to examine in detail diamonds that he bought on the basis of a sampling. One day I was in the office of an important dealer who had purchased hundreds of small stones in Ramat Gan. He had not, at the time, examined every stone. Some were worth less than he had anticipated.

A twelve-hour day for the returned dealer or manufacturer becomes almost mandatory, with hours of paper work at home. The tension is always there. The big stones need very careful study. We have seen, for example, how much time is spent before a large stone is cleaved. After it is cleaved and finished, it must be sold. For example, after the Jonker diamond was cut, it took Harry Winston fourteen years before he sold it to King Farouk. Finally, there is the worry about taxes. Outsiders constantly talk about how diamond people cut corners on taxes. They do. So do any others with a substantial cash flow—restaurant owners, doctors, lawyers, and handymen. It is implicit in American business. What is overlooked, however, is that the I.R.S. is particularly attentive to returns in the diamond business. Sometimes too much so. There was the case in 1977 when Claude Arpels was fined $15,000 for giving two wristwatches, an emerald ring, and a diamond brooch to an I.R.S. agent. Mr. Arpels, pleading guilty to paying the man who was examining his returns, said the agent had demanded the payments. Investigation proved this was so and the agent was dismissed from the I.R.S. and sentenced to three months in prison.

The capacity for concentrated and prolonged work, for resourcefulness and tenacity have brought the major dealers and manufacturers substantial rewards. They have beautiful suburban homes, condominiums on Fifth Avenue, summer homes. Their children go to expensive private schools.

But to maintain their businesses at the required pace they have developed, within the corporate form, the tightest of partnerships. Partners are almost essential to spell one another off on the trips abroad; to have someone watching the home office while the other is away. Because of the secrecy of so many of the operations—either to outwit competition or evade laws—partners in the diamond business have to be so close that the business has given rise to a fascinating phenomenon—the father-son partnerships that seem to defy contemporary behavior in other fields.

Considering that the fathers in this business are aggressive, often domineering, and their sons are usually spirited—that among middle-class and upper-middle-class Jews the strains between fathers and sons have been pronounced in this century, particularly since the 1960s—these partnerships should be stormy and bitter. Some are. But the vast majority are warm, with strong mutual respect and pride between father and son. The diamond partnerships seem to have surmounted the generation and cultural gaps of Jewish families that have been a frequent theme in the plays of the Yiddish theater earlier in this century, and of novels about Jews since then.

Why do these father-son partnerships work so well? One explanation is that the fathers do not try to force the sons to go into the business. The first woman to become a member of the Diamond Dealers Club did so, mainly because her brothers did not want to go into their father's business. In some cases, the fathers even discourage their sons, urging them to find more suitable vocations. Thus Sol Lipiner, who was to become chairman of the board of the Diamond Dealers Club, as well as successor to his father in M. H. Lipiner & Son, was originially urged by his father to do graduate

work in philosophy. He told his son that he was not ruthless enough
for the diamond business. There was something strongly reminiscent
of the shtetl in urging his son to become a scholar, telling him there
was enough money in the business to support him in the less profitable work of philosophy. The diamond people, for all their merce-
nary talents, retain the traditional Jewish admiration for the scholar.

Some leaders of New York's diamond industry explain the
warmth between fathers and sons simply. Lazare Kaplan, founder of
Kaplan International, when in his nineties and watching his sons
run the business, said: "You saw how my sons come and see how I
am. How they talk to me? Leo? George? How they talk to each
other? Never once in all the years did they have words with each
other over who would get this or who would get that. It's because of
my wife. She was the real Jewish mother. . . . She just gave love.
Even the grandchildren feel it. It got passed on to them. . . . So there
will be a continuation."

This, and more complex explanations are offered by George
Solow, whose father started the major manufacturing firm of
J. Solow & Son, and whose three sons have since joined him.

"In the diamond business," he told me, "father and son have to
sit beside one another and work together. If a young man's father is a
doctor or a lawyer and if he wants to do the same, he still has to go
away to college and postgraduate work before he can practice. So
much of his study is away, on his own, at school. But when a son has
to learn the diamond business he has to sit down beside you and
learn from you. He takes an apprenticeship in your shop as you did
with your father. Father and son work side by side. They travel
together. They learn from one another. That's why in this business
so many are chips off the old block.

"One more thing you have to remember about our business.
Here we can never forget about Jewish persecution. It is with us all
the time. We see it in the people who escaped the Nazis on Forty-
seventh Street. We see it in Antwerp and in Ramat Gan. So long as
you have to remember Jewish persecutions you have to think about
the family tie and realize how precious it is."

7

THE
MECHANICS

"Mechanics" they are called on Forty-seventh Street, the grimy men who work out of sight of the public, often under unpleasant conditions, to transform unappealing bits of grayish carbon into the brilliant diamonds calculated to attract large amounts of money in the name of love, sentiment, or investment. Perhaps all three at once. It is the mechanics—cleavers, sawyers, girdlers, cutters, and setters—who shape the stone; remove the dull skin of mine or river bank; facet and polish it; set it in a ring, bracelet, pendant, necklace, earring, or brooch. The rough diamond loses about 50 percent of its weight as the mechanics make it ready for the challenge of such slogans as "A diamond is forever," or "Nature's limited edition." Without the skills of the mechanics, the diamond dealer's daring and shrewdness are wasted. Many diamond dealers have become successful because they served in apprenticeships as mechanics.

The aristocrats of the mechanics—there are some who think their skill so great they should be called artists—are the cleavers. Their work is high drama. A diamond dealer may misjudge the value of a diamond when he sees it in the rough and merely cut the size of his profits. But when a cleaver makes a mistake the most precious diamond can become worthless. It is said that Joseph Asscher, who cleaved the Cullinan diamond, the largest in history, had to be hospitalized for several weeks after the cleaving because the months of tension preceding the critical moment brought on a nervous breakdown.

However, the few cleavers I have known seemed remarkably steady. Lazare Kaplan, considered by many to be the greatest cleaver of this century, was approaching ninty-seven when I talked to him in 1979, and seemed to be quite alert, still turning up at work two or three times a week as head of the famous diamond firm of Lazare Kaplan International. Pastor Colon, who had been trained by Mr. Kaplan, was, in his mid-sixties, star cleaver for Harry Winston & Company, having a full life as painter, sculptor, and needlepoint artisan as well.

For all their prestige, however, the diamond cleavers may be extinct before the end of the century—victims of technology and the triumph of economics over aesthetics, plus the reluctance of young people in a computer age to serve a long apprenticeship to learn this difficult skill. "Cleaving is a dying art," says Mr. Colon. Even such a bustling diamond business as J. Solow and Son, which has "factories" on Forty-seventh and Forty-eight streets, and handles diamonds from its rough state to the preparation of laudatory television commercials, has no cleaver. "When we need a cleaver, which is seldom," says George Solow, "we import one."

Many millions have seen, in movies and in television, the breathtaking moment when the cleaver brings down his mallet and smartly taps a wedge that splits the diamond. But very few outside the diamond world know of the months of intense study and worry that precede the tap of the mallet. Even on Forty-seventh Street there are many who do not know what costly mistakes have been made by experienced cleavers.

A costly mishap in cleaving—possibly a six-digit one—was witnessed by many millions on television in 1968, but they never knew it. This was during the cleaving of the late Harry Winston's 601.25-carat Lesotho diamond. As the mallet hit the wedge, the diamond fell into three pieces instead of two. The unexpected chunk weighed some twenty-five carats. An employee, was standing near the cleaver at the time, scooped it up so quickly that the public never noticed it. Later, when Winston was told of the loss, he said it was a mistake to have concealed it from the television audience. It would have been wiser—and somewhat more dramatic—for the television viewers to have seen how risky a cleaving was.

"We don't cleave as many diamonds as we used to," says Richard Winston, a vice-president of the company and nephew of the founder. "It's too dangerous."

The most famous cleaving job of this century, in 1936, was by Mr. Kaplan and became a superb illustration of the work and risks of the art. This was the cleaving of the 726-carat Jonker diamond. It took much longer to plan this cleaving than for the transactions that brought the diamond from its finder, Jacobus Jonker, a poor farmer-prospector, who sold it to De Beers, who sold it to Winston, who put it on display at the American Museum of Natural History for the public, before asking Mr. Kaplan to cleave it.

Mr. Kaplan studied the diamond for more than a year. He found problems he had not anticipated. More than forty years after the cleaving, he told me that one of the main reasons he did the job for Winston—who, after all, was a competitor—was so his son, Leo, could have the experience of working closely with someone cleaving a magnificent diamond.

"I thought it would not be too much trouble, when I took the job," he said. "After all, the stone had already been studied by experts in Europe for Winston and they even marked it with black ink to show how many stones would come from it."

At first glance, the Jonker ran true to form for alluvial stones. Its thin skin was grayish. It had the tiny surface spots of sand and iron oxide. In one respect it was astonishing. It had no internal flaws. On more careful study, however, Kaplan became worried. The grain of the diamond, he decided, was not running the way it should—not at all as the European experts had marked the stone.

"This stone was a freak," he said. "If I went by the markings the stone would be ruined."

He discussed his misgivings with Winston, who told him to use his own judgment.

At one point, he recalled, he had raised the mallet to cleave, when he spotted a minute crack—called a "gletz"—in the surface. He restudied the stone. Eventually, when he decided where the cleavage should occur, he put the stone into a cementlike substance in a cuplike dop. When the cement was hard he placed the dop in the vise, and with Leo standing by, he began scratching a line of cleavage into the diamond with another diamond set in a handle. Eventually, he had a V-shaped groove. He placed the cleaving wedge over the crack. The blade of this wedge is blunted, to spread the V-scratch when struck. He tapped the wedge lightly with the mallet. The Jonker split exactly as he had hoped.

The main reason that cleavers are becoming rare is the development of the diamond saw. More than 95 percent of diamonds that have to be split are now turned over to diamond sawyers. The saw is much safer than cleaving and requires much less planning. A good diamond man can mark as many as two hundred diamonds a day for sawyers. A single sawyer can operate a bank of 20 diamond saws at once. I have seen three operators maintaining 120 machines. Though it takes hours, sometimes days for a saw to cut a diamond—compared to the instant required for cleaving—the risk of ruining a diamond with a saw is very small with a well-trained sawyer. It takes a year to make a competent sawyer, compared to the many years required to develop a top-notch cleaver.

The diamond saw, which made its slow debut about the turn of the century, is a circular, paper-thin bronze blade, a few inches in

Kimberley Mine, South Africa, at the end of the nineteenth century.

Hope Diamond—45.5 carats, the largest blue diamond in the world.

Cottage industry in diamonds in Surat, India. They are working as diamond cutters.

The diamond sorter is separating the darker stones which are industrial diamonds from the white stones which will become gems.

An assortment of rough diamonds. (COURTESY OF THE DIAMOND INFORMATION CENTER)

Diamonds marked and mounted for sawing. The bottom diamond has already been sawn in half. (COURTESY OF THE DIAMOND INFORMATION CENTER)

Though cleaving has been almost entirely replaced by sawing, it is still used on large and very expensive stones, where great skill is essential. (COURTESY OF THE DIAMOND INFORMATION CENTER)

The final step in cutting a diamond is grinding its facets on a disc impregnated with oil and diamond dust. (COURTESY OF THE DIAMOND INFORMATION CENTER)

In 1934, Sir Ernest Oppenheimer (left), founder of the DeBeers Syndicate, purchased the Jonker diamond—726 carats, the fourth largest in
the world—from Jacobus Jonker (right) for £70,000. Jonker's son
(center) counts the money. (NYT PICTURES)

A shop window on Forty-seventh Street. (BOB SHAMIS PHOTO)

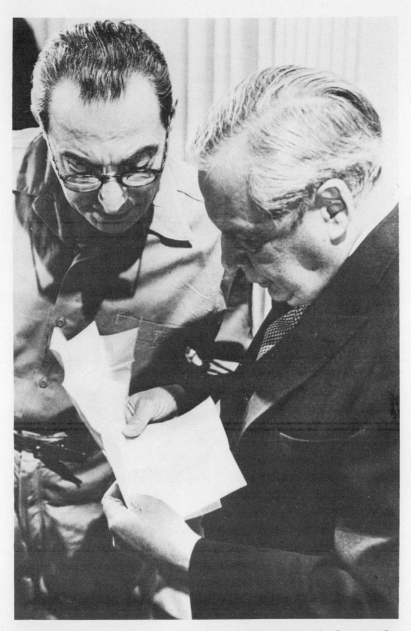

A rare photo of Harry Winston (right) in 1968 with his chief cutter after the cleaving of the Lesotho diamond. (DON HOGAN CHARLES/NYT PICTURES)

A deal in progress on the block. (BOB ADELMAN PHOTO)

Right: A deal is concluded with a handshake and the words "mazel und brucha" meaning "good luck and blessing." Below, an open packet of diamonds and a loupe. (BOB ADELMAN PHOTO)

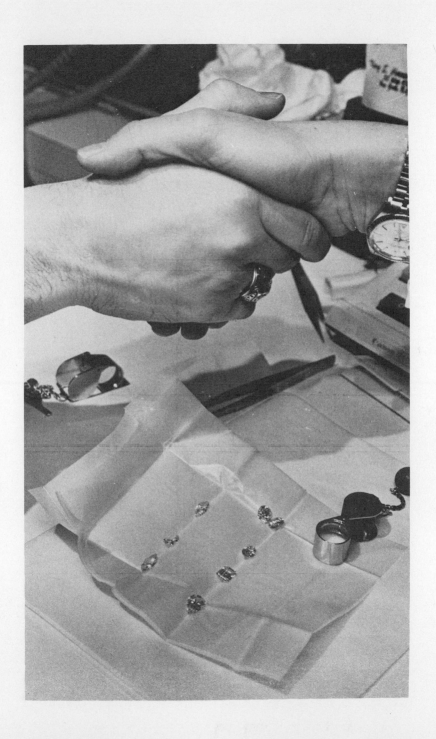

The entrance to the Diamond Dealers Club. (BOB ADELMAN PHOTO)

Diamond merchants. (BOB ADELMAN PHOTO)

A Forty-seventh Street cutter inspects a diamond before grinding.
(BOB ADELMAN PHOTO)

Pinchos Jaroslawicz, the twenty-five-year-old diamond broker, whose brutal murder undermined the honor code of Forty-seventh Street.

Pinhas (Pini) Balabin and Shlomo Tal, convicted murderers of Pinchos Jaroslawicz.

diameter that revolves so quickly it does not seem to be moving. Its cutting edge is treated with a mixture of diamond powder and oil, with the diamond dust as the abrasive. The diamond is put in a cylinder about an inch long and about a quarter-inch in diameter that also contains plaster of Paris. This cylinder is called the pot. When the plaster of Paris has hardened, the pot is locked into the machine and moved into position so that the diamond can be cut along a line marked with India ink. Blades of different size and thickness are used in sawing. The smallest and widest saw is the one used to make a wedge in the diamond. Bigger and thinner blades are used as the diamond is being cut. During the sawing, the operator may change the weights that control the speed of the revolving saw. He will always stop the machine before making any change. The saw is more dangerous to the operator than it is to the diamond. Yet I have seen experienced operators, while warning me not to gesture in the direction of the saw, keep a hand within an inch of the blade.

Sawyers, like all competent diamond workers, know that every diamond is different and that even though most diamonds can be sawed without much trouble, nothing can be taken for granted. The greatest concern of a sawyer, apart from a knot in the diamond, is what they call the diamond's "stress" or "tension." If the tension is too great, a diamond may fall apart during the sawing. A good sawyer can detect such a possibility, and when he is suspicious he will put the diamond under a special microscope called a Polariscope. If he sees a sort of rainbow effect in the stone he knows the tension is too great for sawing. In such situations, the owner will either try to sell the diamond to an unwary dealer or broker, or else have the work done by a wheel—a technique we will be examining shortly.

Sawyers are probably the least independent of diamond mechanics. They work for others as a rule, either for a man who has a sawing shop or for a large company that has its own sawing equipment and operators. The average sawyer makes between $22,000 and $27,000 a year. A few, who are known to be very expert and are used to train others, may get more than $30,000. The best sawyers among those who work for large companies are sometimes promoted to jobs as markers of diamonds for sawing. A good sawyer, pacing back and forth between two banks of machines—a total of forty saws—can detect, amid the steady hum of the saws, the slightest alien click or shrillness that tells him the saw may have hit a knot or that the diamond is tougher than anticipated. He will rush toward the machine, halt it instantly, by kicking loose a lathe, before there is any damage.

I spent some time watching and talking to a good sawyer who has worked for a Forty-seventh Street shop and for a large company. He prefers the latter, for reasons that may or may not be typical of life on Forty-seventh Street, but which are not too unusual.

When he graduated from a yeshiva, he told me, his father approached a friend who had a sawing factory—the term for such Forty-seventh Street shops. He asked the man if he would train his son in this diamond skill. The man said he would do it without charge. But when the youth showed up for work, the factory-owner told him to bring five hundred dollars in cash the next time. He was told that this money was necessary because the law prohibited him from working for nothing. He told the youth that the money would be repaid to him during his apprenticeship as "salary." None of the money was ever paid back. For two years he worked as an apprentice in the shop, sweeping up as well as using the diamond saw. The diamonds he sawed were for dealers and his boss was paid for this work, but the apprentice was not. The money he paid to the owner for the apprenticeship is referred to, on Forty-seventh Street, as "rebbeh gelt,"—money for the rabbi. This is a sarcastic perversion for the legitimate fees paid to rabbis to teach children to read Hebrew, study the Bible and Talmud. After his apprenticeship was completed, the youth took a job as a sawyer in this shop, but soon left to work for a company for less money. He has since received raises and is making more than he would have ever received had he remained with his "teacher."

The sawyer's skill may, like that of the cleaver, vanish before the end of the century. The laser saw has been developed—an instrument that is precise and can apparently cut through the toughest diamond without trouble. It has not been accepted on Forty-seventh Street, partly because of resistance to novelty and capital expense. But more because the diamond loss with a laser is between 3 and 4 percent, compared to the loss of between 1 and 1.5 percent with the bronze saw. The Soviet Union, on the other hand, has been using laser saws increasingly and an important dealer, who has seen them in Russia, tells me that steady improvements are being made and he has no doubt that eventually the diamond loss will be cut back to the point where the laser saw will replace the bronze on Forty-seventh Street.

From cleaver or sawyer the stone goes to the girdler. The basic job of this machanic is to round off the points of the gem, preparing it for the cutter. This process is the most forcible demonstration of diamond against diamond. One diamond is embedded in the opening of a rotating horizontal cylinder. The other diamond is set in the cup of a metal rod. As the cylinder rotates, the girdler presses the diamond in the rod against the one in the cylinder, wearing down the points of each stone.

Though the vanishing cleaver is still the aristocrat of diamond mechanics, the diamond business rests on the cutters. Without good cutters no diamond center can survive. In the hierarchy of Forty-seventh Street, they outrank the sawyers. They give the diamond its shape—brilliant, marquise, emerald, heart, pear, single-cut, oval, baguette. They heighten the brilliance of a diamond by creating facets at just the right angles to push the maximum brightness through the top of the stone by not allowing light to "leak" through the sides or bottom. Strictly speaking, cutters should be called faceters. Cleavers and sawyers are also cutters of diamonds, but on Forty-seventh Street the faceters—the diamond artisans of the wheel—are the only ones who refer to themselves as cutters, or sometimes polishers. They seem to be working almost automatically at times, and say that quite often they can be working and thinking of other things. But like all good craftsmen they take pride in their work, and one of the constant gripes among diamond dealers—and the most highly respected cutters—is that the younger cutters are not as good as those who were trained under a more severe apprenticeship. This may or may not be true.

One of the best cutters on Forty-seventh Street told me that while it was true that workmanship has declined, dealers do not care about perfection. "They want the goods in a hurry." When he first came to Forty-seventh Street from Paris, after fleeing the Nazis, he adhered to the high standards he had learned in a three-year apprenticeship. But he found he was having trouble making a decent living. He complained to the dealers that he was not paid enough.

"I told these dealers it took me too much time to do the kind of job I wanted to do and, for the money they paid me, I was having trouble taking care of my family. They told me that what they paid me was their fee. So I started to turn out the stuff faster. The quality of my work was not as good, but I made a better living. The dealers they didn't care. Or maybe they didn't know. For them my work was good enough. So far as these dealers are concerned, they figure the retailer doesn't know the difference and the retailer's customers certainly don't know. When I do work for Van Cleef & Arpels or for Cartier, I work better. They appreciate what I'm doing and they pay better."

The basic tools of the cutter are a revolving wheel that works like a record player and a dop that is set in a metal handle much like a cartridge in a record player. The wheel, made of cast steel, is installed firmly in a workbench where the cutter sits on a high chair or stool. The cutter places the diamond into the dop. The wheel revolves at about 2,800 revolutions per minute. The wheel is porous and has scratches across the surface as well as circular grooves. Into these scratches and grooves the cutter applies, with his finger, a mixture of diamond dust and olive oil, or sometimes sesame oil, which he keeps at hand in a small dish. As the wheel turns, with a shrill whine, the cutter presses the dop from which the diamond is protruding against the wheel with its diamond dust abrasive and facets the stone. Every few seconds the cutter raises the dop to examine the diamond through his loupe. Sometimes, when the facets are large, a cutter will place flat metal weights on the arm holding the dop, letting the weights keep constant pressure on the diamond against the wheel for a few minutes at a time. Cutters, working on large facets, can have three or four diamonds in separate arms held against the same wheel by weights simultaneously.

The great majority of cutters on Forty-seventh Street work for themselves and generally make upwards of $30,000 a year. Since some of the work is for cash—which can mean less being paid out in taxes, in addition to buying and selling diamonds on their own, good cutters can earn better than $50,000 a year. And the most gifted ones can, if they wish, earn more than $75,000 a year. Since the cutters are really independent contractors—except for the small percentage, usually Hispanic, who work for companies—they do not belong to a union. They have a sort of loose federation that will, occasionally, bargain with a committee from the Diamond Dealers Club for more money. They get paid by the weight of the diamond. One dealer I know pays between forty dollars and fifty dollars a carat. For any stone less than a carat the fee is twenty-five dollars. Another pays fees that start five dollars lower and go five dollars higher. On Forty-seventh Street little work is done on the very small stones called melees. The main work on melees is in Tel Aviv and Bombay.

Though the Forty-seventh Street cutters prize their independence—some fiercely so—their working conditions are among the worst in the city. Their little workrooms are noisy, dirty, and sometimes fetid from the stale air. Windows are rarely opened and the air-conditioning systems are erratic. A fine dust—diamond dust—is so pervasive that it quickly forms a film on the walls. Run a finger along the wall and it comes away black. When a cutter sneezes or blows his nose into a handkerchief, it leaves a dark smudge that is a mixture of the diamond dust and oil with which they work. They insist, however, that the dust does not affect their health. I am convinced that an investigation by health experts would show otherwise. "When a cutter gets cancer," one of them told me, "it is from smoking." Another said: "Cutters die from heart attacks, not cancer."

The diamond dust cannot be avoided. It is as necessary to their work as the diamonds themselves. Only diamonds can cut diamonds, they repeat endlessly.

Since there are often a dozen or so cutters squeezed into such small rooms, the noise of the wheels is penetrating, forcing cutters either to avoid talking or else to talk loudly. Older cutters tell me they don't mind the noise. But some of the younger ones work with radio headphones to their ears. The workbenches are usually side by side and the space between one row and another is barely wide enough for someone to squeeze through.

As the cutters bend over their wheels, diamond dealers and brokers come and go, bringing diamonds to be cut, taking away those that are finished; arguing about prices to be paid; money owed to cutters; discussing how diamonds should be cut to give maximum brilliance with least loss of stone. In some cases, it may be better to sacrifice weight of stone for greater quality. At other times, when cutter and diamond dealer disagree, the cutter will simply shrug and say, "You're the boss." Then, there are times when, after the dealer leaves, the cutter may decide to cut the stone his own way—as a matter of pride in his craft. One cutter may also turn to another for advice. When this happens, it means that the cutter owns this diamond.

Diamond dealers bring their goods to the cutter in the usual folded paper parcels, pressed into wallets. On the paper is written the number of stones in each parcel and their weight. The cutter keeps his own notebooks in which, alongside a code number for the owner's name, he enters the number and caratage of diamonds and, in some instances, specifies the kind of work to be done. The notebooks are usually looseleaf so when the work is done and paid for, the page can be removed, leaving no record for inquisitive people like the I.R.S.

Because diamonds on the wheel, as by the saw, are cut against the grain, the first thing the cutter has to do is locate the grain. This is done by very rapid trial-and-error, putting the diamond to the wheel for split seconds. A good cutter can tell almost at once by the sound of the wheel and the resistance of the diamond if he has found the grain. The stronger the vibration, the shriller the tone, the bluer the patina of the wheel, the more certain he is that he is working against the grain.

The significance of the cutter's skill as a way to learn about diamonds was demonstrated by a deal made between an important diamond dealer and a man with a high reputation for his diamond craft. The diamond dealer's son had finished college, and was about to be taken into his father's business. The father wanted his son to know about diamonds, not just the paper work and bargaining. The diamond dealer asked the diamond savant to become a teacher for his son. The diamond expert said he first wanted to meet the young man. This was arranged. The expert was satisfied that the youth was intelligent and eager to learn. He told the father he would teach the young man. After some bargaining, the father agreed to pay him $2,500 a month for ten months to allow his son to learn from him. The two men shook hands with the usual mazel und brucha. Each month the father gave the teacher $2,500. At the end of ten months he expressed pleasure at how much his son had learned.

Some time later, when I discussed this with the teacher, he told me: "I didn't teach him everything I knew, naturally. How could I. In ten months how much can you teach. But he was bright and willing and he did well. I spent about three hours a month with him. But he learned enough to avoid making mistakes for his father that could cost his father a lot more than $25,000."

There are a number of cutters on Forty-seventh Street who teach apprentices. They do this while they are working a regular day. They charge about $1,500 for the course. The teacher also gets free labor on the stones for which he charges the diamond dealer or broker. Of course, there are times when the apprentice makes mistakes that the teacher has to rectify, so he is constantly supervising his pupil.

One of these diamond-cutting beehives was so typical of Forty-seventh Street that, for several weeks, I visited it two or three times a week, sometimes remaining for several hours, listening to the comments, arguments, and jokes of the cutters; becoming aware of the undercurrents of skepticism and hope; of the tensions between Hasidic and non-Hasidic Jews. All were foreign-born Jews who, with few exceptions, had fled their own countries to escape persecution or death. Some were Hasidim. Others, though rather religious, were not Hasidic. One was anti-religious, outspokenly so. Their attitude toward me, the American-born Jew, the stranger in their diamond ghetto, was unpredictable from day to day. Sometimes they were affable, almost garrulous, smiling as I walked from one busy bench to another. Other times they greeted me curtly, said very little, answered questions tersely or pretended ignorance. Or they might decide to be very helpful, stopping work to make drawings to show how they were faceting diamonds, tracing a stone from rought octahedron, the most common rough form, like two crude pyramids base to base.

I already knew some of the rudiments: that the top flat surface of a diamond is the table and that the diamond is cut to broaden at the middle, called the girdle, then is tapered from girdle to the bottom, called the culet. I knew that the area from table to girdle is the crown; and from crown to culet is the pavilion. I knew that a well-cut diamond has fifty-eight facets, thirty-three above the girdle and the rest below; and that there is a relatively new cut with seventy facets, which is used in special cases.

They explained that for the greatest brilliance the girdle should be parallel to the table and not too thick; that the crown should be only about a quarter of the diamond's depth. They told me that if a diamond is cut too shallow, light "leaks" through the lower part of the stone, making the diamond not only less brilliant, but sometimes less sturdy. If the diamond is cut too deep, light can "leak" from the sides and make the stone seem dark in the center.

Cutters, I came to realize, like most diamond people on Forty-seventh Street, have not bothered to read much about their business. So they were interested in what I had discovered in books, particularly about Jews. When I told them, for instance, that the innovator of modern cutting was a man named either Loedywyck van Berquem or Louis de Berquem who learned to use diamond dust as an abrasive in the mid–fifteenth century and faceted diamonds in geometric patterns, one of them asked at once if he was a Jew. I said this was very likely since he was trained in Paris and then migrated to Belgium, almost certainly to escape anti-Semitism. In fact, in one of the Antwerp diamond clubs, there is a bronze statue showing him holding a diamond to his eye. They were also pleased to learn that the reason the Koh-I-Noor diamond, most famous of the British crown jewels in London Tower, is not well-cut is because Queen Victoria and her consort, Prince Albert, did not wish to use cutters from the Low Countries, and interfered with their resident cutter, though foreign-trained, when he was working. They were intrigued to hear of the controversy over whether or not the ancient Hebrews had diamonds. This argument stems from the Biblical reference (Ex. XXXIX: 1) to a gem in the breastplate of the high priests in Israel. Some say this gem was a diamond. Others contend it could not have been a diamond because the gem bore the name of the tribe and the Hebrews of that time could not have known how to engrave a diamond. They were amused by legends about the powers of diamonds—that they could cure insanity, be an antidote for poison, and that, in the Middle Ages, they were sometimes called "pietra della reconciliazone"—peacemaker between husband and wife.

They taught me how to peer through a loupe and look for tiny spots in a diamond; made me aware of tints in the color of diamonds—yellow, gray, and brown. They knew about the scientific theory which espouses that diamonds were originally created by underground volcanic action that produced the pipes of kimberlite that are currently mined. But they did not know that diamonds in alluvial deposits are probably the result of the long-term erosion of such pipes. Some knew about the efforts that have been made to mine the ocean bed of the Atlantic by De Beers, off South West Africa. They also knew that the mines in Siberia are very productive. But they had never heard of the Russian geologist, Victor Sobolev, who when studying diamondiferous areas in Africa and Siberia, found strong similarities which eventually led to the discovery of many mines in certain sections of Siberia. They knew that even in kimberlite the chances of finding diamonds are slight. But they were surprised when I said that De Beers experts have found that even in diamondiferous soil diamonds are only one part in twenty million.

Though my scraps of book knowledge helped to encourage conversation during my visits to the cutting room, the cutters never completely trusted me. Perhaps because they were flattered that I had been reading about their business, they never asked me to leave, nor did they suggest I stop coming. Still, with the Hasidim saying they did not want names used and the others expressing some concern, I decided not to identify them as I took notes. But over the weeks I spent with them, there grew in my notebooks a mosaic of their world, a ghetto microcosm of Forty-seventh Street.

As with almost every office on crime-fearing Forty-seventh Street, the cutting room could not be entered until you pushed a button. Then you would stand before the inner door, your face framed in the small window it contains. When you were recognized by someone inside, that person would push a button that buzzed, releasing the door lock, and allowing you to enter. Inside, small mirrors had been placed at various points so the door window could be seen from almost any part of the office.

The work area consisted of two connecting rooms, with a total space overall of a small office suite. Crammed into this area were ten workbenches where the cutters would sit on high stools or chairs, their backs tilted forward, their heads bent over screeching wheels. They were so tightly packed that in one part of the room only a slender person could squirm between a bench and the wall. A diamond dealer or broker talking to a cutter could be overheard at an adjacent bench since he would have to raise his voice to be heard over the din. If he wanted to talk privately, he and the cutter would leave the bench and either go off into a corner near the door, or into the corridor.

The office space was leased from the owner of the building by one of the cutters. He, in turn, would rent the benches to other cutters. At least one of these other cutters was in some sort of partnership with him. Neither the lessee nor the other cutters would discuss the rent with me. The cutters would rent the wheels from one of the suppliers on Forty-seventh Street for fourteen dollars. A wheel would only last about two weeks before wearing down and returned to the supplier.

In the weeks I was with them, I never saw any of them go out to lunch. Whenever I offered to bring back a sandwich, they would decline. As a rule, the cutters did not eat lunch. Those who did, either opened a can of tuna, or cut up cheese for a sandwich. They would make their own tea or coffee, sharing a common heater. Food was kept in a small, communal refrigerator. One reason they did not go out to lunch was because some of the cutters, particularly the Hasidim, observed the kosher dietary regulations very strictly. Mainly, though, it was because they had become accustomed, over the years, to working without lunch, a tradition that stems from the sweatshops where workers ate hurriedly at benches or not at all in order to produce the greatest quantity of cut diamonds since they were being paid by the piece.

Not too long after I began my visits, I was astonished to learn that these independent contractors in this highly competitive business often worked cooperatively on the same diamonds. Some cutters were better at a certain phase of cutting than others. So each cutter concentrated on his specialty. For example, one cutter was more adept at girdles, another at working on the table; some were more efficient in small facets and others in large. Very often a diamond would pass back and forth between two cutters, sometimes three. But the diamond dealer would pay only the cutter he had asked to do the job. The proceeds were shared among the cutters who had worked on the stones. In these operations nothing was written down. Yet I never heard them quibble over how the money was shared. When I asked them how they remembered what was owed to whom, they merely shrugged and said it was no problem.

"What we have," one of the cutters explained, "is a sort of assembly line. We can all do almost any kind of work here. But if we concentrate on the things we do best we can get more work done and make more money. The dealer won't complain because for the same price he gets two or three specialists working on his stones, doing them faster and better. This is one advantage of several cutters working in the same place. Any of us can do a whole stone. But we prefer to do part of a stone."

Another cutter, with whom this one had just been sharing work, added: "You can't make nearly as much money if you try to do it all. Everything is very competitive on Forty-seventh Street. To make money you have to produce. To produce you have to specialize."

Sometimes this cooperation extended beyond the little shop to similar cutting rooms in other parts of the building. The only complications I witnessed in the share-the-work process occurred when a diamond was subcontracted by one of the cutters in this room to a cutter elsewhere in the building. When it was returned, the cutter in "my" shop was unhappy. He louped it and said it had a "nest," a tiny spot that can be either white or black. In this case it was white. He said the spot should be removed. The cutter from upstairs disagreed. The cutter from my place argued that the stone now weighed 1.69 carats and that the imperfection could be removed with the loss of only ten points. He said the improved quality would more than compensate for the loss of stone. The upstairs cutter disagreed. The stone was passed to another cutter in the room. He agreed that the imperfection should be removed. The upstairs cutter grumbled, "You should have told me what you wanted in the first place."

Before he could leave in a huff, the first cutter called him back and showed him a diamond ring. "I got it for $650," he said. "I want to make $50. It's a good white." The upstairs cutter louped it. The first cutter said, "Nice quality, 68 points." The upstairs cutter pondered. "I'll need it for a few days," he said. The first cutter agreed and the upstairs cutter departed cheerfully. The first cutter did not own this ring. He had it on consignment form someone who may or may not have owned it. The stone might go through two more pairs of hands, with each making a profit, before it leaves the building. All these profits will go into the final retail price. "It will still be cheaper if you buy from the last person in this building than if you buy in a store," the first cutter told me. This is what is meant by buying a ring from someone in the business. You won't really be getting it "wholesale," but you will be getting a bargain. For example, if I had bought the diamond directly from the first cutter for $50 more than the other cutter was willing to pay, I would still be buying it for hundreds of dollars less than its price would have been in a store.

In search of advice, cutters occasionally go beyond their own shop. One time, an upstairs cutter came into the shop to show one of "our" cutters a four-carat rough diamond. The cutter studied it, summoning his son-in-law with a finger toward another bench. He had trained the young man himself. After a few minutes of silent study, the two older cutters talked for a little while. Then the cutter from my shop picked up a pen and made a rough diagram of the diamond. He drew lines showing how it should be cut. He also drew little circles in the picture to show spots that should be removed. The visiting cutter talked excitedly. The consultant replied clamly. Periodically, he would glance over at his son-in-law to make certain he was paying attention and learning from this.

Anyone trained in the logic of business negotiations would probably find the commerce between cutters and diamond dealers— or brokers—of Forty-seventh Street maddening. Since the cutter cannot be treated as an employee, no dealer, no matter how affluent, can expect subservience. And to the dealer, no matter how lowly, no cutter, no matter how great his skill, is exempt from demeaning bargaining. Emotionally, the encounters make up an often love-hate relationship. Cutter and dealer are bound by years of such interaction that breeds a curious mixture of respect and antagonism. The tightest bond of all is the absolute trust implicit in exchanges of the most valuable merchandise. The dealer has to trust the cutter not to substitute one of his diamonds for a stone of lesser quality—the cutter could easily sell the better diamond without much risk—and the cutter has to trust the dealer to abide by his fee. Their contract is the handshake, the code of mazel und brucha.

The quirks in a cutter-dealer relationship are unpredictable.

There was once a dealer who sought too much perfection in a particular diamond. It was a six-carat emerald-cut, worth at least
$200,000. A lovely white. The cutter did a good job. The dealer
liked it. He paid for it and left. But when he got back to his office he
began to wonder if he should not have a certain blemish removed. It
was so tiny, the sort of thing that is called a "vish"—something that
could be removed with the swipe of a cloth. The dealer had known
about this vish when he brought it in to the cutter but had agreed to
leave it alone. Now he wanted the perfect stone. He took it back to
the cutter. The cutter went back to work. Suddenly the diamond was
in pieces. The dealer came, as the saying is "like on fire." He looked
at his ruined stone. He was furious. He knew it was not the cutter's
fault. But he never gave the cutter another stone.

The story reminded one of the cutters of his own experience.

"I was cutting this stone. Not a big one. But good quality. I
picked it up to loupe it. It slipped out of my fingers. I handle thousands of stones and they don't slip out of my fingers. But this one
slipped. Who knows why. And where does it fall? It falls right in the
little crack where the turning wheel is in the bench. It was shattered.
No matter how experienced you are, when a stone is shattered your
heart stops beating. You stop breathing. It is the terrible nightmare
cutters have. This dealer, he had a reputation for a bad temper. He
was a man who used to be a cutter before he became a dealer. Now
he was an important dealer. And it was my fault. No mistake. I
phoned the owner. He came over. He looked at the pieces. A total
loss. He looked and he looked and he said nothing. Then he said to
me, in Yiddish, "When you chop wood, chips fly."

This evoked from a third cutter a story about his experience. He
was cutting a five-carat stone, also of good quality. Cutting and louping. Cutting and louping. Very careful. Suddenly the beautiful diamond in the dop cracked like salt crystal. The cutter started to turn
the knob that would release the stone. But another cutter urged him
to leave it in the dop, and summon the owner. The owner came. He
picked up the dop and looked at what was probably his best diamond.
He turned the knob and the diamond fell into his hand in little

chips. He put the bits in parcel paper, folded it, and put it in his pocket. He said nothing. Just walked out. The next day he telephoned the cutter and asked if he would meet him at his hotel.

"I went there. I didn't know what would happen. You'll never guess. He bought me a dinner. A real mensch."

Endemic in the relationship between cutters and dealers is the complaint by cutters that too many dealers and brokers are slow in paying for work. The cutters have to badger them in person and on the phone. They have to threaten not to work for these dealers again. Frequently, the cutter, in his pleas for full payment, will say he needs the money. Then the dealer or broker may pay the remainder. It is more likely, however, that he will pay a substantial part of the debt, but also bring in more work, thus making the total amount of the debt as large as ever. Very often, when the cutter demands payment, it is the dealer or broker who complains about his own financial problems.

Some of the intricacies of the cutter-dealer world were highlighted for me the day I was at the cutting shop talking to a cutter we shall call Abe. A dealer arrived, bringing stones for Abe's neighbor, Duvvid. Abe explained to the dealer that Duvvid was out. He did not tell the dealer that Duvvid was subcontracting to an outside cutter diamonds he had taken on consignment from another dealer. The dealer seemed anxious and asked Abe when Duvvid would be back. Abe, who knew this dealer owed Duvvid money for the last cutting job, began to needle him.

"Maybe he's out working for a dealer who pays when the work is finished. There are other dealers, you know."

The dealer laughed and replied, "On Forty-seventh Street it is no trouble to find cutters."

"Sure," said Abe, louping a stone he had just raised from the wheel. "I know there are cutters. And there are cutters. Anybody with a bench and a wheel can call himself a cutter. You don't need a license to ruin a diamond."

The dealer smiled, showing no sign of worry. In his shabby clothes, he looked like another cutter in work clothes. No one would have thought him a successful dealer, who also worked as a contractor, getting cutting jobs from other dealers and turning them over to cutters.

"You're friend Duvvid," said the dealer to Abe, "he does very well working for me. That I can tell you."

"And he waits a long time too," said Abe. "What do you want, the IRS should get all the money?"

The dealer pulled out a wallet. It was thick with bills. He pulled loose a hundred-dollar-bill and extended it toward Abe. The cutter barely touched the bill and let it fall beside Duvvid's wheel. The dealer shrugged and left.

A little while later Duvvid arrived. Abe pointed toward the hundred-dollar-bill and insultingly named the dealer who left it. Duvvid was miffed. It was only a fraction of what he was owed. He grabbed the wall phone and called the dealer. The dealer was out so he left his name. About fifteen minutes later the dealer phoned Duvvid. After a few seconds, Duvvid, with a quick wink at Abe, shouted, "Stop the bullshit. What good is it to me if you have plenty of money in your wallet. I don't have it in mine and I can't support my family with the money in your wallet. I'm leaving right now. I'm coming over to collect. What do you mean you have to leave now and you'll be back later. What's later. A year from now?" There was more bickering until Duvvid said he'd be at the dealer's at 5:30. Duvvid is a burly, aggressive man. He seemed very angry. But as soon as he hung up the phone, he grinned, and he and Abe joked about the dealer. Duvvid was not worried about getting paid. There would be no violence. It was simply one of those unwritten rules of the cutter-dealer relationship. Duvvid had decided the time had come for a show of anger and the payoff—all just part of the business.

This provoked a general discussion among the cutters about the conditions of their work. No security, they said. Right now, it was true, they were busy. But business had been slow in the past and could be slow again. They had their own pension and health plans. They made their own hours. One of the cutters who had worked in

Africa told of the union there. He waved at the grimy walls, the congested rooms, pointed at his filthy work clothes. "There," he said, "the boss supplies you with a clean jacket. Like a doctor's jacket."

Someone argued against unions, recalling cutters in New York who had a union in the thirties, when he was an apprentice. "I got three dollars a week," he said. "And every three months a one-dollar raise. At the end of two years, when I finished my apprenticeship, I was making thirty-five a week. Of course, then I became a journeyman and could get two hundred dollars a week—a good salary if you could get work. I'm better off without a union."

In discussions among dealers, the subject invariably turns to cheating which usually occurs among the biggest dealers. Dealers cheat on weight. Since cutters get paid by the weight of the diamonds on which they work, when dealers send over a large parcel of stones, they will list the weight at somewhat less than the truth. Most of the time it is only a few points on a diamond. This could mean cheating the cutter by as little as fifty cents on the stone. Cutters have an electronic diamond scale in the shop, but they rarely use it. They almost always take the dealer's word for the weight. However, when they have reason to be suspicious of a dealer—they will weigh the stones themselves. When a cutter finds he is being cheated, he leaps for the phone.

"What kind of business you doing?" he demands at once. "If you want to steal, go out with a gun and steal. Don't steal from me."

The dealer's response, is, at first, to challenge the cutter's scales. Then he blames someone who works in his office or says he will have his office scales checked. But the dealer's ultimate attitude is: "Berel, how many years we have known one another. Why should I cheat you. I know you. I know you're honest. If you say that's the weight, then that's the weight. Why argue. It's not worth talking about. I take your word for it."

When the cutter hangs up, he and the other cutters discuss the situation. They understand why the dealer is cheating on such a small scale. As a big dealer, he can cheat by pittances several thousand times a year, and save thousands of dollars. "And tax-free money," the cutters chorus.

One reason the cutters understand the dealers so well is because, like almost everyone else on Forty-seventh Street, they are constantly trying to buy and sell diamonds on their own. Very often they do this in partnership with other cutters, or with a dealer. A good cutter has the advantage of being both a shrewd judge of diamond quality and, equally important when studying a rough diamond, being able to gauge how much will have to be cut. Moreover, the cutter can do this work himself, saving a fee and guaranteeing good craftsmanship.

The cutter is the most vulnerable as a dealer when he gives the diamond to a broker to sell on consignment. One of the cutters in this shop had a four-carat diamond for which he had promised to pay $12,800. He put it out with a broker, telling him he wanted $3,500 a carat, or $14,000. The broker found a customer willing to pay that price. But the broker, instead of making the sale and collecting his 2 percent commission, told the potential customer that the owner wanted $3,600 a carat, or $14,400. The customer held off. The broker said he would go back to the owner and see if there was anything he could do. But the broker told the cutter that the customer would not pay more than $3,400 a carat, making a guess at what the cutter had paid. The cutter told him to take $3,450 a carat and nothing less. The broker went back to the customer and sold the stone for $3,500 a carat. Thus, he was able to pocket $50 a carat, or $200, plus his commission. The broker cheated the cutter out of $200. This is unethical, but not uncommon on Forty-seventh Street. This will work out smoothly if the customer pays in cash. But if he pays by check, the broker will have to deposit it into his own account, withdraw the amount of sale minus what he has embezzled, then pay the cutter in cash. The cutter won't suspect him of any wrongdoing because everyone in the diamond industry—as in any other business—likes to be paid in cash to cut back on taxes.

Once in a while the cutter will learn he has been tricked. This happened with the cutter I have called Berel. He had consigned seventeen emerald-cut stones to a broker. He knew the exact weight of the stones and told the broker how much he wanted for the total. A few days later the broker told him the best offer he had received was about $200 less than what Berel wanted. Berel agreed to the price because it still meant a profit. The day after the deal was closed, a dealer came in to the cutting shop and asked Berel if he had any small emerald-cut stones. Berel said he had just sold seventeen of them and had none left. The dealer remarked that this was a curious coincidence because the day before he had purchased seventeen small emerald-cut stones. He asked Berel the total weight of the stones he had sold. Berel told him. The dealer said this was the same as the weight of the stones he had bought. Berel told the dealer what he had hoped to get for his seventeen stones, and what he had received. He asked the dealer if he would mind telling him what he had paid. He did. Berel realized he had been cheated. He phoned his intermediary and told him he wanted the full price that had been paid.

The broker claimed that Berel was mistaken in his asking price. Berel said he could prove his claim with a cutter who had overheard the conversation at the next bench. This was a bluff but it sounded good. He threatened to take the case to the Diamond Dealers Club, of which the broker was a member. At first the broker told him to go ahead. But eventually he realized that even if the club sustained him, his own credibility in the club and on Forty-seventh Street might be undermined. He agreed to pay the remainder.

Nearly every Friday, shortly before noon, a couple of young Hasidim who were not in the diamond business visited this cutting room. Their purpose was to persuade non-religious Jews to say the traditional early morning prayer of devout Jews while binding the left arm with a leather thong, the ritual known as laying "t'fillim" (philacteries). Each week they would press the anti-religious cutter, and he would always refuse. One day, after the two young men had failed once more and left, one of the devout, but non-Hasidic cutters in the room offered the non-religious cutter fifty dollars to lay t'fillim. He refused, saying, "Religion is a racket." The Hasidic cutters in the room said nothing. The exchange had touched a pervasive, but seldom discernible tension on Forty-seventh Street—the antipathy between the Hasidic and non-Hasidic Jews.

Because Hasidic and non-Hasidic Jews worked so closely in this cutting room, the undercurrent could be felt more easily there than among the dealers or in the jewelry exchanges where the contacts were of much shorter duration.

Two incidents, both over trivia, made this feeling very clear. One day, the anti-religious cutter was drinking Perrier water from a bottle, as was his custom. The Hasidic cutter who had leased the premises asked him if he might taste it.

"There's nothing left," said the non-religious cutter gruffly. "Anyhow, even if there was, you couldn't have any."

"Why not?" asked the Hasid.

"It's not kosher."

"Water is kosher."

"Not this water. They put carbonation in this water and the carbonation is not kosher."

"I say the carbonation is kosher and so the water is kosher."

"What makes it kosher for you," snapped the anti-religious Jew, "is that it would be free."

The Hasid joined in the laughter by the non-Hasidic Jews and, pointing at his own head, he said, "He is very clever that one, with someone else's money."

Several days after this repartee, there was an exchange between the same Hasid and another non-Hasidic cutter. This one, however, was a rather devout Jew. The Hasid had just told him that beginning next month the rent would be increased. The cutter looked on him with contempt and said, "Do you want to get rich off me?"

"If you think I'm making so much money," retorted the Hasid, "would you give me $500 to be part-landlord?"

This was a cleverly phrased question that walked the tightrope of Forty-seventh Street ethics. He did not say that he would *give* him a partnership for $500 because if the cutter agreed, he would have no choice but to give it. By putting the offer in the form of a question and if the cutter agreed, the $500 could then be used as the opening gambit of a prolonged negotiation.

But, the cutter refused and the Hasid said, triumphantly, "You see. You know I don't get rich from the rent."

One of the religious, but non-Hasidic cutters, in discussing the Hasidim with me one day, said, "These Hasidim, they look upon us other Jews as the fallen ones. As for non-Jews, the Hasidim despise them. They think that only Hasidim have the truth. I do not like them. But there are exceptions. There are some who will never discuss religion. Them I respect." As he was talking, one of the Hasidic cutters rose from his bench and left the room. The non-Hasidic Jew said, "That Hasid who just left the room. Him I would trust with every penny I have."

When I asked the anti-religious Jew about the Hasidim, he said, "Their word is good. But you have to listen very carefully to what they're telling you. Still, you never have to worry about them paying a debt."

At times, the anti-religious cutter deliberately tried to irritate the Hasidim with ribald tales about his sex life while being driven from one country to the next during the war. After comparing the women in these lands, he ended by saying, "But I never slept with a Jewish woman." Then he paused, making sure he had the attention of nearby Hasidic cutters, and said loudly, "I wouldn't sleep with them. They think they have a gold mine between their legs." The Hasidim pretended they had not heard.

The deepest antipathy on Forty-seventh Street is between the Hasidic and Israeli cutters. The Israelis are almost proudly atheistic when they are in the presence of Hasidim. They have carried over from Israel the anger they often felt toward the very devout Jews who would sometimes stone Israelis who drove on the Sabbath or who said Israel should not be recognized as a state because the Messiah had not returned before its formation. It is generally believed among non-Hasidic cutters that a Hasid who has rented a cutting room will not rent space to any Israeli unless he is Hasidic.

The world of the cutter, like that of the sawyer, is threatened by new technology. The Soviet Union has developed lasers for this work. A laser is also being used in the diamond district to remove tiny black spots from diamonds. Dealers who have been to the Soviet Union say the Russians have gone far beyond this level of achievement and currently have lasers working with computers. In Israel, highly automated machinery is being used, operated by women who can be trained in a few months. The cutters of Forty-seventh Street know about these developments, but profess to be unworried. They say their work is far superior. Still, in a world where quality seems to have become less important than cost, time would seem to be against them.

In the diamond business it is sometimes said, "A setter can work in a closet." His workbench is not much larger than a desk in an elementary school. As he sits before it, in a low chair, he seems to be almost an outgrowth of his bench. Protruding from it is an open drawer with a metal bottom that covers his lap. This is to catch gold dust and filings that fall from ornaments of jewelry as he plants diamonds and other precious stones into them. In some shops, the floor is covered with a metal grille and the setters are told to shuffle their feet against the grille before they leave so the gold dust can be scraped loose and swept from the floor each day. In other shops, the setters wash up in a special tray that drains off into one or two barrels. Gold dust is caught in the barrels.

Unlike the cutting room, the setter's workshop is quiet, the loudest noise being the somewhat soothing buzz of the flexible drill that works very much on the principle of a dentist's drill. The setter also uses an assortment of small, razor-sharp chisels, with wooden handles. These are made of strong steel and used to shave gold or silver. In addition to the usual loupe, the setter has a head loupe that is worn with a band around his head. Younger setters, whose eyes are keen, rarely bother with head loupes. When the setter works, he embeds the jewelry item into a kind of shellac and lets it harden. The shellac is cupped in the top of a short stick called the shellac stick. The shellac stick is set into a semicircle of wood, called a bench pin that acts as a vise. Over each bench is a movable fluorescent light. Workers usually work in silence and when they converse they don't have to raise their voices. Music from a radio is the customary background in a setter's shop.

Most setters are either Italian or of Italian descent. There used to be a substantial number of Jews, Germans, and Frenchmen in this field. But they have died out and their sons have either gone into other fields or, in the case of Jews, have gone into phases of the diamond business considered more lucrative. In the diamond ghetto, Italian setters have a fine reputation for craftsmanship and some of them work as designers of jewelry as well—a tradition that goes back to the Renaissance.

The large majority of setters work in small shops as subcontractors. Many of the young setters are the sons of friends or relatives of shop owners. At one point, the federal government, in an effort to teach skills to minorities, asked some shop owners to train them. The owners said they would do so if the government would bond the young men. The government refused, so the owners refused to teach.

"How can you take a chance on someone you don't know?" a shop owner told me. "We have gold and diamonds around all day long."

One of the established setters in the diamond district is Sal Greco, who owns a shop and has been in the business since 1958. He learned the trade while working after school. Since then, he has trained many youngsters referred to him by friends or relatives. He supplies the bench and tools. He gets the work for them. At first he pays about forty dollars a week. Then, every few weeks he gives them a raise. After a couple of years, they use him as a contractor. He gets the work for them, setting the fees with the manufacturer. The worker gives him a percentage and keeps the rest. There are some setters who work as absolute independents, just renting a bench in a shop, and getting their own work. Mr. Greco figures it takes between ten and fifteen years for a man to become a first-class setter.

Like the good cutters, Mr. Greco is saddened by the speedup in production required for profit and a good living. "Everybody who gives you work wants it done in a hurry. You can't do the best if you have to turn out stuff in a hurry, I don't care how good you are."

Among the setters, as in other aspects of the diamond business, there are no receipts. Everything is negotiated on trust. The setter gets an envelope of diamonds from a manufacturer and is told what is wanted. If there are diamonds left over, they are returned. If they need more diamonds, they ask for them. No arguments take place.

Setters are among the first to detect new trends in jewelry and any offbeat developments. They were, for instance, among the first people in the business to realize that the soaring price of gold in the late 1970s would bring about a trend toward lighter jewelry—to save on the purchase of gold. Also, the legalization of gambling in Atlantic City was greeted with pleasure by setters. They knew that a gambler who has made a killing at the casinos could be persuaded by his wife or girl friend to use part of his winnings to buy her a gift in the jewelry shops, and that much of the jewelry in Atlantic City is supplied by New York's diamond-area setters.

Setters, like other mechanics of Forty-seventh Street, take fliers in diamonds. They will buy a diamond from a manufacturer or dealer, and hold it until they hear someone is looking for such a stone. If the profit is right, they sell. There have been times when the dealer who sold a diamond to a setter has bought it back at a higher price. The dealer may even recognize the stone. The mechanic will not gloat openly. For mechanics, like everyone else in the diamond industry, find it easy to be gracious when faced with profit.

8

THE MURDER

For anyone not involved with the diamond people it is almost impossible to comprehend the impact the Jaroslawicz murder had on them. It sent a shudder through the diamond business of the nation, from lowest apprentice mechanic to multimillionaire dealer. It reverberated through the diamond network of the world. This murder may prove to be the diamond crime of the century for the United States, possibly for the world. There have been many diamond robberies on Forty-seventh Street over the years and those who work there accept this risk as an unhappy fact of the business, like the shattering of a diamond in cleaving. One plans against it, takes all the precautions. But sometimes it happens. As for murder, there have been diamond dealers from Forty-seventh Street killed elsewhere. Yet discretion and intelligence can guard very effectively against such an extremity. But the murder of Jaroslawicz was the first time

that a diamond dealer had been killed for diamonds on the Street.
Almost as staggering was the suspicion among the diamond people—
long before there were any arrests—that the murder was an inside
job. Many of them would have preferred to believe the wild media
rumors that claimed the killing was by infiltrators from organized
crime, or even by some fictitious "Israeli Mafia." That way the
blame could be pinned on outsiders. Murder by one of their own was
an offense of Biblical proportions that shook the foundations of their
industry. What was the use of the handshake and the mazel und
brucha ritual, if you never knew whether or not the hand you shook
might kill you?

This was the horrible thought that first began pulsing through
the minds of the diamond people when Jaroslawicz vanished. It became more oppressive when his body was discovered on the block.
"And by Jews," was the fearful, headshaking, whispered refrain, as
though every Jew in the business clairvoyantly knew who had done
it, and had been stigmatized by this crime. Anger and shame were
the sources of the vengeful fury that drove dozens of Hasidim to the
Criminal Courts Building in downtown Manhattan every day of the
trial to pronounce moral judgment in the corridors, and sometimes
even in the courtroom. They were like the chorus of a Greek tragedy. As the details of the grisly murder were slowly assembled and
revealed during the trial, there emerged a mosaic of the curious
crossbreeding of money, idealism, and tradition that shapes life in
the diamond Ghetto. The strange trail of the murder showed how,
even when it was to their own advantage to confide in the police,
these secretive people withheld essential information from the authorities until their own Diamond Dealers Club urged them to cooperate with the police and the district attorney.

On the morning of September 20, 1977, Pinchos Jaroslawicz, a
gentle, frail diamond dealer with a sweet smile and trusting nature,
began work by going underground, as usual, to a large vault beneath
a building on the northwest corner of Forty-seventh Street and Fifth
Avenue. The security man inside the iron gate recognized him and

pushed the buzzer to release the lock. Jaroslawicz unlocked one of the small compartments in the vault, removed his safe deposit box and, standing at a high table with other dealers, began removing and checking parcels of diamonds. He stuffed the parcels into a long zippered wallet chained to his vest, squeezed it into his pants pocket, and left. He worked quickly. He was as other diamond men who met him that day were to recall, in a great hurry, even by the standards of Forty-seventh Street, where the pace is always frantic.

He had a great deal to do. He was carrying more than one hundred diamonds worth between $600,000 and $750,000. Most of the diamonds he was holding were on consignment. He hoped to sell them for the owners and collect a 2 percent commission of the total price. Many of the diamonds, he realized, he would not be able to sell in the immediate future and he intended to return those to the owners. Also, he wanted to make the rounds of diamond dealers to see what else they had that he could take on consignment and sell quickly. It was not unusual for Pinky or P.J., as he was known to many, to be handling hundreds of thousands of dollars worth of diamonds at one time.

The little diamond man was about five feet, five inches tall, weighed less than 120 pounds, and had an excellent reputation. When he took diamonds on consignment, he would either sell them, return them, or get a time extension. If he could not keep an appointment on time, he telephoned. He did not indulge in any tricks to make an extra profit. He did not lie. He was utterly trustworthy.

On this Tuesday, he was in a special hurry, as were others on the Street. This was a very short work week. The following evening would be the start of Yom Kippur. As a devout Jew, he planned to leave about midday the next day in order to be home in plenty of time to wash thoroughly, eat a meal before sundown fast began, and leave for the synagogue for the most solemn of Jewish holidays. Like most Orthodox Jews, he planned to observe the holiday on Thursday as well. Since he normally did not work a complete day on Fridays in order to be in the synagogue for the start of the Sabbath services, and never worked on Saturdays—the Jewish Sabbath—this Tuesday was, for religious Jews, the last full workday of the week.

Ironically, the Yom Kippur holiday was instrumental in trapping his killers. For that reason, the crime became known to the diamond people as the Yom Kippur Murder.

No one will ever know everything that Jaroslawicz did the day of his death as he raced through work. But enough information was dredged up very slowly, over many weeks, by the police and by the assistant district attorney, Peter Stevens, to show he had unshakeable faith in his colleagues, and even in those who killed him.

From what was eventually learned by the authorities about this day, it is possible to trace a pattern in the life of a broker-dealer on Forty-seventh Street. For all his gentleness, he was, like most others in the business, a very hard worker.

It is known, for instance, that he saw David Tauber earlier that day and spoke to him on the phone several times. Tauber worked at the Louis Glick Diamond Corporation at 20 West Forty-seventh Street, one of the most important firms on the block. Tauber was so highly regarded by Louis Glick, for whom he had been working for some fifteen years, that he had been given a separate business with his boss's son-in-law, selling diamonds "to privates" —the term for retailers. Tauber would put out diamonds on consignment to brokers for his company. Sometimes he would sell them to dealers or buy diamonds from them. The distinction between a broker and dealer seems, at first, to be significant. Some dealers say it is critical. Strictly speaking, a dealer owns the diamonds he buys and sells. A broker does not. In practice, however, the distinction is often slight. A broker may buy diamonds on his own account. And a dealer will sometimes take diamonds on consignment. It is very common on Forty-seventh Street for someone to be a broker on some of the stones he is carrying, and a dealer in others simultaneously. Thus, during the trial, Jaroslawicz was referred to by witnesses in the business as both a broker and a dealer. Most of his work was as a broker, however, though he was also a member of the Diamond Dealers Club.

Jaroslawicz, in his dealings with Tauber that day, was working as a broker. Of the thirteen diamonds he had on consignment from Tauber, he returned two before he was murdered. The last time he talked to Tauber on the phone was between 5:15 and 5:25 P.M.—less than an hour before he was killed. He said he wanted to return some more diamonds. He was just across the street and could be there in a few minutes. Tauber told him he had just closed the office safe. So Jaroslawicz said he would bring the diamonds in the next morning. He never appeared, of course, and the firm received some $40,000 in insurance money for its share of the stones that vanished.

The longest period of time that Jaroslawicz seems to have spent with anyone was with Marc Blickman, who worked for the prestigious diamond firm of Orthman and Glickman, at 7 East Forty-eighth Street. This may have been the only time he left the block that day. Blickman recalled that Jaroslawicz had many diamonds in his wallet. For half an hour they examined one another's wares, discussing prices. The windup was that Blickman took a few diamonds from Jaroslawicz on consignment and Jaroslawicz took, on consignment as well, one diamond worth $13,500.

Jaroslawicz also visited a cousin, Manny Jaroslawicz, who at that time worked as a diamond grader on Forty-seventh Street. A grader evaluates a diamond by considering its size, clarity, and imperfections. Like almost everyone else on the Street, his cousin also did business buying and selling diamonds, taking them on consignment as a rule. On this day, Jaroslawicz had come to return some diamonds he had taken on consignment from Manny. At the time of his murder, Pinky had other diamonds from his cousin in his wallet worth $35,000.

By 4:30 Jaroslawicz was in the Diamond Dealers Club at 30 West Forty-seventh Street. He went there almost every working day like many brokers and dealers who are members of the club. It served as his only office. He was there to buy, sell, trade, and see if anyone was looking for him. He also went there to say his afternoon prayers—Mincha—in the small praying room.

On this particular day, something happened in the prayer room that illustrated the curious interplay of religion, business, and the frenzied pace of Forty-seventh Street. The incident, which seemed of little importance at the time, was so significant at the trial that the jury, when deliberating on a verdict, asked to have this section reread. When Jaroslawicz entered the prayer room, he was approached by another member of the club. The gentleman asked him if he could give him $100 bills in exchange for $2,500 in bills of smaller denominations, mostly twenties. Jaroslawicz handed him a stack of $100 bills without counting them. He received a much thicker pile of twenties and some fifties back. He did not count these either. He began praying, a matter of not more than ten minutes, since he knew his afternoon prayers by heart.

Then Jaroslawicz became more anxious than ever. He knew it was important to get back to the vault before 6:00 P.M. and put the diamonds in the safe deposit box. So he telephoned Leo Schachter, a diamond dealer across the street, to say he would be unable to return his diamonds that day and would see him about ten the next morning. This was now about 5:15. Jaroslawicz had twenty-two diamonds on consignment from Schachter. The diamonds were worth more than $100,000, but Schachter was not worried. He trusted Jaroslawicz so much that he kept no records of the diamonds he passed to him on consignment.

Several minutes later, Jaroslawicz dashed into the lobby across the street at 15 West Forty-seventh Street, where he met Hekmatollah Kalatisadeh, a gem dealer, who had an office on the twelfth floor of that building. Quickly, Jaroslawicz dug an emerald out of his wallet that he had taken on consignment from Kalatisadeh, and handed it to him. Then both men trotted to the elevator.

"He was really in a great hurry," the gem dealer recalled. "He was talking and running and, in the meantime, he was preparing to give me the goods."

Also in the elevator was Nico Swaap, a diamond cutter, who worked in Room 1502 on the fifteenth floor. Nico got out on his floor with Jaroslawicz, and saw him walk quickly down the hall, and knock on the door of Room 1504, where Shlomo Tal worked as a diamond cutter and broker. This was about 5:30. Swaap did not wait to see what happened. He entered his own office and left a short time later.

This was the last time Jaroslawicz was seen alive.

The difference between the reactions of the wives of Shlomo Tal and Jaroslawicz when their husbands failed to come home on time that night was revealing. Eva Tal was accustomed to the easy ways of her swarthy, thirty-one-year old husband. "Philanderer" was the word his own lawyer used during the murder trial. Whenever he was a few hours late, she did not think he had been injured or killed. She was convinced her stocky, aggressive husband could take care of himself. So she was not surprised when he wandered in several hours late without an excuse. But when Pinchos Jaroslawicz did not arrive at his Brooklyn home for dinner, his wife became worried. She knew he liked to go directly home from work so he could have dinner with her, and spend time with their two-year old daughter before she was put to bed. So when her husband was more than an hour late, she became alarmed. She phoned his father, Nathan. He telephoned a brother, Philip. The two men drove out to her home. Then, they accompanied her and a couple of friends to the local police station to report him missing.

But they were not satisfied with just telling the police. They realized that it was difficult for the officers to become too upset about a grown man who was a few hours late for dinner. So the Jaroslawicz brothers and their friends drove to the diamond district, getting there between 10:00 and 10:30 P.M. The Street had been closed for repairs so they parked nearby and walked hurriedly through the block. Wherever a building was open and they could see lights, they knocked on the doors, hoping that they could learn something to help them find the young diamond man. They did not go to 15 West

Forty-seventh Street. They learned nothing. But what proved to be important was that they saw men repairing the Street and noticed it was closed to traffic.

The next morning, when the subterranean vault at Forty-seventh Street and Fifth Avenue was opened Jaroslawicz's father and wife were waiting. So was David Borochov, who had an office in that building where he bought and sold diamonds, and manufactured jewelry settings. Pinchos Jaroslawicz had thirty-two of his diamonds, worth between $90,000 and $100,000, that were not insured. The safe deposit box was taken from the safe and opened. It was empty. Now it seemed almost certain that something terrible had happened to Pinchos Jaroslawicz. They knew that, if he had been able, he would have returned the diamonds to the safe before it was closed for the night. Diamond men rarely carry their goods around with them after work.

There was little more they could do that day. Many people from the block were not at work because the day before Yom Kippur is a half-day. Those who did work were eager to clear up their business and leave by noon. Shlomo Tal was one of those who had come to work that morning. He also left shortly after noon.

Nathan Jaroslawicz and his brother, Philip, did not give up the search. On Sunday, September 25, the first day after Yom Kippur and the Sabbath holidays, they were on Forty-seventh Street before 9:00 A.M. to do their own police work. The result was one of the most stirring events ever seen on Forty-seventh Street. A volunteer search party of about one hundred persons, including many of the bearded, black-clad Hasidim, was organized. The police had been alerted about seven in the morning. Media people were also on hand. The search party was broken into groups of four or five that went into every building on the block. The hunters were not satisfied to ride elevators. They walked every step of every staircase. They knocked on every door. They went out on rooftops and down into musty cellars. They trudged through littered backyards. For nearly six hours they searched. They found nothing.

They broke into only one office—room 1504 at 15 West Forty-seventh Street—Shlomo Tal's office. Once again they found nothing. However, the fact that they broke into this office showed that the grapevine of diamond people had already fed information to them of which the police knew nothing.

Not too long afterward, Tal's wife phoned the police. Someone had called her to say the door of her husband's office was seen ajar. She told the police her husband's office had been burglarized. When she reached the building, she rode up in the elevator with two officers. They found her husband's office locked. She gave them permission to summon the superintendent and take the door off the hinges.

With Mrs. Tal, the police entered the inner room. It was made up of two tiny rooms, connected by a doorway. Tal's workroom was about ten feet by four-and-a-half feet. It had three workbenches and a tool bench. The police saw nothing to prove that anything had been stolen. No charges were filed, though it was known that the glass of the inner door had been smashed by one of the search parties so they could open it from the inside.

On September 28, 1977—eight days after Jaroslawicz disappeared—the police designation of his dossier was changed from missing person to homicide.

About 2:00 A.M. on September 28, Police Officer Joseph Wukich, of the 112th Precinct in Queens, was on the midnight to 8:00 A.M. tour on RMP—radio motor patrol—with his partner Carmine LaFaso. They spotted a station wagon about one hundred feet from the service road of Grand Central Parkway, one of the major arteries of the borough, a road that could be used if one wanted to abandon a body and get out of the borough—or city—in a hurry. Queens has, for years, been a popular dumping ground for the disposal of bodies by organized crime. The largest of the city's five boroughs, it still has many open areas and its middle-class residents go to bed early.

The rear lights of the station wagon were on. There was no apparent reason for anyone to park a car so far away from any residence. Officer Wukich, with nearly seventeen years on the force and four in the 112, decided to investigate. He saw a man prone on the floor of the section just behind the rear seat. The doors were locked. He banged repeatedly on the door. The man sat up and opened the door. He asked for his driver's license and registration. Officer Wukich recognized the name. Shlomo Tal. The police had been looking for him ever since the first report of his office being broken into.

In a classic police understatement, Officer Wukich said, "There is an awful lot of people looking for you."

"Yes, I know," replied Tal.

Tal told Officer Wukich the first installment of a story that was to become increasingly dubious. He said that on Sunday morning about ten o'clock—five days after the murder—he had left his wife and three children at their home in Plainview, New Jersey, to go to work. He was driving and had started to slow down a short distance from his home when two men in the street ordered him to halt. They kidnapped him in his own car and forced him to drive for three days in Queens and Long Island. Where the officer found him, he said, the men had given him a liquid containing a drug, and then abandoned him asleep.

Officer Wukich asked him if he was carrying any diamonds.

In response, Tal went to the front of the car and reached underneath the front seat. He pulled out a small leather pouch containing diamonds.

Officer Wukich notified his sergeant.

Sergeant Frederick Ronca drove Tal to the 112, where Tal telephoned his wife. Before hanging up, he handed the phone to the sergeant. Tal's wife asked him when her husband would be home. The sergeant said he did not know.

Then to Detective James Gallagher, a man who has heard many strange tales in twenty-four years on the force, Tal told the second, and even more fanciful installment of why he had been abducted, beginning with the murder itself.

On September 20, about 5:15 P.M., Jaroslawicz had telephoned Tal to say he would be right over to pay $2,850 for stones he had sold for him.

But an hour before he arrived at the dingy office, Tal said, two other men came to the inner door. They were masked. The first one had a gun. They ordered Tal to push the buzzer releasing the lock. Although Tal had $30,000 worth of diamonds on his workbench, he pushed the buzzer to let them in. The men ignored the diamonds on the bench. Instead, they waited for Jaroslawicz.

When the little man arrived, they ordered him to turn over his diamond wallet holding more than $600,000 in diamonds. They also took his money. Then one of the gunmen picked up a two-by-four and knocked him unconscious with a blow to the head, and then strangled him.

They ordered Tal to tie him up with wire. Then said, "Look. One word from you and you, your wife and your lovely kids will get it." They told him to go home and wait until he heard from them.

When they left, Tal did not go directly home. First he went to a Long Island motel for a romp with a woman friend from Pennsylvania.

After reaching home later that night, he received a telephone call. He recognized the voice as belonging to the taller of the two killers. He was ordered to get into his car, drive to Manhattan, and park it at the busy intersection of Sixtieth Street and Second Avenue, leave the door unlocked, and walk a few steps away. He did so. When he looked back a few minutes later, the two men were in the car. They told him to take the wheel and drive off. At Forty-eighth Street and Second Avenue he was ordered out of the car and accompanied the taller thug to his office.

In the office, he was told to fold the small corpse and encase it in the garbage bags they brought with them. The body was stiffening. The tongue was protruding and black. He was told to force the corpse into a box about the size of a child's coffin that was underneath an unused tool bench.

Finally, he was told to clean up the blood on the floor. Then they left. By this time, it was between 12:30 and 1:00 A.M. They walked back to the car, and he drove the two killers to Seventy-sixth Street and Madison Avenue. They warned him once more to keep quiet and left the car.

The next day Tal went to work. He said he did not bother to look in the box, which was covered with a wood and plastic ventilator cover. He assumed that the body was there. He left for home shortly after noon. The following day was Yom Kippur, so he went to the synagogue.

The day after that was a Friday. He went to work as usual. During the day, he was visited by an insurance adjuster and a couple of Jaroslawicz's friends. They asked Tal if he had seen him the day he disappeared. He said he had not. The next day—the Sabbath—he did not work.

On Sunday morning he was kidnapped.

After Tal finished telling this story, he was taken to police headquarters in Manhattan. While he was being questioned there, a police officer was sent to his office to look for the body. When he reported he could not find it, Tal led a police detail to the office. He pointed to the box under the tool bench. Detective Aaron Grossman moved the bench, and loosened the cover from the top of the box. He tore a hole in the green plastic bag and poked a finger through the hole. In his report he wrote: "I felt the toes of the deceased and it was affirmed that the body was there."

Nearby, under another workbench, the police found a second garbage bag. It contained, along with bloodied pieces of wood, a calculator, checks, and bank notes made out to Pinchos Jaroslawicz, his empty diamond wallet, his prayer book, and a yarmulkah in which his name was embroidered in Hebrew characters.

9

THE TRIAL

In the opinion of the diamond people, there was no doubt that Tal had committed the murder. His story about the masked killers was dismissed angrily as desperate fabrication. Yet six months passed before Tal was charged with the murder. Accused with him was Pinhas (Pini) Balabin, a man the police had never heard of when the body was found. It took another six months to get to trial. This, in spite of strong pressure put on top police officials by the diamond community and on the police, in turn, by the brass. But the delays were not the result of police negligence or the usual clogged court calendars. The time was needed to build a case based almost entirely on circumstantial evidence. Even after both sides had rested and were preparing to deliver summations, the prosecution, in an astonishing and heatedly contested argument, won the right to reopen its case, and put on the stand a man who had fled the country rather than testify.

Inherent in murder trials built on circumstantial evidence is the reluctance of jurors to convict solely on such evidence. The eye witness may be more fallible than a well-wrought chain of objective circumstantial evidence. But an eye witness usually carries more weight with a jury. To overcome prejudice against circumstantial evidence in a murder trial, the prosecutor and police must follow every lead, in the quest for endless details, in order to assemble an overwhelmingly logical sequence that will withstand the aggressive questioning expected from the defense.

In this case, the assistant district attorney, Peter Stevens, faced a special problem—the distrust and animosity that had existed for many years between the diamond people and the police was preventing him from getting all the facts. The men and women of Forty-seventh Street considered the police corrupt. The police thought the diamond people were dishonest. Each had stories to support its own side.

A favorite among diamond people was the story of the young man who robbed a diamond merchant in a building on Forty-seventh Street, and was spotted as he darted along the block toward Fifth Avenue. Police officers on duty on the block, alerted by cries from the crowd, pursued the thief and caught him before he had gone two blocks down Fifth Avenue. The police said he had no diamonds. The diamond people refused to believe the thief had passed the stones to a confederate while running. They were convinced the police had confiscated the diamonds as booty.

On the other hand, there is the story told to me by a detective. The detective said he worked on a case in which a diamond dealer claimed he was robbed in his office of diamonds worth many thousands of dollars. He was fully insured. The detective said that long after the insurance money had been paid, he learned—but could not prove—that the "victim" had arranged the robbery and, after collecting the insurance, had sold the diamonds at his leisure. Some of the diamonds were recut by cutters and sold to dealers in the same building.

There was also a story told to me by dealers that revealed their distrust of district attorneys as well as the police. A diamond dealer had been told to turn over some diamonds to the police as evidence to be used against a man who had forged a check to buy them. As months passed, the diamond dealer became worried about his diamonds. The police told him they had to retain custody of them until the case went to trial. The diamond dealer inquired at the district attorney's office. There, he was told that the diamonds were no longer needed for the trial. So the diamond man once more asked the police for his diamonds. Again he was told the diamonds were needed for the trial. He told them the district attorney's office had said the diamonds were not needed. The police told him he was mistaken. The diamond man, wondering if both the district attorney's office and the police were in cahoots, told the police he would go to the police commissioner's office if they weren't returned. They told him to go right ahead. But a short time later they telephoned and told him to pick up his diamonds. He did.

This condition of mutual suspicion was aggravated in the Jaroslawicz case when the police were incapable of finding his body in a tiny room until Tal pointed it out to them. But hostility had existed between Jewish diamond merchants and the police long before there was a Forty-seventh Street. For many of the Jewish diamond dealers, it was rooted in centuries of persecution, in which the police had been the spearhead and obvious symbol of pogroms. There were hundreds of diamond workers on Forty-seventh Street who had fled the Nazis and many who had lost relatives and friends in Hitler's concentration camps. To them, the police were, to some extent, symbols of anti-Semitism. Among the police, a residue of anti-Semitism was fanned by the animosity of the people on the block.

The diamond people may have justly criticized the police for failing to charge Tal with the murder right away, but they also withheld information that could have made such a charge stick.

Caught in the middle was assistant district attorney, Peter Stevens. Some months after the trial he said, "This crime became, for me, a study in the reluctance of the Street to confide in the police or in any authorities."

From the beginning, Stevens was convinced that Tal was a liar and, at the very least, involved in the murder. The police, once the body was found, were skeptical of Tal's story. Nevertheless, they gave him the benefit of the doubt and even found him a secret apartment where he and his family could hide from the "real killers" who, he feared, would kill him for talking to the police.

Stevens, under pressure from the diamond community to charge Tal with the murder, settled, at first, for holding him as a material witness.

"I did not believe Tal's story," he later told me. "But at the same time you don't lock up a guy for murder right away on what we had. I wanted to put a hold on him until we could check him out. Bail would be an indication. If Tal, as he told us, had indeed been threatened by men who he said were murderers, why did he put up bail?"

The first step, Stevens realized, was to persuade the diamond people to confide in him and the police. Unless they did so, it would be impossible to gather the information necessary to establish a murder case with circumstantial evidence. Many weeks passed. No help came from Forty-seventh Street. He was frustrated to the point of desperation.

Finally, he was saved by the Diamond Dealers Club, of which Jaroslawicz and his friends, and many Hasidim—and nearly all important diamond dealers in New York City—were members. The club let it be known to its members—and thus to the whole block—that it was essential for the diamond people to help the police and the district attorney's office in this case.

"What changed everything," Stevens told me, "was when the Diamond Club told the people in the Street to talk to me; told them not to hold out any more."

Only when the diamond people became cooperative did the

police learn of the close friendship between Tal and Balabin; how Balabin and Tal were together for much of the day of the murder; how Balabin was not at work during the days when Tal claimed he was "kidnapped." Information supplied by the diamond people opened new avenues of investigation for the police who were eager to make up for their initial sloppiness, and made possible the indictment of Tal and Balabin for the murder of Jaroslawicz. Equally important, the men from Forty-seventh Street—dealers, brokers, cutters, graders—who had always avoided a courtroom, took the stand during the trial, supplying not only information, but also the credibility so important in a murder indictment sustained by circumstantial evidence.

The usual confrontations that are the highlights of murder trials—a witness identifying the killer; the defendant under cross-examination—were not part of the Jaroslawicz trial. The defendants did not take the stand; there were no eye witnesses to the murder. There were no witnesses at all for the defense. In this murder trial, revelations and offstage emotion were the highly dramatic moments that rose amidst efforts to answer the key questions raised by the murder: Why was the body of Jaroslawicz not disposed of at once? What sort of men were Tal and Balabin? How could the case be built for conviction?

The religious overtones that marked the murder descended on the trial, without warning, in the opening remarks of Assistant District Attorney Stevens to the jury. He explained why the murdered man's body had remained wrapped in garbage bags in Tal's office for eight days. The prosecutor knew this point was essential for the jury, but he could hardly have anticipated its impact on the spectators. For this was not a courtroom audience of buffs, loiterers, thrillseekers, lawyers between cases, and law students. In fact, with the city's three major newspapers on strike for almost the entire trial, the crowds were not large. But those who were there were very special. It was made up largely of devout Jews, most of them Hasidim—bearded, glowering, black-suited, black-hatted men who believed in Old Testament vengeance.

For them, as they sat on the pewlike courtroom benches, not unlike those of many synagogues, and heard the prosecutor tell the jury how Yom Kippur had made it impossible for Tal and Balabin to dispose of the body quickly and avert suspicion, it was as though the Almighty had intervened to smite the sons of Cain. It was a confirmation of the words of their daily prayers; the opening words of the Jewish prayer for the dead: "Yisgadal veyiskadash shmay rabaw"— exalted and hallowed be God's name. It touched off the first of several waves of angry murmurs that eventually exploded in the corridors in episodes that nearly caused a mistrial.

Tal and Balabin, the prosecutor told the jury, had returned to Tal's office on the night of September 20, 1977, a few hours after the murder, intending to get rid of the body. To their astonishment, they found that the street where they had planned to park their car was closed off. This block that should have been quiet and dark, was brightly lighted and bustling with street repair workers. The reason was the imminence of Yom Kippur, the ideal time to do repairs on Forty-seventh Street.

By the time the holidays had ended, it was too late for Tal and Balabin to try to carry out the body of their victim. It would have been impossible to do so without being observed. Yom Kippur, the voice of atonement in the Jewish religion, was making them pay for the murder.

During the trial, from the testimony of friends of the defendants, as well as from the diamond people and police, the defendants emerged as utterly selfish, conceited, cruel men who were contemptuous of society and particularly of women.

There was the testimony of Chaim Bratt, young, shifty, less than two years in the city since leaving Israel. He had shared an apartment with Balabin and Benny Shabtai, both ex-Israelis, in the good residential district of East Sixty-ninth Street near Second Avenue. Tal, another ex-Israeli, had often come to their apartment and when Bratt visited Tal's office, Balabin was always there.

He had good reason to remember September 20, the night Jaroslawicz was killed.

Balabin had come home about 7:30 that evening, with a girl friend named Dorothy Caggiano. He left with her and returned half an hour later by himself. Balabin then went into the bathroom with Bratt and, the witness said: "He told me that he killed Mr. P.J. He told me that he is going to have a lot of money and if the police would ever come and question me I should stick to my story that I saw him coming home with the girl.

STEVENS: Did he say how he killed him?

BRATT: He told me he hit him over the head and strangled him.

STEVENS: What did you do after that?

BRATT: I had a date, and together with Benny Shabtai the girls came over and we went out.

The next time the witness saw Balabin, was on Friday, after the Yom Kippur holiday.

"He told me," the witness testified, "Sunday is a very important day for him. He told me he would have to get out the body from the building and he thinks he is going to have a problem because they are tarring the road on Forty-seventh Street."

A couple of months later he testified that Balabin discussed the murder again: "He told me the police did not know what they were doing and they would never catch him."

Balabin was worried about something else. "He told me he has a problem with the elevator man. He is not sure if he saw him, or whatever, and if he will have a problem with him he would try to get away with him [to do away with him]."

At a later time, the witness said, when he and Balabin were sharing an apartment at 400 East Eighty-fifth Street: "I came home after questioning by the police, after I had been held by the police for two days and I was very angry with Pini [Balabin]. And I told him that I am very angry with him and I'm getting bothered by the police all the time, and I was telling him why was he telling me all these things. I don't want to know about it. He told me he was sorry, but it is too late now and I should stick to the story that I saw him with a girl that evening coming home and that's what I should tell the police all the time."

The witness said he told Balabin at that time that Benny Shabtai was also being questioned by the police and he did not know what Shabtai had told them.

During this conversation, Balabin promised him that if he had any problem about immigrating he would arrange for him to marry a Puerto Rican girl and thus become a citizen.

When cross-examined by Balabin's attorney, Abraham Brodsky, Bratt was asked why he had not talked to the police about this murder. He said, "I didn't believe the person is telling me things like this. I didn't believe him."

Brodsky then pointed out that when he went before the grand jury he did not talk about the strangling. Not until he was questioned by the FBI did he tell the story.

Bratt told Brodsky that he told the full story to the FBI because the FBI told him that if he lied to the grand jury he would go to jail.

"And that's when I decided to come out."

Another witness whose testimony showed a sinister side of Balabin was Ellen Mae Riley, a young woman with an episodic career in department stores that included dismissal for shoplifting by Alexander's. She said she and Balabin were "very good friends," and was also on good terms with Tal, had been intimate with Bratt, to whom she gave gold chains for him to sell. The chains, she said, were "given" to her by a manufacturer.

She testified that a few nights before Jaroslawicz was murdered, she was with Balabin, Bratt, and Shabtai in their apartment. Balabin was talking about going to Harlem to make "a very big deal." She gave him a gold bracelet for luck.

On the night of the murder, she was in the same apartment with a girl friend, planning to go on a double-date with Bratt and Shabtai. A week later she was at the apartment with Balabin. She testified as follows:

"I asked Pini how he was and so on. How things were going for him, and he said everything was fine. Then after that he spoke about killing. He said he got a very great sensation out of killing. He had no fear, you know. It didn't bother him whatsoever."

Q: What did you do at this point?

A: At this point, I didn't move at all. I didn't take my eyes off him. And I just let him continue on talking.

Q: What did he say?

A: He said that there was some problem trying to get rid of the body.

Q: Did you ever have a conversation with Pini concerning the police investigation?

A: Yes, I did.

Q: What did he say?

A: They were, you know, several different times. Most of the time it would be in a coffee shop. We would have coffee and talk. That's basically about it.

Q: And what did he say about the police investigation?

A: That he had the police beat. That it was, you know, it was sort of like fun. That he had no worries whatsoever."

A diamond cutter who worked in the same room with Balabin remembered that on the day of the murder a young woman had called for Balabin. Dorothy Caggiano, a secretary, and the woman with whom Balabin had come home that night, told of their date. On the evening of September 20, she met him at his office shortly after six o'clock. They walked from Forty-seventh Street to his apartment at Sixty-ninth Street and Second Avenue, about a mile and a half away. His two roommates were already there. She dropped off a package, and left with Balabin. They went around the corner and had a few drinks in a tavern. They returned to his apartment for about an hour. Then he put her in a cab. He had arranged this date with her the day before with a phone call.

This testimony was considered significant by the prosecution because it demonstrated that the day before the murder, Balabin was already planning an alibi for the slaying, and that the girl's appearances with him at the apartment and a tavern were intended to prove he was with a date at the time of the killing. The prosecution, pinning down the time of their meeting, showed that Balabin could have committed the murder and still have kept the date. The perfunctory nature of the date was also an indication that it was hardly romantic.

One of the most exciting developments of the trial was kept from the jury by Justice Aloysius Melia. In a discussion held in his robing room, the prosecutor recounted Bratt's testimony that Balabin told him he might have to "get away with" [do away with] an elevator operator he thought had recognized him when he returned to his office late on the night of the murder.

On December 6 the prosecutor told Justice Melia, more than three months before any murder arrests had been made, the elevator man who had been on duty during the night of the murder was working the night shift again. At about 6:30 A.M. he was approached by a white man he considered Israeli or Greek, but whose face he could not see clearly. The man shot him three times without saying a word. He was not robbed, though he was carrying eighty dollars and wearing a watch. The prosecutor argued that this information should be admitted as corroboration of Bratt's testimony. Justice Melia refused, calling it "too remote," adding, "It well may be that Balabin is the one who had the shooting gun, but that's too speculative and too prejudicial."

As testimony piled up, showing Balabin and Tal as callous and vicious individuals, the Hasidim became so angry they made unflattering remarks about the defense lawyers in the corridor. One day, just as the court was emptying for luncheon recess, they were so abusive toward the lawyers that Tal's lawyer, Steven Hyman, before the jury had returned, moved for a mistrial. He said that there were "at least two or three jurors" within hearing distance when the Hasidim were shouting obscenities and that this demonstration "very well may have tainted a jury." The judge, who had observed this demonstration, said he did not think the words were clear but offered to poll the jury. The defense lawyers disagreed among themselves so the poll was never taken and the trial carried on.

Justice Melia then spoke coldly to the spectators about "mob rule" in a democracy, saying: "Those of you who do not wish to follow the rule of law and common decency not only are not welcome, but will not be permitted on this floor. The spectacle in the corridor outside this courtroom at the luncheon recess is not justice. It is a desecration of justice and a credit to none of us. . . . This is not the market place. This, with the help of God, will be a court of law and I mean to see that it is so conducted."

Less sensational were details that became links in the circumstantial chain. For example, the link in the form of Tal's rubber check. A diamond man testified that a check from Tal for a few hundred dollars had bounced and that he had complained about this to Tal the day of the murder. Another diamond man said that Tal had told him on the phone he was anxious to see Jaroslawicz that day because Jaroslawicz had promised to pay him for the diamonds he had sold for him. From another witness came the information that Jaroslawicz, a few hours before he was killed, had given a diamond dealer some $2,500 in $100-bills in return for a thick pack of twenties and fifties. Bank employees told of Tal's deposit of more than $2,800 in cash the day after the murder, and a film from the bank camera showed he required about four minutes to count the stack of bills before making the deposit.

None of these details, separately, created excitement in the court. But when the jury was deliberating on a verdict, it asked for a rereading of this sequence.

Another example was the investigation of garbage bags. Police went to Balabin's apartment building and the porter led them to a pile of green plastic garbage bags in the laundry room, similar to those in which the body was wrapped after the murder. Experts testified on the detailed similarity between the bags in the laundry room, and those used for the murder. Balabin told the police that both he and Tal used these bags from time to time, but not for hiding bodies.

Police skepticism became known during the trial when texts of their interrogations of Tal and Balabin were read to the jury. As Tal neared the end of questioning, a detective asked, "Do you think this [your] story makes sense?"

Tal replied, "I don't know if it makes sense. I'm just telling what happened."

Toward the end of the police interrogation of Balabin, a detective said, "Pini, you don't trust us. . . . You're trying to bullshit us and you can't."

The most damaging witness against the killers was a man no one expected to see in court, Benjamin Shabtai. Assistant District Attorney Stevens had entered a stipulation in court, the day before both sides rested, that the whereabouts of Shabtai were unknown.

The next week the prosecutor asked the court to reopen the case to hear testimony by Shabtai. He said that just before the trial began, Shabtai fled the country and had just been brought back, after District Attorney Robert Morgenthau had agreed to pay for his return. Justice Melia, despite objections by defense counsel, ruled in favor of the prosecution on the grounds that Shabtai had gone before the grand jury and the defense counsel had seen the grand jury testimony.

Shabtai was as shady as the others in the Tal-Balabin clique. A former roommate of Balabin's, this Israeli had worked as a croupier and dealer in Swaziland, but was fired for "behaving badly at the table." In the United States, he admitted during cross-examination, he sold "phony" Cartier watches "by the thousands."

On the night of the murder, he testified, he, Bratt, and two girls were chatting and laughing in the apartment they shared with Balabin. Balabin arrived about 7:00 P.M. with Dorothy Caggiano. After about an hour and a half, Balabin and Dorothy left. Approximately fifteen minutes later Balabin returned alone.

STEVENS: "And when he came back did you have a conversation with him?"

SHABTAI: "After half an hour, when we were talking, he called me to my room and he told me: 'I want to tell you something.' I said: 'What is it?' So he told me: 'I committed a murder.' "

STEVENS: "Did you ask him any questions at this time?"

SHABTAI: "No. I just told him: 'Pini, what are you talking about? You got nothing else to tell me? What is this nonsense.' And I walked out. I didn't believe him."

The next time he saw Balabin was the day after the Yom Kippur holiday.

STEVENS: "And did you have a conversation with him?"

SHABTAI: "Yes. He told me it's a different case to take the body out of the office. And because the Street is full of FBI and people are walking in the Street."

STEVENS: "Did you say anything to him at this time?"

SHABTAI: "I still didn't believe it. So I didn't have to say anything to him, except that I don't know what you are talking about. I didn't believe it at the time."

Subsequently, he told Balabin that the doorman had informed him of the FBI coming to the building, and checking on the plastic garbage bags with the super. "I asked him: 'Did you use anything like a plastic bag or anything like that.' So he said yes."

In cross-examination by Brodsky, the witness said he had repeatedly told the police he knew nothing about the crime but had told the truth to the FBI "to save my skin."

In redirect examination by the prosecutor, Shabtai said that after he learned the detectives were checking into the plastic bags, he said to Pini: "The detectives were here and they were down in the basement to look at the plastic bags. So I asked him, 'Did you use the same plastic bag for the crime?' So he said yes. So I said, 'You're in trouble.' So he said, 'No, I'm not in trouble because most of every apartment building in New York used the same company or the same bags or plastic bags, the same thing.' He's not worried at all."

The defense summations were brief. Brodsky asked the jury to use "common sense" in judging Balabin. He said the police believed that Tal and another man had committed the murder. He said they picked up Balabin because he was a friend of Tal's. "And so the scenario is written." He called Balabin "humble, honest, and forthright" in statements to the police. He challenged the credibility of Shabtai and Bratt, calling the former a seller of phony watches and the latter a loan shark.

Hyman's case was even more difficult since the body was found in his client's office, and Tal had admitted to being a witness to the murder. Tal's story, he said, "may not make sense, but it does not mean there is guilt beyond a reasonable doubt. Why would a man guilty of murder point out the body to the police after the police had been to the office and had not found the body? As strange as Tal's story might sound, the police had not refuted it.

"Tal," he said, "was set up by the murderers. He was the patsy."

Assistant District Attorney Stevens, in his summation, addressed himself to the question that had become increasingly obvious during the trial: Why did Balabin tell his roommates about the murder?

"He had just pulled off a homicide and robbery, in which he had stolen something like $600,000 or $700,000 worth of diamonds," Stevens told the jury. "He was bragging about it.

"Two: Who was he talking to? He was talking to his roommates. His friends. He was confiding in them in some respect.

"And three: At this time he was confident, confident that he and Tal would get rid of Pinchos Jaroslawicz's body and that there would never be a solved homicide."

He then raised other questions for the jury to consider: How would the mysterious masked men know that Jaroslawicz was coming to Tal's office? How would they know there was a two by four in that office? Why would they allow a witness to live?

"This was a planned execution of Pinchos Jaroslawicz."

Justice Melia, who had instructed the lawyers for both sides not to raise the question of circumstantial evidence during the selection of jurors, stressed this aspect of the case. Circumstantial evidence, he told the jurors "consists of a chain of circumstances which lead from the proof of things that were seen and known, down to the establishment of the unknown or unseen facts; the unknown and unseen is the actual killing."

Thirty-two hours after the jury retired, it returned with a verdict of guilty against both defendants. Justice Melia, in imposing the stiffest possible sentence—twenty-five years to life—said in a final statement: "This was cold-blooded murder for greed."

10

DIAMONDS VERSUS INFLATION

Two diamond dealers were discussing the most important subject on Forty-seventh Street in the autumn of 1979, and perhaps for many years to come—how the rising popular fever to purchase diamonds as a hedge against inflation was driving up the price. The man whose office it was, sat behind his desk, fingering dozens of diamonds, occasionally holding one up between thumb and forefinger, switching on the fluorescent desk light, peering at it through his loupe. The visiting dealer talked. But the more he talked, the more absorbed the man became in his diamonds. When the host dealer talked, the visitor would look bored, glance out the window, or at a shelf, as though intrigued only by the electronic scales. The two dealers were playing one-upmanship with stories about diamonds versus inflation.

Finally, as though convinced he had exhausted his host's best tales, the visiting dealer played his trump tale with great assurance: "I saw something today I never thought I'd see on Forty-seventh Street."

No response. The host dealer unfolded a parcel of diamonds, as casually as though he were doodling while listening to a tedious telephone call.

"I just saw a red diamond, right here on Forty-seventh Street," repeated the visiting dealer. He waited. Red diamonds are quite rare. Even when they turn up, they are usually a rather insipid red.

The fingers that were folding the paper wrappers around the diamonds stopped. The host dealer said, "Yeah?" It was a mixture of curiosity and skepticism.

"Yeah." With emphasis. Then, almost aggressively, "Three carats. Flawless. Absolutely flawless."

"A pink?" (Attempt at putdown.)

"No. No pink. Red. Red like a good Burmese ruby."

"I'd like to see it."

Silence.

From outside the double set of secured doors a voice cried down the dim corridor, "Hold the elevator."

The man who wanted to see the red diamond continued thinking for a few seconds. Then he said, "Can you tell me where I can see it?" (Insistent. No longer skeptical. Not challenging. Certain that the other dealer was not exaggerating.)

"No. I already told you too much."

"I'd like to see it."

"I shouldn't even talk about it. I talked too much already."

"I would like very much to see it. Not to buy it. I just want to see it."

"It's leaving the country."

"When?"

"Today."

"Come on. I just want to see it."

"How much," he said, teasingly, "do you think it is, per carat."

Silence. The dealers looked into one another's eyes, as if they were involved in a bargaining session. Then the man who wanted to see the red diamond said, "A million. A million a carat."

The visiting dealer gaped. "How did you guess?" he asked with genuine astonishment, unexpected among these people who are experts in feigning emotion or disinterest.

"I figured if I had such a diamond, what would I want. And I thought, 'Such a diamond is worth a million dollars a carat.' " He became silent. When he spoke again it was with sudden passion.

"In my whole life I only saw one red diamond. And that wasn't flawless. Now some Arab buys a flawless red diamond. For him it's a few minutes of oil. He puts this perfect red diamond in a vault and lets it make money for him."

A few days later, at one of the busiest exchange booths on Forty-seventh Street, the phone rang. A doctor from the Midwest was calling to ask the booth man if he had a good diamond for about $25,000. The booth man, who rarely sells retail and then only for very special customers he has known for a long time, offered a few suggestions and, before hanging up, said, "Okay, I'll hold it. But I can't hold it more than a week." Three days later the doctor was at the booth. He looked at the diamond. "You say it's good quality," he said. The booth man nodded, "Very fine." The doctor said he would take it. The booth man asked how he wanted it set. The doctor said he didn't want it set. "Just put it in your vault," he said, "until you hear from me." He paid the booth man. The two talked about one another's families for a while and the doctor left.

About the same week, Morton Sarett, president of the nationwide Jewelry Industry Council, was threading crowded Fifth Avenue, near Forty-seventh Street, with the quick step so characteristic of the diamond area, when his sleeve was plucked. He turned to face a prominent diamond dealer, one of those with a Fifth Avenue office in the Fifties, who tend to be condescending toward the hurly-burly and congestion of Forty-seventh Street.

"I just left ——," the diamond dealer told Mr. Sarett, naming another respected diamond dealer. "He was offered $100,000 for a one-carat stone." He waited for this to take effect. Mr. Sarett showed the expected surprise. Then, with calculated calm, the diamond dealer added, "And he refused. He refused." His calm broke. "It's wild, I tell you. Wild!"

Not too long afterward I was with Howard Herman, the fourth-generation diamond dealer, whose enormous acquaintanceship among dealers, brokers, cutters, setters, and assorted dabblers in the diamond business, makes him an ear for stories on Forty-seventh Street. He told a dealer the following:

In the spring of 1979, a dealer purchased a diamond for $16,000. He did not try to sell it. Just put it in the vault and waited. In the late summer he removed it and sold it immediately to another dealer. The price was $22,000. A week later it was sold at the Diamond Dealers Club. The price was $29,000. Three days passed. It was sold to still another diamond dealer. The price was $32,000.

When the story was finished, his friend remarked: "If that stone ever leaves the Street, half a dozen people could go out of business."

The same year the super-diamond for the super-star appeared—the 69.42 carat diamond that Richard Burton had given to his then-wife, Elizabeth Taylor, in 1969. At that time it was reported to have cost $1.1 million. The marriage ended, time passed and the actress wanted to sell it. Her asking price was said to be $4 million. In June of 1979 she succeeded. Henry Lambert, the diamond dealer was the purchaser, said he paid $3 million for the pear-shaped stone. By the fall of 1979 he had sold the diamond at a price he did not disclose, but which he described cheerfully as "a profit, of course." Not too long afterward, he spent more than a million dollars to acquire another pear-shaped diamond. This one, 111.59 carats, he claimed to be the largest natural coffee-tinted diamond ever found and the twenty-fifth largest diamond in the world. "Quality diamonds," he said, "continue to increase in value. They are extremely desirable investments as well as fabulous decorations." Insiders in the diamond business said privately that they believed Lambert was either part of a syndicate in these transactions or perhaps working for such a syndicate on a commission basis. There was even some skepticism about the prices. But this sort of suspicion is traditional in the business and can never be ascertained.

The key word for the diamond business, as of 1979, was, indeed, "wild." Many thousands of Americans had decided to follow the example of rich Europeans, Japanese, and oil-swollen Arabs in buying diamonds as a defense against inflation. This development, while profitable for dealers, sent billion-dollar quivers down the crystalline spine of the industry, from the muted luxury salons of Fifth Avenue to the noisy booths of Forty-seventh Street. It was the major subject of conversation in the office suites of top dealers, and among the Hasidim who had no offices. It reverberated in the diamond marts of Antwerp, London, Tel Aviv, Johannesburg, Amsterdam, Hong Kong, and Bombay. It threw the industry into controversy. Some dealers feared eventual disaster. Others dismissed the calamity-howlers as fools. And, as might be expected, there were those dealers who, while they deplored this new turbulence, were secretly selling diamonds to companies and persons who acquired them for the diamond investment business.

On Forty-seventh Street, diamonds for investment escalated the excitement to something approaching pandemonium, particularly as Christmas fever came on. Old ladies, who had never intended to sell diamonds they had been holding for fifty years, were crowding Forty-seventh Street with young couples seeking engagement rings. The elderly semi-retired men and youths who worked as errand boys were on the prowl for a diamond that could be bought and sold at a profit. The line between investment and speculation had become almost invisible.

One dealer said, "Our policy now is to buy anything that we think will make a profit." This, at a time, when the industry was professing to be maintaining a very low profile, avoiding any accusation that it was becoming more concerned with the sale of diamonds for investment than for jewelry.

Even De Beers Consolidated Mines, Ltd., whose domination of the world diamond industry has earned it the nickname of the Syndicate, was concerned about the investment splurge that it could not quite control. The normally low-keyed Harry F. Oppenheimer, chairman of the board of De Beers, in the staid 1979 annual report of the flourishing company, warned:

"While the use of diamonds as a store of value is, I believe, likely to continue at a higher level than in the past, the trading of diamonds at prices unrelated to those that can be currently sustained in the jewelery market is a threat to the stability of the trade."

In five years the price of quality diamonds had soared some 300 percent. One-carat stones that dealers had sold for between $37,000 and $40,000 in November of 1979, were being sold for $50,000 in February, 1980. Rings, brooches, necklaces, bracelets—some of them of fine workmanship—were being taken apart for the resale of loose diamonds for investment during inflation. Diamonds that, under ordinary circumstances, would have been sold by dealers to famous jewelry establishments to be mounted in exquisite settings and sold at high retail prices for adornment, were being sold loose only to be interred in the darkness of safe deposit boxes.

Retailers, some of them sizable, and even some retail chains, had moved into the diamond investment business, making special offers in price for those who made substantial purchases. Banks in Switzerland, France, and Belgium were offering diamond investment services. A Chicago bank offered diamonds instead of interest on some savings certificates.

No one knew how many millions of dollars Americans were swapping for diamonds to fight inflation. One of the best studies of this development on a world-wide basis was made by the Economist Intelligence Unit in 1978. They estimated the American investment at that time to be between $150 and $200 million. Other estimates, in more widely read publications that were not as reliable, estimated the American investment to be as high as $500 million, and claimed that perhaps 20 percent of gem diamonds being sold in the United States—largely via Forty-seventh Street—was for investment. How much of this money was a form of tax evasion and how much for legitimate investment—or a combination of both—no one could guess. It was certain, however, that never in the history of the United

States had there been such a plunge for investment diamonds by Americans.

The grave danger of this boom was that the buyers of these diamonds knew nothing about diamonds and very little about the differences between buying diamonds as opposed to buying gold or collectibles. People chattered about "diamond certificates" that had emerged from relative obscurity into public consciousness. But they really did not understand what the certificates were based on, how reliable they were, how wide the differences were between one kind of certificate and another.

Even worse, the "investment diamond" firms upon which they were almost entirely dependent for guidance, knew very little more than they did.

The result was inevitable. Thousands of Americans were being duped in their purchases of diamonds for investment. This is supported by official investigators in New York, California, Arizona, and Florida, and by undercover inspectors from the post office who are among the most assiduous diggers into the operations of shady diamond investment companies. Such companies have gulled customers with multicolored brochures, glib telephone sales pitches, and fictitious offices with addresses in Wall Street, Fifth and Madison avenues.

Nevertheless, these countless examples of chicanery in the diamond investment business do not mean that diamonds are not a smart way to beat inflation. It is very possible that if diamonds are purchased intelligently, and with expert advice, they may be among the best repellants of inflation. In fact, some pension funds, in late 1979, were exploring the possibility of putting money into investment diamonds. There is a solid history, going back many generations, to support the premise that quality diamonds can be a good defense against the economic and political turbulence that can follow uncontrolled inflation.

David Robbins, who investigated diamond frauds for many months as a special deputy attorney general in New York State, told me:

"Sometimes the investors have paid close to the retail price for what they thought they bought at 'wholesale' prices. More than 50 percent of the cases we have looked into show excessive pricing. I don't doubt that if you could be sure of getting quality stones at a good price and could hold them for three years, you would probably come out ahead. And certainly some of these companies are on the level. But the more I look at the ripoffs, the more I think that if you want to buy diamonds for investment you could do better buying on Forty-seventh Street from someone you can trust than buying from investment companies."

Many of the complainants, he said, were doctors and dentists. A substantial number were small businessmen. "People who have a lot of cash." Some of the diamond investment companies, he said, were making a good deal of money legitimately. Most of the companies that go into the business, he said, intend to be honest. "They just get greedy. They find that people are so gullible they can't resist the bigger profits of ripoffs."

What about the customers? Are they involved because it is a good route to tax evasion? Mr. Robbins laughed. "Call it tax deferral," he said.

As of December 31, 1979, New York State was the only state requiring diamond investment firms to register. Some companies chose to leave the state rather than register. The reason is obvious. Registration requires the officers to fill out a form giving his or her background by answering such questions as: Have you ever been suspended or expelled from membership in any securities exchange, association of securities dealers, investment advisers, or counsel? Have you ever had a license or registration revoked as a dealer, broker, investment adviser, or salesman? Have you ever been enjoined or restrained by any court from issuing, selling, or offering securities; handling or managing accounts; rendering securities advice or counsel? Have you even been convicted of a crime? Have you ever used aliases? If so, give them. And so forth. The state also requires a photo taken within the preceding six months.

The development of the diamond for investment trend in the

United States grew slowly. As it began to boom in the mid-seventies, there were some media exposés of fraudulent companies and crackdowns by state authorities. For a while, the trend seemed to subside. Then in 1979, as inflation rose in the wake of sharp oil price increases, investments in diamonds soared again. Mr. Robbins, though fearful of the victimization of purchasers, is hopeful that companies are becoming more responsible and that, as state attorney generals assume regulatory functions, the worst sort of operators will find it increasingly difficult to function.

Juan Albornoz is reluctant to be as optimistic. He is one of the post office inspectors who, over and over again, has to trace complaints to abandoned offices, littered with piles of telephone books, and rented furniture. He is torn between pity for the victims and rage against the con artists. He listens to tales of the elderly, small business men, owners of retail stores, and veterans of the Vietnam war, who saved their money and lost it all perhaps in a single investment. These people do not buy out of greed, but out of fear that their savings will be wiped out by inflation. "Yet one of the greatest problems in fighting such frauds," says Albornoz, "is that there is little public sympathy for the victims. They are regarded as fools who should have known better."

"Generally, the people we have talked to," he continued, "are intelligent. I don't understand how they were taken in by the nonsense that they were buying diamonds wholesale. And so often they did not think of the fact that they have no way of being able to sell the diamonds, and when they do sell them, it will be to someone who is certainly not going to pay retail prices or anywhere near it."

He told me of the investor who paid $70,000 for a few diamonds. When he sold them, he received only $12,000—a loss of $58,000. There is also the story of the old man who paid $3,000 for a little box of tiny diamonds.

"If he can get fifty dollars [for them], it will be a lot," he said.

He spoke of what has come to be known as the "Catch-22" of the diamond investment scam.

"You buy a diamond. You are told the weight. It comes in a

plastic container. If you take it to an appraiser to judge the color or clarity, he can't do this properly unless he removes the stone from the container. But if he does this, then the company that sold you the diamond says it is not obligated to take it back."

In fact, the company has no intention of taking it back in any case. Their talk that by removing the diamond from the container you have voided the insurance is also untrue. If the diamond was insured at all, it would be the company that was insured, not the customer. Once the customer receives the diamond, the insurance has ended.

There is another deal that such companies arrange when the post office inspectors close in on them. The officers of the company say they know nothing about misrepresentation by their sales force to customers. They will even produce papers signed by the salesmen or women promising not to misrepresent the merchandise. The salesman will say he has nothing to do with the quality of the diamonds. He just sells. He doesn't select the diamonds. He does not judge them.

One time, Mr. Albornoz went through an entire carton of telephone bills recovered from an investigation of what proved to be an empty office. He selected telephone calls from the bills which were more than twenty minutes long, assuming the telephone numbers would lead to past sales of diamonds. Of those people he called, the ones who had purchased diamonds had no complaints.

"None of these had even had the diamonds appraised," he said. "They just put the diamonds into their safe deposit boxes and planned to leave them there for a few years. Several years from now they may want to sell the diamonds. Maybe to send a kid to college. Then they will learn that the diamonds are worth much less than they paid for them."

Basically, the telephone selling pitch by fraudulent companies is divided into three phases: the opening; the drive; and the close.

In opening, the salesman will be rather low-keyed. He introduces himself, says he is not calling to sell anything, he just wants to tell you about investments being made in diamonds. He will quote briefly from the *Wall Street Journal* or some other financial publication. Then he will say that if you are interested, he will send you his company's literature on the subject. On the basis of your re-action, he will make a notation on a card that indicates whether you are worth a followup.

The second phase begins about a day after he thinks you have received the literature. He will not wait much longer than that be-cause he does not want you to have too much time to think about it, or consult with others, particularly a lawyer. In fact, salesmen for these companies are instructed not to sell to lawyers, media people, or government employees. In this second phase, he asks what you think of the literature. Then he gets around to the kind of money you should invest.

The close is sometimes assigned to a person who is expert in the hard sell. He will say that he is sorry but the diamonds he had offered to sell you for $17,000 have already been sold. They went for $19,500, he will tell you. But, he adds quickly, he has "a direct line to persons handling a new shipment that we're expecting in a couple of days, and I can get you a good buy at $19,000. I have only until Friday [or some day about three days away]. I can't hold them beyond that date. I will give you first shot." He asks for the name of your bank—giving the name of his company's bank as a prelude. The sure sign that he is closing in for the kill is when he tells you to "take your pen out" to total figures he will rattle off to you. You and he do simple arithmetic together and you are pleased that you both reach the same answer. He talks about the transaction last week and you both figure out how much you could have made if you had been in on it. "I can't guarantee we'll do as well with the new batch of diamonds," he will say. "The price of diamonds keeps going up. We both know that."

The salespeople, many of whom have had training in acting or announcing, receive special instructions for certain anticipated ques-tions. For instance, if a potential customer, obviously leaning toward purchase, says he would like to discuss the matter with his wife before making a definite commitment, the script of one company is:

"(Talk low and softly, as though you're whispering a secret in his ear). 'Mr. ——, let's be honest. Did you ever meet a woman who didn't love diamonds? Matter of fact, when buying stocks or commodities, and they go the wrong way, all you have to show for it is a piece of paper, whereas with diamonds you always have what you bought. We have many clients who actually use the stones, enjoy them for many years, and have the freedom of converting them back into cash anytime they need. Let's face it. There are not many things you can invest in, use and enjoy, and then ten years later get back far more than you paid. Now all women love a surprise gift, so let's register these diamonds in your wife's name and keep it a secret from her, and a few weeks from now she'll wake up one morning and find three sparkling diamonds on the breakfast table. And I'm sure she won't complain. Am I right Mr. ——? Now get a pen or pencil and I'll tell you exactly how we'll handle the transaction. OK?' (Be sure to get the wife's first name.)"

Officers of diamond investment companies that have registered with the New York State attorney general's office, concede that there have been many abuses by fraudulent or irresponsible firms. But they insist that diamonds can be a wall against inflation.

Michael Freedman, president of Gemstone Trading Corporation, in his handsome office suite lined with wall maps of the nation, produced for me a number of checks and statements to show that persons who had purchased diamonds from his company a couple of years earlier had resold them through his firm as well. After the company had deducted a commission for resale, the individuals still made considerable profits, far beyond the rise of inflation.

Mr. Freedman recognized that those from whom his company bought diamonds had to make a profit, just as his own company did. This meant two markups. The post office inspectors told me that some markups in the diamond investment business are far in excess of 50 percent, sometimes well beyond 100 percent.

When I asked him if a person with friends in the diamond business could do as well or better by buying diamonds through them, he replied, "People come to me and say: 'Can't I do better on Forty-seventh Street?' I tell them: 'Sure. If you know someone.' Very few of our customers are from New York. Even less are Jews from New York. So many New York Jews have a friend or relative in the business. Our market is Mr. and Mrs. America who don't know someone in the business."

From mid-1977 until the latter part of 1979, he said, more than one hundred diamond investment companies had opened and closed.

"The fly-by-night companies outnumber the legitimate ones," he said. "Here we are. Our company is only five years old and we are already a granddaddy in the business. But I think the industry is maturing and the public is getting smart."

One interesting development that occurred about this time was a diamond investment company that crossbred Wall Street and Forty-seventh Street. At that time it was the only diamond investment company on Forty-seventh Street and was, to my knowledge, the only diamond investment company with its roots in the diamond business. The company, called NYDEX (short for New York Diamond Exchange, Inc.), was registered with the attorney general's office. It worked on a flat 10 percent commission basis. It would not handle any order for less than $10,000, or sell any diamond that was less than $6,000 a carat. It preferred not to sell diamonds priced higher than $30,000 because resale was easier with that ceiling. The firm was headed by Faivel J. Jaroslawicz, a member of the Diamond Dealers Club. It was his nephew, Pinchos, who was murdered on Forty-seventh Street in 1977. One of the few benefits of this tragedy was that it called attention to the fact that this family adhered strictly to the mazel und brucha code of the diamond industry. The other two officers of the company, sons of the president, were Isaac and Manny. The former had Wall Street brokerage training and the latter was an expert with diamonds.

Each of these companies conceded that unless it had quality diamonds, it could not offer a reliable guard against inflation to its customers. Each had a solution. Mr. Freedman's company had an arrangement to buy what he called the bulk of its diamonds from a very reputable diamond firm in Antwerp—a firm so well established that it was one of the elite that was supplied directly by De Beers at the sights. The Jaroslawicz firm had the advantage of having as its president a man who was respected on Forty-seventh Street, and a member of the Diamond Dealers Club.

But what would happen if the Syndicate, having already indicated its displeasure with the mushrooming business of diamonds for investment, were to cut off supplies of quality diamonds to dealers who sold to diamond investment firms; perhaps even shared in the profits of diamond investment companies? In reply, some officers of diamond investment firms said there were reliable reports that De Beers had changed its attitude and now looked with sympathy upon the sale of diamonds for investment, provided the companies were legitimate.

This was emphatically denied to me by the official spokesman for the De Beers operations in Europe, David Neil-Gallacher.

"Our official policy," he said, "is that diamonds we sell are for use in jewelry. But we cannot prevent persons who buy from us from selling to investment firms."

That the Syndicate is so helpless is not taken seriously on Forty-seventh Street. Dealers point out how easy it is for De Beers to cut the allocation of diamonds to anyone on its list if it is offended by the behavior of that dealer. It has the ultimate threat—one which no dealer will risk—that of being cut off their list entirely and thrown into the wild scramble of buying diamonds on the open market. Not to mention the enormous loss of status that comes with being stricken from the list.

"We know," says Mr. Neil-Gallacher, "there are many people who have invested successfully in diamonds. There is no doubt that if you buy good quality stones from a reputable dealer, and keep them for a reasonable time, you can make a profit. What is a reasonable time? You would need to expect to keep them seven to ten years. By its very nature, any investment is something that is going to be sold. With diamonds you do not know when you will sell. But very likely you will sell in an economic recession. That is exactly when the demand for diamonds eases off. You would then have a situation when large quantities of stones are being sold at the same time."

Such a situation is not far-fetched. In France, early in 1978, as the election approached, there were insistent reports that polls showed the Left would triumph. There were also suggestions that if this happened some industries would be nationalized. Many rich men and women invested heavily in diamonds. They even dipped into the funds they needed for business, which indicated they were considering the possibility of fleeing the country. When the Left failed at the polls, there was a rush to resell the diamonds. Buyers were in a strong bargaining position. Prices offered were considerably less than were asked. Losses were great to many of those who had invested.

There are other possibilities that could be even more menacing for those who have bought diamonds for investment. One of the strongest forces driving Americans to make such investments is the loss of confidence in the dollar. As it slumped in response to the soaring price of imported oil, it created havoc with the nation's balance of trade. Assume that the United States were to make big oil discoveries offshore; or work out practical methods for the substantial use of solar energy; or make a practical electric automobile long before the mid-eighties. Even in 1979 there were many exciting ideas for the use of solar, wind, and thermal energy. The nation has always shown a great aptitude for mechanical inventiveness. Any of these developments could strengthen the dollar. When the dollar gained back its strength, those who had bought diamonds for investment would be selling simultaneously. The price would tumble. This is a prospect that frightens many diamonds dealers.

Lazare Kaplan, founder of the important diamond firm of Lazare Kaplan International, recalled vividly what happened when diamond prices collapsed within a year of the fall of the stock market in 1929. He was wiped out. Suddenly there was no longer a market for diamonds. Those to whom he had sold diamonds on credit could not pay off their debts. He was only able to rebuild his business because his son, Leo, had $300 in a savings bank, which he withdrew and gave to his father.

"With that $300 I was able to get going again," he recalled. "That shows you how low diamonds fell."

Both Kaplans agreed that such a collapse could not occur in 1980. Since the crash, De Beers has set up its own elaborate system for controlling the prices of rough diamonds.

Leo Kaplan—he still keeps his canceled bankbook—has a warning, however, for those who buy diamonds to resist the erosion of inflation.

"You can't use the sharp rise of diamonds of the last five years as a criterion," he says. "Over the long run, diamonds have tended to appreciate at the rate of about 7 or 8 percent a year."

Allen Ginsberg, president of the international division of Zale, which was grossing more than $500 million a year from jewelry sold through its 1,200 retail outlets, said: "The people who buy diamonds for investment have to understand that the people who sell to them have to make a profit. And they should also realize that most of those who sell to them do not know very much about diamonds."

Some dealers say that since only quality diamonds are of investment grade and that to resist inflation one has to be able to hold onto diamonds for a matter of years, only the rich can really afford this kind of hedge.

Legitimate diamond investment firms brush these fears aside as unfounded, exaggerated, or a vestige of the distant and irrelevant past. If that is so, how do legitimate investment companies protect their customers?

With very few exceptions, the officers of diamond investment firms know very little about diamonds. They draw their customers from advertisements they place in publications read by persons interested in investment; from speaking at investment seminars; from lists of persons who invest in stocks and bonds and collectibles; from word-of-mouth; and from names of those who have been selling their stocks.

The basic ignorance of both diamond firms and their customers about the subject in which they are investing, brings us to a fundamental difference between investing in diamonds and in gold, or some established collectible. With gold, 14 carat, or 18 carat, whatever the carat, that is the quality of the metal and the quality will be the same everywhere. But with diamonds, the word carat is merely the weight of the diamond—142 carats to the ounce. As we have seen, every diamond is different and the range in quality can be prodigious. The next problem is that there is no recognized market for diamonds. Gold is bought and sold on established exchanges. Paintings are bought at auctions or from reputable galleries. There are ways to learn the price range for paintings by a particular artist. But for diamonds, there is no exchange. The experts keep their knowledge to themselves.

The vast majority of diamond investment firms, since they lack knowledge and an official public exchange, have two forms of protection. First is to buy from dealers they can trust. This is hardly a guarantee. Anyone with even a casual knowledge of the tough bargaining in the diamond business knows that a dealer tries to get the best price he can for his merchandise. He does not consider himself obligated to teach a purchaser how to judge a diamond. This knowledge cost him many years—and some serious losses—to learn. It is expected that a diamond dealer will praise his own merchandise. Caveat emptor, like the diamond, is forever, so far as the diamond business is concerned. Diamond dealers, among themselves, have a code of honor. But that does not necessarily apply to diamond investment firms. Even with their code, diamond dealers enjoy outwitting one another.

So trust in the dealer is certainly not enough to bring quality diamonds to diamond investment firms.

The second defense is more important: the diamond certificate. In recent years, technological advances have made it possible to examine diamonds more carefully than in the past and companies have been created to perform this service for dealers, jewelers, and the public. The best-known of these companies—and the one considered the most reliable in the United States—is the Gemological Institute of America, which has its East Coast laboratory at Forty-seventh Street and Fifth Avenue.

Any responsible diamond investment company will want G.I.A. certificates for the diamonds it buys and sells. This certificate gives the diamond's weight, shape, cut, measurements, and proportions; it gives an opinion of its polish and symmetry, and grades the stone for clarity and color. A reputable investment company will sell only those diamonds that are within certain ranges of weight and quality, and these are indicated on the certificate. In weight, the customer's best opportunity for a good investment is to buy a diamond that weighs between one and two carats. In color, the diamond should be in one of the classes from D to H. In clarity, it should range from flawless through VS. The growing demand for investment diamonds in this range has forced some diamond investment companies to lower their avowed standards and sell diamonds that are less than a carat in weight, with color classifications down to I and J, and even lower; and to clarity classifications of SI.

One thing the G.I.A. certificate does not do is place a monetary value on the diamond. The G.I.A. has seen too wide a range of diamonds to become involved in the highly subjective and often deceptive hassles in pricing diamonds. As it is, the G.I.A. is not perfect. There can, for instance, be honest differences of opinion among experts about the exact color or clarity of a diamond. The line between a diamond that has D or E classification for color can be very fine—and the difference can be expensive.

Robert Crowningshield, vice-president of G.I.A. and head of its eastern division, who is highly regarded for his integrity on Forty-seventh Street, concedes that there are instances when dealers, after getting a G.I.A. certificate for a diamond, are dissatisfied and resubmit the diamond without saying it has already been certified. Sometimes, he says, the second certificate is different from the first one. A very important diamond dealer told me that on the basis of many such experiments, he has found that differences in certificates for the same diamond can occur in one out of three cases. He contends that the experienced experts of the diamond business are much better at making the partly subjective judgments of color, clarity, and cut than the relatively less experienced persons who work in the laboratory.

Mr. Crowningshield, who has been in a good position to see the rapid growth of the purchase of diamonds for investment, believes that the overall quality of diamonds being sold has been going down. This may be because dealers are keeping their best stones in inventory or are selling them privately at better prices than they can get from investment companies. Or it may be that so many of the good quality stones are being sold that the rise in prices has brought forth poorer stones for the investment market.

The G.I.A. official told me the story of a man who bought a diamond for $8,000 in the early 1970s. This man knew something about diamonds, was shrewd and had acquaintances on Forty-seventh Street. In 1979 he decided to to sell the diamond. He took it to investment firms. The best offer he got was $17,000. On Forty-seventh Street, he was offered from $11,000 to $22,000.

Because diamond investment companies know that their business could expand considerably if the public had some way of knowing the value of diamonds, a few officers in such firms have tried to work out a basic scale. One of these scales was placed as an advertisement in the *Wall Street Journal* at weekly intervals by NYDEX. It gave what it felt to be the going prices for a round brilliant—the most prevalent investment diamond cut—of one carat, for the color categories of D, E, F, G, and H, and for the clarity scale of flawless to VVS2. This showed a range, after being broken down into these categories, from $37,000 down to $6,600. But there is no way of proving that these ratings are any more accurate than the considered judgment of the officers of that company. It is likely that such figures would have more acceptability if posted by the Diamond Dealers Club. But the club, far from leaning in that direction, has avoided the subject. For one thing, the attitude of the Syndicate carries overwhelming weight at the club.

How do diamonds compare with other investments by standards outside the industry? A report in June of 1979 by Salomon Brothers, which was intended to show that stocks were a good investment because they were so low in price, placed diamonds in eighth place—below gold, Chinese ceramics, stamps, rare books, silver, coins, and Old Master paintings. Diamonds were ahead of oil, farmland, housing, foreign exchange, bonds, and stocks. Stocks were at the bottom.

What this report did not consider was that diamonds have some very special advantages for investors. They are not subject to the wild fluctuations of gold or the whims of taste that can change the value of a painting. They can contain vast value in very little space. Millions of dollars worth of diamonds can fit very easily into a tiny pocket. They are the hardest of substances. These qualities are particularly important for those who wish to conceal them and vital to those who feel it may become necessary to leave the country in a hurry; something that Europeans, particularly Jewish ones, learned long ago.

But none of these attributes of diamonds is worth much for those who buy through untrustworthy companies. Since the representatives of the fraudulent diamond investment companies may often be more persuasive than the more responsible salespersons from legitimate ones, the problem for the would-be investor is how to avoid the shady company. There is no guaranteed way. But there are some sensible precautions.

1. Before making any commitment, check with the attorney general's office.

2. In purchasing a diamond, favor a round brilliant cut, between one and two carats; do not go below H in color or VS1 in clarity.

3. Have the right and opportunity to have the diamond appraised independently before purchase.

4. Be sure, before buying diamonds for investment, that you can afford to tie up these funds for a few years, at least. Diamonds, unlike Treasury notes for instance, do not pay interest while they await maturity. The best pulling power of diamonds seems to be in the long run.

There is one contingent in the diamond business that is usually disregarded by those who are eager to sell diamonds for investment; those who believe the best investment value of a diamond is in its beauty as a jewel. One of the most fervent believers in this point of view is Claude Arpels, head of the American division of the luxury jewelry stores of Van Cleef & Arpels. He looks with some sadness on the trend toward buying diamonds unmounted to be buried for investment. To him precious stones are meant for exquisite settings and the joy of adornment. Here is an aesthetic value that can be incalculable over the long pull, just as the Cellini chalice in the Metropolitan Museum of Art is priceless far beyond its gold and precious stones.

"I have noticed," he told me during the height of the 1979 diamond investment fever, "that my customers want better quality. Is this because they want a better investment? We don't sell our pieces for investment, you know. In the old days, grandmothers passed on jewelry as heirlooms. They did not sell. I have a customer who, every Christmas for many years, has bought two or three important pieces. He now has as many good pieces as we do. He will not sell. He did not buy them for investment. But they are very fine investments. When I see our customers looking for quality again, I like to think that they are buying them once more to pass along as heirlooms. And if they are, these may be the best investments of all."

II

THE ELITE

When you emerge from the congested, one-block Diamond Ghetto of Forty-seventh Street onto Fifth Avenue and turn north, you are not aware of any sharp incline. You do not feel any sudden ringing in the ears, as in a swiftly rising elevator. The sidewalk becomes less crowded, but remains quite flat in the ten short blocks along Fifth Avenue from Forty-seventh to Fifty-seventh streets where the leading diamond retailers in the nation are located. In addition to Rockefeller Center, St. Patrick's Cathedral, Saks-Fifth Avenue, and Bergdorf Goodman, you will pass the elite of the world's retail diamond business—Tiffany & Co., Cartier, Harry Winston, Inc., and Van Cleef & Arpels. From these establishments that sell to the wealthy and the famous, even the clerks look down on Forty-seventh Street, as if from a mountain peak, and speak of it with disdain. Here the gems are treated as works of art, not "goods." You will see no "sale" signs in their windows, so carefully ornamented with only a few choice jewels. The prose of their catalogues is as rich as their carpeting. Their marts are "salons" and "boutiques." Their buyers are not customers but "clients," who can study six-digit gewgaws at leisure in private rooms on antique tables covered with black velvet. These are the most sacred temples of "high jewelry," where harsh bickering about prices is in poor taste.

The attitude of Forty-seventh Street toward Fifth Avenue may be envious, sometimes malicious, but certainly not humble. Many of the diamond people are convinced that the once great gap between Fifth Avenue and Forty-seventh Street has narrowed considerably and that this trend will continue. They know there are many more millionaires on Forty-seventh Street than in Fifth Avenue companies. In fact, many on the Street still refer to Harry Winston as Harry Weinstein, his name at birth. They have watched these Fifth Avenue stores drift into lower-priced merchandise to capture a larger share of the middle-class and lower-middle-class markets. They know that Winston sells substantial quantities of diamonds to diamond investment firms, in addition to selling diamonds loose to individuals for investment. They know that Tiffany, Cartier, and Van Cleef & Arpels take jewelry on consignment and sell it for commission. All of this the diamond people of Forth-seventh Street do as well.

To the block, the strongest confirmation of their belief—although snob advertisement exists to the contrary—that Fifth Avenue and Forty-seventh Street are coming closer together has been the debut of Fortunoff, the jewelry-store chain, with its name in letters more than a foot high, it's hard-sell approach, and its indifference to the reticence of Fifth Avenue elegance. Inevitably, a joke about the new Fifth Avenuenik is told on Forty-seventh Street with great relish.

There was once an old and very rich Jewish lady who realized the time had come to talk to her rabbi about death. She told him that when she died, she wanted the funeral service in his temple. He smiled. She said she wanted to be cremated. He stopped smiling. He told her this was not in keeping with Jewish tradition. She insisted. She reminded the rabbi that she had given generously to the temple and might remember him in her will. The rabbi said he would consult with scholars and get back to her. Several days later he told her that cremation was out of the question. When she remained adamant, he asked her why she wanted to be cremated. She replied, "When I am cremated I will have my ashes scattered in Fortunoff's on Fifth Avenue. That way I know my daughter will visit me twice a week."

Behind the aplomb of Fifth Avenue are signs of great change in the world of high jewelry. Clients who can afford expensive pieces are buying more modest pieces because they are afraid to attract attention, lest they be robbed. This is supported by figures from N. W. Ayer, which handles advertising and publicity for De Beers in the United States. Its statistics show that while the sale of diamonds to women in 1978 increased to $2 billion from $1.9 billion in 1977, and in units from 6.4 million to 6.9 million, there was a decline in overall caratage. The once gentlemanly competition among Fifth Avenue salons has become more cutthroat. In 1979, for the first time since its founding in 1837, Tiffany was bought by another company. Once a dying enterprise until Walter Hoving took charge in 1955 and rebuilt its profits, it is now the property of Avon—a company which became well-known when it started selling cosmetics door-to-door. Cartier, on the other hand, just a few years earlier, had a great celebration when its Paris, London, and Fifth Avenue stores came together again, is now part of a holding company called Cartier-World, with Joseph Kanoui, a Swiss financier, as chairman. Such financial shenanigans are scorned on Forty-seventh Street, where each company, dealer, broker, or cutter is fired with independence. As for the big customers of the Fifth Avenue salons, they are no longer rich Americans. They are Arabs, Japanese, and West Germans, who buy just as heartily from Forty-seventh Street merchants as they do from Fifth Avenue retailers, and who usually have the stones sent to them via Antwerp or Switzerland.

It is conceivable that Fortunoff, a strange blend of Forty-seventh Street and Fifth Avenue standards spawned in the suburbs, is indeed the wave of the future in high jewelry. If so, it will not be the first time that the most fashionable jewelry stores have made dramatic changes.

Charles Lewis Tiffany, founder of the oldest and most famous of Fifth Avenue's jewelry stores, and known for most of his life as the "King of Diamonds," would have found the competitive spirit of Forty-seventh Street stimulating. They, in turn, would have appreciated how he progressed from stationery to diamonds. A canny and energetic New Englander, he and a boyhood friend, John P. Young, chose a terrible year to start. Panic and riot were sweeping New York in 1837 and financial failures were epidemic. Nonetheless, with money borrowed from Tiffany's father, they opened a stationery store on Broadway near City Hall, that also sold assorted bric-a-brac ranging from umbrellas to desks. When they realized there was a market for Oriental items, they walked over to the waterfront and haggled with seafarers back from the Far East for merchandise to place in their store on consignment. From the beginning, however, Tiffany laid down an extraordinary policy for the time—the price of every item in the store was to be clearly marked and no bargaining over price was allowed.

The Tiffany road to diamonds began with paste jewelry. But Tiffany never deceived his customers. He told them it was cheap costume jewelry from Germany, the sort of merchandise which, not many years later, he would not have allowed in his store. In the early 1840s, he sent his partner to Paris and bought an enormous quantity of superior paste diamonds. They sold well. He decided the time had come for a flier in real diamonds. Again his partner went to Paris. This was 1848, when the revolution forced Louis Philippe and his Queen, Amelie, to flee in such haste that they left behind the crown jewels. At once, Tiffany's partner and a young assistant bought up diamonds at very low prices from royalists who had nothing else to sell. Then they learned about the crown jewels that had been found by the police. When Tiffany's men left France, some crown jewels were missing.

No one has ever said that Tiffany went into the diamond business as a fence for royal jewelry. But the definitive work on the company, *The Tiffany Touch*, by Joseph Purtell, says: "No official suggestion has ever been made as to precisely what happened to them [the missing jewels], but a few discreet lines in a Paris newspaper of the time record that Tiffany's had acquired a store of diamonds during a buying trip to Paris—including some of the French crown jewels."

Back in New York, far from hiding the jewels and selling them secretly, as any efficient fence would, Mr. Tiffany, who was friendly with reporters and enjoyed publicity, told of his great acquisition of precious diamonds. It was in these stories he was dubbed the "King of Diamonds."

Tiffany's venture into high-class silver was largely the result of his flair for publicity, in addition to his friendship with P. T. Barnum. When two of Barnum's celebrated midgets, General Tom Thumb and Lavinia Warren, were married, Tiffany made a silver horse and carriage for the couple, displaying it well in advance of the wedding in the store front window. The public's interest in silver induced him to enter the silver business more seriously. Here, he firmly established the Tiffany reputation for quality and integrity. He specified that his silver be 925 parts silver out of 1,000, which was far superior to the usual merchandise in this country, on a par with English sterling.

The House of Tiffany became pure Tiffany in the early 1850s, when Mr. Tiffany bought out Young and another partner he had acquired. By that time, Tiffany's—a four-story building on Broadway near Spring Street—had bought the Atlas-supported clock still over its door, and become a tourist stop. Tiffany also made a discovery to rival diamonds—Oriental pearls. They were more expensive than diamonds since they were worn in strands down to the waist, sometimes costing more than a million dollars. But the price was within easy reach for post–Civil War multimillionaires and their wives. In 1870, Tiffany built an iron-fronted building on Union Square that was hailed as a "Jewel Palace." American presidents and foreign royalty competed for Tiffany diamonds, pearls, and silverware with families like the Vanderbilts, Astors, Belmonts, Goulds, Rothschilds, J. P. Morgan, and Diamond Jim Brady. The discovery of diamond mines in Africa in the late 1860s and 1870s simply meant increased sales for Tiffany's. When the Metropolitan Opera House opened in 1883, the blazing diamonds that gave the first tier the name The Diamond Horseshoe were largely from Tiffany's.

In 1902, at the age of ninety, Tiffany died. No other Tiffany ever headed the business. But its growth continued, under persons trained by the founder, and in 1905 Tiffany's put down fresh roots on Fifth Avenue and Thirty-seventh Street, its new home a replica of the Palazzo Grimani in Venice. They did not even bother to put the name of the company on the building.

Though the oldest son of the founder, Louis Comfort Tiffany, had little to do with the store's continuing success, he made an impression of his own with his Tiffany glass. Slowly his work was appreciated and even celebrated, but eventually it became passé and his glass-making studio went bankrupt. When he died in 1932 at the age of eighty-four, his inherited fortune had shriveled from some $13 million to less than 1.5 million. This Tiffany, even more than his father, believed in the combination of the functional and the artistic. But he lacked his father's business sense. His survivors considered his glass so ugly they gave it away, unloading it on secondhand dealers and even destroyed it as junk. Tiffany lamps that could be bought in the 1950s for less than $100 sold in the 1970s for more than $100,000 each.

The stock market crash of 1929 and the Great Depression of the 1930s hit Tiffany's hard. But, stubbornly, despite losses, it continued to pay dividends to stockholders out of its reserves. When it made its next move, in 1940, to its present home, Tiffany's was in a purely functional, seven-story box of granite and limestone. World War II improved its business, but Tiffany's had been badly hurt by the popularity of cultured pearls and growing competition from Cartier, Van Cleef & Arpels, and Harry Winston. Its poor showing after World

War II brought on fights for stock control and ended in the victory of
Walter Hoving as chairman in 1955. Hoving had previously been
an executive at Macy's Montgomery Ward and president of Lord &
Taylor. At Tiffany's, he made changes and ran sales. He brought in
new designers, including Jean Schlumberger. He called attention to
the store's low prices for good value. Between 1961 and 1970 he
tripled its sales.

"Aesthetics," he said, "if properly understood will almost always
increase sales." And to a decorator hired to work on the windows, he
said, "Make the windows beautiful and don't try to sell anything."

By 1978, though Tiffany's was offering diamonds valued from
$250 to more than a million, the average purchase was between
$500 and $2,000.

In the 1960s, Tiffany's introduced the concept of "diamonds by
the yard," created by Elsa Peretti. These were necklaces of small
diamonds on gold chains that sold for as little as $125. They were
ideal for the highly informal spirit of the 1960s—worn with jeans as
well as to the opera; by young and old; sold in Japan as well as in the
United States. They became, in a way, almost as famous as the "Tiffany setting"—the six-pronged ring claw that reveals so much of a
diamond and is one of the reasons that Tiffany's is probably the best-
known seller of diamond engagement rings.

"We literally revolutionized the diamond business with the
"diamonds by the yard,' " I was told by Henry D. Platt, a great-great-
grandson of the founding Tiffany and president of the company.

By the end of the 1970s, the Tiffany association with great
wealth had altered considerably.

"We depend on large volume," Mr. Platt told me toward the
end of the 1970s, "not just catering to the very wealthy. The focus of
our direction is toward the great middle class. Not with the very rich.
We don't follow the taste of others. We set the standards. We offer
the diamond, the workmanship, the design. We don't take marketing polls. We do not feel we must find out what the public wants.
We raise the taste. I am always astonished at my friends, good business men and women, who are impressed by talk of 'discount' and

'wholesale' in diamonds. Why people buy jewelry that way I'll never know. They are usually taken to the cleaners when they do that. We have been around all these generations because we have kept our reputation for fair dealing."

Will the Tiffany emphasis on what Hoving called "aesthetics" remain unalloyed with Avon in charge? The Tiffany management insists that Avon will not interfere. By Christmas of 1979, when the aisles between Tiffany's diamond showcases were a bedlam of customers, a tall scaffold was rising along the Fifty-seventh Street wall of Tiffany's. Three new floors are being added. The official explanation is that the space is being provided for Tiffany craftsmen and other employees. But on Forty-seventh Street, where Hoving is disliked intensely, the gleeful conjecture is that somewhere on these new floors will be space for Hoving's new bosses—people from Avon who believe in marketing polls and limitless mass markets. Will the Tiffany craftsmen who are permitted to take their time in making jewelry find that the new regime will bring about a speedup that, as on Forty-seventh Street, will sacrifice quality for quantity? Tiffany says no. On Forty-seventh Street, they say yes.

Among those who shop along Fifth Avenue there is a tendency to think of Cartier and Tiffany as very similar. Both date back well into the last century. Both do a brisk business in silverware, dishes and stationery, in addition to jewelry. Both have a tradition steeped in royalty and wealth. Both have a famous diamond named after the store. The signature of each adds value to a jewel. But there is an important difference.

The House of Cartier is Paris-oriented. In its Fifth Avenue establishment, at the end of the 1970s, it had one major designer. In Paris, it had sixteen. If Tiffany were to lose its Fifth Avenue operation, it would be out of business. But Cartier without Fifth Avenue would still have operations in some ninety countries, and its headquarters in Paris would probably continue to flourish. Tiffany, for all its reputation, and its foreign-accented sales help, consciously dislikes Forty-seventh Street. Cartier, being European in view, thinks of itself as different from Forty-seventh Street, of course, but bears it no more animus than it would toward Antwerp, from which so many on Forty-seventh Street came. Besides, from time to time, since Cartier-Fifth Avenue has no cutters, it draws upon Forth-seventh Street, particularly its Paris-trained craftsmen, to work on its diamonds.

The special pride of Cartier is its pioneer work in Art Deco design for jewelry. At the Fifth Avenue mansion, Louis Cartier is considered the father of Art Deco jewelry, the so-called classic look. The revival of Art Deco in the late 1960s was a boon to Cartier's, just as, when, during the 1940s and 1950s, Art Deco was out of favor, Cartier's was hurt. One of the major innovations of Nathalie Hocq, when she succeeded her father Robert in 1978, as president after he was killed in an automobile accident, was to research the designs of Cartier jewelry early in the century and have them reworked for the 1980s.

An essential ingredient of the Cartier atmosphere is its elegant Fifth Avenue residence at Fifty-second Street—a classic Renaissance mansion that has been designated an official landmark building of the city. The interior, with its spacious aisles between showcases and display tables—another difference from the more crowded Tiffany— is in keeping with the exterior. How Cartier's acquired this structure is one of the favorite tales of its colorful history that dates back to 1847.

In 1908 when Pierre Cartier, a grandson of the founder, came to New York to set up a branch for the Western Hemisphere, Fifth Avenue in the Fifties was choice terrain for residences of the very wealthy. So he picked a mezzanine along Fifth Avenue in the Fifties for his business, which, after all, would be among the rich, a number of whom had shopped in the Paris and London branches of the House of Cartier. It was the appearance of such little businesses, a mere trickle of sedate commerce, that persuaded the Vanderbilts to move uptown to get away from the taint of tradesmen. Whereupon Mrs. Mazie Plant, wife of a financier, Morton P. Plant, decided that their home, at Fifth Avenue and Fifty-second Street, was in a declining neighborhood and urged her husband to move uptown. But she loved the house they were in. Mr. Plant suggested they pick a new site and have a duplicate house built.

Though Mrs. Plant thought business was polluting her environment, she enjoyed the proximity of Cartier's. One of the prize possessions of the new Cartier branch was a long double strand of pearls. The price was one million dollars, but she coveted them. She told her husband she wanted the necklace. He said that what with the new home he could not afford this luxury. She insisted. He resisted. Somehow, in conversations between Mrs. Plant and Mr. Cartier, an idea evolved. The result was a most extraordinary barter deal. The house was swapped for the pearls. In 1917, the residence became Cartier-Fifth Avenue. Apart from installing display windows on the street floor, Cartier made few changes in the interior. The high ceilings were retained. So was the beautiful paneling of the main floor, the marble of the ballroom floor upstairs. The entrance, which had been on Fifth-second Street, was shifted to Fifth Avenue.

The House of Cartier, which became a world symbol of established order, was almost literally born in guns. Pierre Cartier, early in the nineteenth century, was not content merely to make guns, however. He also decorated them. His son, Louis-Francois, who was taught goldsmithing, preferred jewelry and by 1847, was concentrating primarily on making it. Within three years, his Paris boutique was catering to the extravagances of the Second Empire. His display at the Paris exposition of 1867 won favor with the nobility and, though the Franco-Prussian War and the collapse of the Empire nearly ruined him, he was, with his son, Alfred, well on his way back in business in time to take advantage of the gold strikes in Africa.

Alfred had three sons, Pierre, Louis, and Jacques, whom he encouraged to study painting and sculpture. The Cartiers made friends with the Worth family, already famous as couturiers. After Louis married one of the Worth girls, he and his father set up their most famous shop on the rue de la Paix, in 1897. It was, naturally, close to the Worth atelier, with its clientele of European royalty and

American nouveau riche so that those who bought gowns at Worth did not have to go far for Cartier jewels. The House of Cartier opened its London branch in 1902 and was already so beloved of royalty that King Edward VII ordered twenty-seven diadems from them for his coronation that year.

Louis Cartier needed diversion from jewelry. He became fascinated with clocks, bringing to them his feeling for beauty. Then, in 1904, because a friend who was a balloonist needed a timepiece that would not force him to dig in his pockets for a watch while aloft, Louis Cartier developed the wrist watch. From jewels, clocks, and watches the Cartiers, through the inspiration of Jeanne Toussaint, branched into handbags, suitcases, toilet kits, cigarette holders, ashtrays, wallets, desk ornaments, and stationery. Cartier was at least as prodigious, when it came to Fifth Avenue, as was Tiffany.

Because of its international range it weathered the stock market crash and the depression much better than did Tiffany's. In fact, it expanded during that period. But World War II and the Nazi invasion of France began a new phase in the history of Cartier's. Jacques and Louis Cartier, though never taken by the Nazis, died in 1942 shortly before the liberation of France. After the war, Pierre, the last of the brothers, retired. The next generation of Cartiers did not have the flair for the business. The three Cartier branches broke apart, preparing the way for the next ruler, Robert Hocq, a French industrialist. He took over the Paris branch in 1972 and, within four years, had reunited it with the London and New York homes to touch off a gala champagne preview and supper with a stunning retrospective of jewelry from Cartier's private collections in Paris, London, New York, and Monte Carlo. Also on display were articles borrowed from museums and private collections—for the benefit of the American Cancer Society—at the New York branch.

Hocq, like Hoving, was a businessman. He developed the boutiques known as "Les Must de Cartier," attached not only to Cartier branches, but planted in department stores considered worthy of such Cartier merchandise as luggage, lighters, clocks, pens, handbags—descendants of the so-called Department S, conceived during Louis Cartier's era. The S was for Select. It now stands for Soir as well. Cartier's, like Tiffany's, was looking for what it called "a broader segment of the market," selling at "more accessible prices." Cartier's was displaying, among its jewelry, private items it had taken on consignment and was selling on commission. Customers did not know which of these jewels were part of the Cartier stock.

Officially, representatives of the new Cartier regime could talk of Nathalie Hocq's love of jewelry, design, and the company's aim "for the top of the pyramid in our clientele." The fact was the distance between Forty-seventh Street and Fifth Avenue was indeed narrowing. The control of all Cartier operations under its holding company, Cartier-World, headed by Kanoui, the Swiss banker, was seen on Forty-seventh Street as a confirmation of this trend.

Rare on Forty-seventh Street are those who are in the diamond business for aesthetic reasons. Occasionally, you find this pure love of jewels when speaking with one of the older store owners or with some veteran behind a counter in a diamond exchange who advanced through a boyhood apprenticeship of working on diamonds. But in the vast majority of cases, when a dealer, broker, store owner, booth man, or mechanic says a diamond has beauty, he means it is worth a good deal of money. He can become very excited about an unusual diamond, but this emotion is more the glitter of profit than of facets.

When I began visiting the top jewelry salons of Fifth Avenue, I thought I would find some pure passion for gems. At Tiffany's and Cartier's, I did hear this sometimes in the voices of customers or in the conversation of craftsmen. Yet, just as beauty was obscured on Forty-seventh Street by tension, competition, and the joy of driving a bargain, so, in Tiffany's and Cartier's, aesthetics were buried under business—the multiplicity of showcases of diamonds, piles of crockery, masses of silver, stacks of stationery. I recall vividly the sarcasm of a fine craftsman on the upper floors of Cartier's as he assembled diamonds and platinum into jewels to please some rich vulgarian who had strayed into the place. Just as clearly, I can remember the joy of a Cartier executive who had returned from a shopping spree on

Forty-seventh Street with some beautiful pieces of silver. Basically, however, Cartier's and Tiffany's, in their bigness and success, are no longer under family control. It is no wonder that Tiffany's had become part of Avon's cosmetic business and that Cartier's is in the embrace of a holding company run by a Swiss banker.

I finally found what I sought at Van Cleef & Arpels, a very low-keyed, intimate salon and boutique on Fifth Avenue and Fifty-seventh Street, diagonally across from Tiffany's. This is still an exclusive family business run by the Arpels—the Van Cleefs are no longer involved in the firm. But it is scarcely what you would call a momma-poppa store. When you enter its small salon, with the poised and well-groomed saleswomen near unostentatious desks, it is a dramatic contrast to the rows of showcases in Tiffany's. Behind the salon are the private rooms. Clients who come here usually call ahead to give some idea of what they want, rather than arrive in droves off the street as into Tiffany's and Cartier's to browse or spend part of their lunch hour.

Claude Arpels, who is in charge of the Fifth Avenue branch of the Paris-born operation, seems genuinely sad as he contemplates a future in which diamonds would be just another kind of investment rather than a thing of beauty. He talks of diamonds and then, suddenly, he asks Mrs. Angela Forenza, a vice-president, to bring "the ruby." She returns soon with a ring in which an 8.95-carat Burmese ruby is surrounded by diamonds. He looks silently at the dark stone with the smoldering lights.

"This is more beautiful than diamonds," he said. "I think I will be sorry when it is sold."

He seems sincere when he speaks of the beauty in quality rubies, emeralds, and sapphires, in some cases finding them more exciting than diamonds. He said he has refused $500,000 for the ruby ring and thinks it's worth twice as much. I asked him what he would do if he were offered a million for the ring. He shrugged. "What can you do? I am in business." He seems to feel toward this jewel as an artist does when he has to sell a painting he loves.

I was subsequently told that he refuses, at times, to sell jewels to women that he felt did not become them or they would not know how to use. He has, for instance, told a woman who wanted to buy a pair of long—and expensive—earrings that she could not have them because she was too small for them. In his desk, he keeps a piece of material against which he sometimes rubs gems to make sure they won't catch on a woman's dress. I was not surprised that he, unlike Cartier's, refuses to sell diamonds for investment.

Perhaps it is because Van Cleef & Arpels is so much smaller than Tiffany's and Cartier's that the aesthetics which Hoving espoused are so much more palpable here. At Van Cleef & Arpels everyone is very proud of the fact that the tiara that Napoleon gave to the Empress Josephine, though frequently on display on a sort of recessed small stage in the Fifth Avenue window, is not for sale. People here are gleeful, but think it only natural that it was the Van Cleef & Arpels design for a crown for the Queen of Iran that won a world-wide competition and that the firm's skills fashioned the 1,646 gems from Iranian vaults into one of the most beautiful jewels of the century.

Leon Arpels and his three sons, Julien, Louis, and Charles, built up the tradition of the company with Alfred Van Cleef around the turn of the century. By the 1920s it was competing with Cartier's for prime customers, and wealthy Americans began to urge them to set up a branch in New York. Finally, Julien sent his son, Claude, to the United States to explore the situation and be prepared to open a place in New York. In the late 1930s, Claude Arpels put out the family shingle in a small office in Rockefeller Center which did not worry Tiffany's and Cartier's too much. But at the 1939 World's Fair in New York, the exhibit of Van Cleef & Arpels made a big impression and, in 1941, the firm took its present space as a tenant in the Bergdorf Goodman building. Over the years, though the company has opened new branches in Palm Beach, Beverly Hills, the south of France, Geneva, and Tokyo, it has remained the only one of the elite jewelry retailers on Fifth Avenue that does not own and occupy an entire building, fearing that the loss of intimacy would undermine its taste. It has made one concession by opening a small bou-

tique next to the salon, where gifts for less than two hundred dollars
have the signature of the house. Perhaps the greatest tribute to Van
Cleef & Arpels is the fact that on Forty-seventh Street it is spoken of
with respect.

Tiffany, Cartier, and Van Cleef & Arpels added tradition and
elegance when they came to Fifth Avenue. Harry Winston, when he
moved into his six-story travertine mansion at Fifth Avenue and
Fifty-eighth Street, brought excitement to the industry. He was the
upstart with the gambling spirit, the courage of Forth-seventh Street
and the passion for expensive diamonds who was more than a match
for his Fifth Avenue competitors. Not since the founding of Tiffany
had anyone seized upon diamonds as a business with such ferocity
and aptitude for publicity. This dynamic little man—five feet, four
inches, tall—claimed that his vast insurance premiums forbade him
to be photographed. But his company was quicker and more re-
sourceful than other Fifth Avenue jewelry establishments in utilizing
television as free advertising for his wares and reputation. Further-
more, while Tiffany, Cartier, and Van Cleef & Arpels are retailers,
albeit of quality, Winston, Inc. is all of that and much more. Harry
Winston was a dealer, one of the most enterprising in diamond history. His company boasts, with justification, that it is alone among
Fifth Avenue's elite to process a diamond from rough to finished
jewel itself. It sells not only to its own customers—they did not
bother to call them clients here—but also through department
stores, mail-order houses, and retail chains as large as J. C. Penney.
It also makes considerable sales of loose diamonds to diamond investment firms.

Some of the diamond mavens of Forty-seventh Street, probably
out of envy, say that Winston did not know as much about diamonds
as he said. They tell of a time when he acquired a large and very
fine, rough diamond, but wasn't quite sure how to have it cut,
despite his company's experts. He arranged a cocktail party in his
building to which he invited some of the shrewdest diamond judges
from Forty-seventh Street and Fifth Avenue. During the festivities,
the conversation, as he undoubtedly must have anticipated, focused
on his newest diamond. He brought it forth and it was passed

around, with each of the men commenting on it, suggesting the best ways to have it cut.

Whether or not Winston arranged the party because he needed advice or because, with his sharp promotional sense, he wanted to stir up great interest in this diamond, thus building the potential price, is hard to say. However, on at least one occasion he underestimated the quality of one of his finest diamonds after it had been lauded by his top expert, who urged him to buy it after seeing it in the rough in London. Lillian Ross, in her two-part profile on Winston, in *The New Yorker* in 1954, reported that after he had purchased the stone and it was brought to him, he was still "lukewarm" about its worth. Subsequently, he extolled it.

Whether Winston was in the very top rank of diamond experts or not may be argued, but he was certainly enormously knowledgeable and successful as a diamond merchant until his death in 1977. He would, indeed, become upset when it was suggested that in his business he was a daring gambler. His knowledge, he insisted, as much as courage, is what minimized risk in his world-wide operations. In the other elegant salons of Fifth Avenue, there was a tendency to look down on his bursting self-assurance, so suggestive of Forty-seventh Street, as being a bit boorish. He was known to refer to himself, when musing about a diamond, in the third person. By his standards, however, his Fifth Avenue rivals were stodgy. To the American public, he became the best-known figure in the diamond business and the wealthy customers paid at least as much attention to his diamonds as to those of other Fifth Avenue salons.

Winston's enthusiasm was enormous. In this, he was certainly closer to the spirit of Forty-seventh Street than to Fifth Avenue. In talking to Miss Ross for the profile, he was probably not indulging in hyperbole when he said of the diamond business, "I love the diamond business. It's a Cinderella world. It has everything! People! Drama! Romance! Precious stones! Speculation! Excitement! What more could you want?"

His wife recalled that even on their honeymoon he talked mainly about big diamonds he wanted to buy.

Winston was unique among the Fifth Avenue gem princes

because he was born and raised in New York City. Hoving had come to this country from Finland when his father, a doctor, decided he did not want to live in a Soviet fiefdom. French executives ruled the other two Fifth Avenue salons. Winston was born poor and remained so for much of his early life. He grew up in a five-story walkup on West 106th Street. His father had a little jewelry store on Columbus Avenue. When Harry was seven his mother died and a year later, his father, who had asthma, moved to Los Angeles and opened another jewelry shop. The business intrigued Harry much more than school, so he dropped out at age fifteen. As an adolescent, he was already traveling through the towns of southern California selling jewels from a suitcase, sometimes in saloons.

Before he was out of his teens, his father returned to New York and started another small jewelry store. This time Harry decided to try the diamond business on his own. With a little money he had saved, he rented a small office in midtown and formed a one-man company with the ambitious name of Premier Diamond Company.

Though Winston did not like to be thought of as part of Forty-seventh Street—he never had an office on the block—he spent a number of his most formative diamond years among the driving men there, particularly in the Diamond Dealers Club. The restlessness, energy, intensity, capacity for concentration, and working without lunch, were all Forty-seventh Street traits that remained with him long after he became addicted to dark, well-tailored suits.

The path that took Winston to Fifth Avenue went from his office in mid-town to a brownstone at 7 East Fifty-first Street, just across from St. Patrick's Cathedral. There, during the 1950s, with his Syndicate sighthold and wealthy clientele, he was already competing strongly with the Fifth Avenue salons, though they did not like to think so. In 1960, however, they no longer had any choice. That was when he moved into the Fifth Avenue mansion at Fifty-eighth Street. The spirit of Forty-seventh Street had finally pushed its way into Fifth Avenue.

Harry Winston's personal impact was so strong that, when he died, at the age of eighty-three, word soon began circulating Forty-seventh Street that his Harvard-educated son, Ronald, would not be able to maintain either the volume or the quality of business. Ronald soon became aware of the rumors and, about a year after his father's death, announced that business would continue, but in a different style. He was seeking a share of the boutique market. He had already introduced a line he called "poesie," that included gold bracelets and necklaces with small diamonds. They were not cheap, with some priced as high as $15,000. But they were far lower than the salon gems that usually sold for six digits.

Even more significantly, Ronald Winston says he is looking for investments in South American diamond mines. This would make his company less dependent on the Syndicate, particularly in the quest for high-quality diamonds. His father, as you will recall, had tried this in Africa but was cuffed badly by the Syndicate. That Winston's son should have resumed this search is particularly interesting because the Winston company is the only one of the Fifth Avenue firms with a Syndicate sight. Tiffany, Cartier, and Van Cleef & Arpels deal very little in rough diamonds and have to scramble for their cut diamonds among De Beers outlets and from dealers, including some from Forty-seventh Street. Their other sources are estates and old customers. Winston, Inc. already has a larger supply of diamonds than any of its Fifth Avenue competitors, probably more than all three combined.

Ronald Winston's new plans do not suggest, in 1980, that in an invasion of the boutique market, the company, whose street plaque boasts "rare jewels of the world," is now only interested in luggage, dishes, stationery, or even silverware. The Winston salon is still the most intimidating on Fifth Avenue. A security guard stands just inside the closed door, several feet from the street door. There is only a small street trade which Winston hopes to increase substantially. In the great majority of cases, during Harry Winston's regime, a client telephoned ahead before being admitted to the muted salon, where wall cases displayed a magnificent sampling of Winston gems, and where elderly salesmen sat at expensive desks to make sales or show jewels in private rooms at the rear.

By the time Ronald succeeded his father, the company had salons in France and Germany, and diamond-cutting factories in Israel, France, Germany, Portugal, Puerto Rico, and Arizona. It had even trained American Indians in Arizona to become cutters. The teacher, incidentally, was from Forty-seventh Street.

Diamonds for investment had also become increasingly important to Winston's.

"Up to 1976, maybe 1977, about 40 percent of those who bought jewelry here were thinking of investment as well as adornment," I was told by Richard Winston, nephew of the founder and a vice-president. "Today [this was late 1978] I'd say it is 90 percent. When you buy from us you know we own the piece and that the only markup on the piece will be ours. We don't handle stones on consignment. We sell diamonds to investment firms from our loose stones and when we sell to them we get paid on delivery. No credit.

"Customers no longer care as much about the design of jewelry as they used to. The design has become simpler than it used to be. In the old days when a man bought jewelry for a woman he figured that if it was sold some day it would bring back maybe about half of what he had paid. Now he thinks in terms of making a profit on the resale. We tell our customers we are always interested in buying back our pieces if they want to sell."

The standards of design, he said, have changed for Fifth Avenue, which has prided itself on being so far above those of Forty-seventh Street. Jewelers are creating more informal jewelry, he told me, using more gold and less platinum because gold is considered less formal.

"Jewelry," he said, "is being made so that people wear it at dinner, or even lunch, not just at gala events. We use less ornate settings. Also, you have to realize that the very wealthy are looking for a low profile. They are afraid."

The line between Forty-seventh Street and Fifth Avenue is becoming blurred.

12

DIAMONDS
OF LEGEND

Implicit in the glittering charisma of Forty-seventh Street is the history of celebrated diamonds combined with legends of bloodshed and intrigue that have furnished countless plots for books, plays, movies, and television. In the minds of millions, the idea of diamonds is as much associated with crime and mystery as with love and beauty. Stories of the greatest diamonds of the world encompass the murder of royalty, the theft of egg-sized gems from the eyeballs of temple idols, the looting of national treasuries, and the disappearance of crown jewels. War, revolution, and scandal are joined with insatiable vanity, avarice, and lust for power in the tales of these diamonds. Legends of "curses" have been embroidered so colorfully into their provenance that the gems have often been more interesting than their owners.

Behind diamonds with names like Koh-I-Noor, Great Mogul,

Cullinan, Orloff, Empress Eugenie, Florentine, Hope, Sancy, and Regent are the lives of rajahs, shahs, kings, queens, tycoons, and adventurers. A Russian noble once sought to regain the favor of an empress with a diamond; a French cardinal became the patsy in an astonishing con game in which the most famous diamond necklace in history vanished; a diamond found by a peasant was given to a blacksmith as a fee to repair a plough.

Because of such lurid and romantic stories, diamonds have become so symbolic of power, glory, and glamor that the craving to possess them has frequently been more important than their romantic or monetary value. It is this aura of greatness that draws so many young people to Forty-seventh Street for just a mere chip of the gem for an engagement ring. Diamonds make them a part of this special heritage which, until this century, had been reserved for only the most wealthy and influential.

No diamond has done more to create memorable settings than the Koh-I-Noor, which went from ancient Indian legend to become the most famous of British crown jewels via conquest, trickery, torture, mystery, extortion, and finally, as a tribute to Great Britain itself.

The mythology says that this diamond goes back some four thousand years to its discovery along a riverbank in India. There are some who say that this was the diamond worn by a war chief in the Indian epic poem, *Mahabharata*, written in Sanskrit about 200 B.C. According to others, the diamond remained for hundreds of years in the hands of various ruling families until, early in the fourteenth century, when, in a war, the stone was seized from the rajah of Malwa. How much of this story is true, no one knows.

The clouds of conjecture clear early in the sixteenth century when the Sultan Baber, conqueror of India and founder of the Mogul Empire, was so proud of acquiring this diamond that he left the following written account:

"Bikeramjit, a Hindu, who was rajah of Gwalilor, had governed the country for more than one hundred years. In the battle in which Ibrahim was defeated, Bikeramjit was sent to hell. Bikeramjit's family and the heads of his clan were, at the time, in Agra. When Humayun (Father of the Sultan Baber) arrived, Bikeramjit's people attempted to escape, but were taken by the parties which Humayun had placed upon watch and put in custody. Humayun did not permit them to be plundered. Of their own free will they presented to Humayun a *pishkish* (gift) consisting of a quantity of jewels and precious stones. Among these was the famous diamond that had been acquired by Sultan Alcaddin. It is so valuable that a judge of diamonds values it half the daily expense of the whole world."

For about two centuries, with the Moguls in control, the diamond remained in the family. But in 1739, the Koh-I-Noor acquired a new owner, Nadir Shah, the Persian who invaded India and seized Delhi. How *he* got the diamond is another strange tale.

In a paper prepared in 1929 Oliver C. Farrington, curator of geology at the Field Museum in Chicago, wrote that the diamond had been inserted as one of the eyes of the ruler's Peacock Throne. When the victorious Nadir Shah examined the throne, the diamond was missing. His investigation led to the harem women. They told him that the dethroned ruler, Mohammed, kept the diamond in his turban. Nadir Shah told the defeated man he would restore his territory. At the ceremonies for this generous act, Nadir Shah suggested to Mohammed that, as a gesture of undying friendship, they exchange turbans. Mohammed could not very well decline. As soon as Nadir Shah returned to his tent, he unrolled the turban. The diamond fell out. Its light was so brilliant that Nadir Shah, in delight, exclaimed, "Koh-I-Noor" meaning "mountain of light."

Nadir Shah took the diamond back to Persia. His nation was torn by uprisings and assassinations. Nadir Shah was among those murdered. The diamond was fought over by his successors and acquired by his grandson, Shah Ruhk, governor of the city of Mesha. One of those determined to gain possession of the diamond was a relatively minor ruler named Aga Mohammed. He attacked and captured the city of Mesha, and ordered Shah Ruhk to turn over the treasures. The shah said he no longer had them. Mohammed had him tortured. This brought forth a number of gems, but not the

Koh-I-Noor. So Mohammed ordered the shah's head shaved and topped with a close-fitting crown of plaster. Boiling oil was then poured on the shah's head. This persuaded the shah to surrender a beautiful ruby, but not the Koh-I-Noor. He insisted he no longer had it.

Meanwhile, Ahmed Shah, founder of the Afghan Empire, decided he would like to get hold of the Koh-I-Noor. He relayed word to Shah Ruhk that he would help him regain his freedom. The price would be the diamond. Shah Ruhk agreed. The alliance triumphed and the diamond went to Ahmed Shah, who left it to his son, Taimur Shah. He bequeathed it, in turn, in 1793, to his son, Zaman. The curse became active again. Zaman was deposed, imprisoned, and blinded by his brother, Shuja ul-Mulk. Zaman refused to surrender the diamond. He had embedded it in plaster in a wall of his prison cell. The plaster began to crumble. One day a guard brushed his hand against the wall and felt a sharp prick. He saw a gleaming point. He dug, and found the diamond and brought it to Shah Shuja ul-Mulk.

Soon Shah Shuja ul-Mulk became so well known that England sent Mr. Mountstuart Elphinstone to his country to act as ambassador. At the reception for the British dignitary, the shah wore his brightest jewels, with the Koh-I-Noor pinned to his breast. Not too long afterward he was driven from his country, taking with him the diamond and the brother he had blinded. They found refuge with Ranjit-Singh, known as the "Lion of the Punjab." Their host, determined to get the Koh-I-Noor, treated them warmly. But the guests refused to show their gratitude by surrendering the diamond. He applied so much pressure that eventually they sold him the diamond for about $40,000 and a small annuity.

The new owner had the diamond set in a bracelet that he wore only on special occasions. Upon his death, the bracelet was put in the national treasury at Lahore. At least one of his successors was murdered, but the stone remained in the treasury until the British became interested.

By 1849, the British, having annexed the Punjab to their conquests in India, made the diamond a stipulation in the victory terms. The Koh-I-Noor was to be given to the East India Company as partial indemnity for the cost of the Sikh wars. The following year, they presented the diamond to Queen Victoria to celebrate the 250th anniversary of the company's creation by Elizabeth I. In 1851, the Koh-I-Noor was shown to the public as one of the natural wonders of the world at the Crystal Palace Exposition in London.

At that time it weighed 186 carats. Diamond experts consulted by Queen Victoria felt that the quality of the diamond, particularly its grayish tint, could be improved if recut. The original Indian cutters, who knew little about faceting and were reluctant to cut away pieces of the stone, had done almost nothing to improve its beauty. In 1852, the work was entrusted to Mr. Voorsanger of Amsterdam, taking a total of thirty-eight days, with the cutter working twelve hours a day. The final product weighed 108.93 carats.

The queen, to please her Indian subjects, promised to wear it on important occasions. Since then it has been said that only a queen can wear it. She passed the diamond on to her daughter-in-law, Queen Alexandra, who wore it at the coronation of King Edward VII. Nine years later, when a new crown was designed for the coronation of Queen Mary, the Koh-I-Noor was made the major stone. Then, in 1937, it was placed in Queen Elizabeth's crown for her coronation. On state occasions, the diamond is withdrawn from the Tower of London crown jewels and worn by her.

In 1905, a diamond was found that was so valuable no one could afford it—the Cullinan. In earlier centuries, the diamond would have been the spoils of war. But by the twentieth century, the rules of the diamond business had changed. This huge, almost flawless gem was found in the Premier mine of the Transvaal—a country which, at that time, bordered South Africa—only three years after the mine had been discovered. It was the biggest diamond ever found, weighing 3,106 carats. The magnitude of this diamond—the size of a small fist—can be appreciated when we realize it takes 142 carats to make a single ounce. This diamond was more than sixteen times the weight of the Koh-I-Noor, even before the

Koh-I-Noor had been cut, and it was of much finer quality. The blue-white diamond, named after the mine owner, Thomas—eventually, Sir Thomas—Cullinan, was deposited in a Johannesburg bank and the public was permitted to admire it before it was sealed in a tin box and sent off to the company's London office for sale. There, each time it was taken from a bank to be shown to a possible purchaser—or syndicate—it was insured for $2.5 million. When it became clear it was too expensive to be sold, suggestions were made that the public buy the great diamond by subscription and donate it to King Edward VII as part of the crown jewels. One estimate given for the public's subscription was close to ten million pounds—more than fifty million dollars at that time. The British public, though fond of its king, was not enthusiastic about this idea.

Then some Transvaal officials suggested their government buy the diamond and give it to King Edward VII in gratitude for the constitution England had given them. After considerable argument, this idea was approved by the Transvaal Assembly by a vote of 149 to 119. Sir Thomas Cullinan accepted a much lower price than he had been seeking in London. The assembly bought the diamond for the equivalent of $750,000.

On November 9, 1907, the king's sixty-sixth birthday, a pageant suitable for the greatest diamond in history and one of the most sensational birthday gifts ever bestowed was staged. Sir Francis Hopwood, former lieutenant governor of Transvaal and assorted British officials in a royal carriage, escorted by men from Scotland Yard, carried the diamond to the castle at Sandringham for its presentation in the drawing room. On hand, in addition to the king and queen of England, were the queens of Spain and Norway.

The next dramatic event was more problematic: cleaving the most valuable diamond on earth. Cleavage was essential because the stone contained one internal flaw. The job went to the prestigious Amsterdam firm, J. Asscher & Co. The three Asscher brothers sculpted a clay replica for study. They decided the cleavage should go through the flaw. The traditional V-shaped nick was made in the gem. A special knife was created for the cleavage. Joseph Asscher, in the presence of his brothers and three representatives of the British government, placed the knife blade in the V, and raised the mallet, knowing, as he brought it down, that a mistake might mean the diamond would shatter. As the mallet struck, there was a gasp. The blade had broken. A second blade was put in the V and struck. The diamond broke cleanly. The next step was to make smaller stones from these two pieces. Three cutters were assigned to the task from 7:00 A.M. to 9:00 P.M. Each night, after work, the diamonds were placed in a strong room and guarded by four police. The head of the firm and ten of his men carried the diamonds to and from the room. During the night, a watchman made a mark on the wall of the room every half hour. The walls, made of iron and cement, were two feet thick. The safe inside the room was hidden behind a mahogany cupboard that had handles. But the locks, nine of them, were concealed by a sliding panel. The steel door of the safe was eight inches thick. Another similar safe was also in the room. It contained nothing.

The result of the cleaving, cutting, and polishing was nine major gems—ninety-six small ones and 9 carats of polished bits. The largest was 530.20 carats, pear-shaped with seventy-four facets, representing the biggest cut diamond in the world. It was named the Great Star of Africa. The second largest, a sixty-six-faceted square cut brilliant, was 317.40 carats and called the Lesser Star of Africa. The larger of the two was set in the imperial scepter and is kept in the Tower of London. The second, also in the Tower, is part of the imperial state crown. A third stone, pear-shaped and 94.40 carats, was set in Queen Mary's crown, along with another square brilliant of 63.60 carats. The fifth major stone, heart-shaped and 18.80 carats, was set in a brooch for Queen Mary. At the coronation of George VI in 1936, Queen Mary wore this brooch in her crown in place of the Koh-I-Noor, which had been set in the crown of Queen Elizabeth. The sixth stone, which became part of an emerald and diamond necklace worn by Queen Elizabeth II, was an 11.50-carat marquise. At the time, it was given to Queen Alexandra by King Edward VII. The seventh diamond cut from the Cullinan, an 8.80-carat marquise, became a pendant on a diamond brooch for Elizabeth II. The eighth, a 6.80-carat brilliant, is the center stone of this brooch. Finally, a 4.39-carat pear-shaped gem was set in a ring with a claw setting for Queen Mary, and inherited by Queen Elizabeth II.

This job also brought the largest fee in history. King Edward VII kept only the two greatest diamonds and gave the others to Mr. Asscher as his fee. He then bought the other seven major diamonds for the royal family. The cost was not made public. In addition, the queen of the Netherlands conferred the knighthood of Orange Nassau on Joseph Asscher. The firm presented as gifts to King Edward the knife and mallet used in the cleaving.

Inevitably, in any reading about famous diamonds, one encounters the name of Jean Baptiste Tavernier, the French gem merchant and traveler who was probably the first European to see some of the most striking diamonds of India. He left detailed accounts of many of them in his book *Travels in India*. It is largely because of him that, for centuries, a controversy has boiled among diamond historians about the diamond known as the Great Mogul. Tavernier wrote that he saw it in 1665 when it was owned by the Great Mogul of India. He said it was as large as an egg "cut through the middle." No one doubts that he saw this diamond and described it accurately as being rose cut and weighing more than 279 carats. The question is: Can it be that the Great Mogul is the same as another diamond, now a prize of the Soviet treasury, called the Orloff? There are even some experts who think that what Tavernier saw may have been the Koh-I-Noor. Tavernier recorded that the diamond he saw, when in the rough, weighed more than 780 carats.

The Great Mogul, like the Koh-I-Noor, during the course of invasion and pillage, fell into the hands of Mogul rulers in Delhi. One of these potentates imported an artisan from Venice to shape the diamond. He did a job that so infuriated the ruler he threatened to have him killed. He was persuaded, instead, to fine the craftsman 10,000 rupees—the man's life savings. After the seventeenth century, no one saw this diamond again. At least, not as the Great Mogul—which leads us to the Orloff.

The Orloff became the most celebrated of Russian diamonds. It was placed in the imperial scepter directly beneath the Russian eagle. Like the Great Mogul, it came from India and was about the same size and shape. Its storied background was even more exciting than the Great Mogul's. It is said that early in the eighteenth century a French soldier, determined to steal it from the eye of a temple idol in India, won the friendship of the Hindu priests by showing deep interest in their religion. Then one night, he pried loose the diamond eye and fled to Madras, where he sold it to an English sea captain for two thousand pounds. The skipper is said to have sold it in London for twelve thousand pounds.

The rest of the story is less bewildering. The diamond surfaced in Amsterdam in the latter part of the eighteenth century, around the time Count Orloff was also there. He was in despair because he had been supplanted as the favorite of Catherine the Great by Potemkin. He sought to regain her affections with a fabulous jewel. A letter from the Hague, dated January 2, 1776, is quoted by Edwin W. Streeter, a British expert who is generally considered to be the first diamond historian:

"We learn from Amsterdam that Prince Orloff made but a one-day stay in that city, where he bought a very large brilliant for the Empress, his sovereign, for which he paid to a Persian merchant there, the sum of 1,400,000 florin Dutch money."

There is one more complication in the tale of the Great Mogul-Orloff mystery. A diamond, somewhat smaller than the Orloff, perhaps about 120 carats, of Indian origin, is also part of the Russian crown jewels acquired in the late eighteenth century. One theory is that Orloff, after failing to sway his empress with the first diamond, gave her a second.

Another version is that an Armenian merchant named Shaffras acquired this second diamond as follows: He tried to buy it from an Afghan soldier who had stolen it, but did not have enough money. The soldier sold it to a Jew. The Armenian was unable to buy it from the Jew. So he and his brother killed the Jew. The Armenian then killed his brother and sold the diamond to the empress. A variant of this story is that the Armenian did not kill his brother, but that his brother went to Amsterdam and sold the diamond to Orloff.

Cattelle, the diamond historian, in trying to unravel these complications, writes in his book, *The Diamond:*

"It is evident from these accounts that there is no certain knowledge of the transactions. Beyond the facts that Count Orloff bought a large diamond in Amsterdam in 1775 and that Shaffras sold a large diamond in Russia, the stories are open to question throughout. All we really know about the Great Mogul is that Tavernier saw it in Delhi in 1665; Delhi was sacked in 1739; and loot [was] carried off by Nadir Shah, the Mogul probably among it. In 1747 Nadir was assassinated and a number of his large jewels were stolen by Afghans, who were his favored personal attendants. Some years later, two large India cut stones appeared in Europe with confused histories of romance, one of them similar to Tavernier's description of the Great Mogul, and were sold between 1775 and 1791 to the Russian crown for large prices, the exact amount being unknown, though variously stated in definite figures. One of these is the Orloff and the Orloff is probably the Great Mogul."

There is confusion about the diamonds. But there is no question about the outcome of Count Orloff's plan. It failed. Potemkin remained the beloved of Catherine. She even gave him diamonds.

Another gem, first named the Pitt and then the Regent, a 410-carat diamond of mysterious antecedents, survived scandal, crime, and celebrity in both England and France before finding glory as a cushion-shaped brilliant of 140.50 carats in the Louvre. An Indian stone, it is said to have been stolen from the Golconda mine in India, or found in a street in that area at the turn of the eighteenth century.

One tale about the Pitt that has won considerable acceptability is that somewhere along the line, a slave stole it, slashed his leg and concealed the rough stone beneath the bandage. To gain passage on a ship, he offered half the value of the stone to a British skipper. The captain took him aboard, possessed himself of the diamond, and tossed the slave overboard. The captain sold it and, the story goes, became a notable roisterer before hanging himself.

Meanwhile, William Pitt, grandfather of the noted British prime minister, was trying to make his fortune as a merchant in India. In his eagerness, he clashed repeatedly with the East India Company, but was finally hired by them. In 1702, when Pitt was supervising the interests of his company in Madras, an Indian merchant named Jamchund appeared with the diamond. Pitt acquired it for some twenty thousand pounds. Soon there were rumors that the acquisition was tainted by skullduggery on his part. The gossip became rife in London. It is certain that before he acquired the diamond he did not have that much money. He was in correspondence with Sir Stephen Evance in London, at the time, who he was apparently representing in trying to buy diamonds on a fee-basis. In 1702, Pitt wrote to Sir Stephen saying he had run across the finest diamond he had ever seen, but that the price was enormous. Sir Stephen replied that what with England engaged in war with France, "There is noe Prince in Europe can buy it soe would advise you not to meddle in itt." Pitt was to spend a good deal of his life claiming that he had obtained the diamond honorably. He contended that he acquired it by prolonged and skillful bargaining. He became known in England as Diamond Pitt. The acquisition of the diamond left him in such need of money that he sent it to London to be sold. No one could afford it. The cutting of the stone alone cost some six thousand pounds, and there were squabbles over commissions between Pitt and some British nobles.

It took Pitt fifteen years to sell the diamond. The purchaser was Philippe, the duke of Orleans, regent of France during the minority of Louix XV. The payment procedure was curious. Forty thousand pounds were to be deposited as a partial payment in England before the diamond was sent to France. This was approximately one-third of the total. If the deal fell through, five thousand pounds were to be forfeited. The diamond was taken to Calais by Pitt, two sons, and a son-in-law. There, they were met by the king's jeweler who gave them some boxes of gems that he said were from the French crown; the rest of the money would be paid in three installments.

The first payment was the last for a while. When Pitt's sons demanded the remainder, they were told that France could not be held responsible for a transaction arranged by the regent. Eventually, about 125,000 pounds was paid. The diamond was worn by Louis XV in his crown at his coronation in 1722. At times, his queen wore it in her hair and years later Marie Antoinette, queen of Louis XVI, used it to adorn a black velvet hat.

In 1792, when France was preparing to sell crown jewels to prop up its shaky currency, the jewels were stolen under mysterious circumstances. Most of them were "found" a short time later. This included the Pitt, which, by this time, was known as the Regent. Twice thereafter, the Regent was pawned with bankers to raise money. Finally Napoleon, as first consul, redeemed it and, at his coronation as emperor in 1804, had it set in the hilt of his sword. When Napoleon was exiled, his second wife, Empress Marie Louise, kept the Regent. However, her father, Francis I of Austria, returned it to Louis XVIII of France. In 1825, the Regent was worn by Charles X at his coronation and he kept it in his crown until the reign of Napoleon III, whose wife made it into a diadem.

When the French crown jewels were put up for auction in 1887, the Regent was withheld. It was put on exhibition in the Louvre. During World War II, before the Germans captured Paris in 1940, the Regent was removed to the Chateau Chambord and concealed behind a panel. After the war, it was restored to the Louvre.

Another diamond with murky beginnings was a 51-carat oval cut brilliant that Napoleon III bought for his empress Eugenie as a wedding present. This was the one that was said to have been found in India by a peasant who turned it over to a blacksmith as payment for repairing a plough. The blacksmith was even reported to have thrown the diamond away before picking it up again and selling it to a merchant. In trying to explain this behavior in a country where the poor wandered along the riverbanks dreaming of finding an alluvial diamond, Cattelle suggests that the peasant and blacksmith were both fearful of owning a diamond since all diamonds were property of the ruler by law.

The diamond was eventually sold to Catherine the Great and she made it famous by wearing it in her hair at her coronation. While Orloff was shopping for gorgeous diamonds for her, she gave this diamond to Potemkin, his successor. It was sold by the grandniece of Potemkin to Napoleon III. After the Franco-Prussian War ended the French Empire in 1870, the diamond was sold to the gaekwar of Baroda for $75,000. It was then sold to a Mrs. N. J. Dady of Bombay, and has been missing since her death.

For complexity and romance, nothing short of a libretto for a Mozart opera can match the tale of the Sancy diamond in its course from sixteenth century Turkey to France, to England, back to France, to Spain, again to France, and then to England. It was possessed by kings, a cardinal, and was the gift of William Waldorf Astor to Nancy Langhorne when she married his son, and is known, at times, as the Astor Sancy. But its greatest adventures preceded its acquisition by Astor. The pear-shaped, 55-carat diamond got its name from Nicholas de Barly, baron de Sancy, who bought it in Constantinople late in the sixteenth century and brought it to France. There, the diamond won fame when it was borrowed by Henry III, who considered it the perfect ornament for the cap he wore to cover his baldness. During the reign of Henry IV, when the king needed money—and de Sancy was superintendent of finance—the diamond was borrowed once more. The story is that the emissary, carrying the diamond to a banker as collateral for the loan, swallowed it when attacked by highwaymen. He was killed. De Sancy ordered a search for the body. When it was found, it was cut open and the diamond removed.

In 1604, while de Sancy was ambassador to England, he is said to have sold the diamond to James I. It is mentioned in the inventory of English crown jewels of 1605 as "one fayre diamond, cut in fawcetts, bought of Sancey." During the reign of Charles I, when England was torn by civil war, Queen Henrietta Maria, wife of Charles

I, took many jewels, including the Sancy, to France and put up the Sancy and another diamond with the duke of Epernon for a loan. The loan was not repaid and the duke kept the diamonds until he sold them to Cardinal Mazarin, then chief minister of France. The cardinal, upon his death in 1661, willed these and sixteen other diamonds to the French crown on condition that they be forever known as the "Mazarin Diamonds." In a 1691 inventory of French jewels, the Sancy was given top billing.

During this period in England, another diamond was reported, called the Sancy. It was entrusted to the earl of Worcester after the execution of Charles I in 1649. He handed it over to Charles II in 1660, at the time of the Restoration. But in 1688, when revolution deposed James II, he took the Sancy and other jewels to France and sold the Sancy to Louix XIV. In the 1791 inventory of French jewels, the Sancy was said to have weighed thirty-three carats. But in the 1691 inventory, it was recorded as fifty-three carats. After the theft of the French crown jewels in 1792, the Sancy was not recovered. Yet three years later, when France pledged some diamonds to the Marquise of Iranda in Madrid for a loan, there was a diamond that weighed between fifty-three and fifty-four carats. Some authorities believe this was the Sancy. The loan was not repaid and, by 1809, it was the property of Prince Godoy and was later believed to have been acquired by the Spanish Bourbons. In 1828, it was sold by a French merchant and, by 1865, its travels had brought it to its first home—India. Two years later, it was back in France, on display at the Paris Exposition by a French jeweler, and the weight was still just under fifty-four carats. In 1906, the diamond that Mr. Astor bought was almost exactly this weight. It received the final imprimatur of legitimacy in 1962, when it was exhibited as the Sancy in the Louvre as one of the highlights of a show called "Ten Centuries of French Jewelry."

The Sancy may have been the first major diamond to be bought by an American, but it was the Hope diamond that became the most famous, not only for its history, but for its association with a "curse." One of the finest examples of a blue-white diamond, the 44.5-carat brilliant with the sapphire tint, was bestowed with its curse in the seventeenth century after it was said to have been filched from the eye of a Hindu temple goddess in India by the discerning and opportunistic Tavernier. He may have bought it at a very low price from soneone who did the actual dirty work. It is very likely that the curse had already been applied to this diamond by earlier, powerful rulers who owned it as a means of discouraging thievery by those who were willing to risk decapitation, but were fearful of a fate that might follow them into the next world. In support of this theory, the Jewelry Industrial Council of the United States suggests that Tavernier's envious, and less enterprising competitors in Europe, may have hoped, by circulating talk of the curse, to make the diamond more difficult to sell. The curse-believers say that Tavernier was eaten by wolves on a trip to Russia. Since the French gem merchant and traveler was some eighty-four years at his death, it is more likely he was killed by old age and a savage Russian winter. By then, he had sold the diamond to King Louis XIV. At that time, it weighed 112 carats. The king's jeweler, by making it heart-shaped, reduced it to 67.5 carats. It is difficult to see how the curse afflicted the king whose life was filled with so much success that he became known as the Sun King. But the curse-school points out that the king lost interest in his mistress not too long after she began wearing the diamond. In fairness to the diamond, it should be recalled that King Louis XIV often shifted mistresses. In any event, he lived to seventy-seven and died of smallpox during a major epidemic. Another royal owner of the diamond did so poorly that he is often cited in support of the curse. This was Louis XVI and Marie Antoinette who were guillotined at the time of the French Revolution. Yet even here, an argument can be made against the power of the curse. During a strange jewel heist in 1792, a year before he was beheaded, the diamond was stolen. While others of the crown jewels in this "theft" were "recovered," this diamond disappeared. In 1830, it turned up for sale in London, somewhat changed. It was now oval and cut down to 44 carats. It was bought by Henry Philip Hope for $90,000. When owned by his nephew, Henry Thomas Hope, it was displayed at the

Crystal Palace Exhibition of 1851 as the Hope diamond, though there was little doubt that this was the gem stolen in France. Once more, the diamond can be associated with misfortune. Lord Hope married an American musical comedy star, May Yohe, whose beauty and talent had made her a sensation in London. He gave her the diamond as a wedding present. Several years later, leaving him— and the diamond—she ran off with an American army officer. Lord Hope squandered most of the family fortune and had to sell the diamond. Miss Yohe lost her lover, was unable to rebuild her career and, for a time, worked as a scrub woman until a third and rather happy marriage. The curse won strong support early in this century after its acquisition by Abdule Jamid II, sultan of Turkey. By 1908, he was faced with revolution and sold the diamond.

At this point, the Hope began its American career. In 1911, after its acquisition by Pierre Cartier, it was sold to Edward B. McLean, and became one of the greatest attractions in the colorful social life of his wife, Evelyn Walsh McLean, who wore it regularly without ill effect at her lavish Washington parties. Mr. McLean, however, died in a mental institution. His son was killed by an automobile and a daughter succumbed to an overdose of sleeping pills. Mrs. McLean died in 1947 of pneumonia, at the age of sixty. Harry Winston, the American diamond merchant, bought it for $179,000, some $25,000 more than McLean had paid for it. In 1958, the diamond dealer donated it to the Smithsonian Institution where it is viewed annually by millions of tourists, attracted as much by the legend of its curse as by its beauty.

Diamonds with many names have figured importantly in affairs of state. A beautiful yellow diamond known best as the Florentine, was also called, because of its adventures, the Tuscan, the Grand Duke of Tuscany, the Austrian, and the Austrian Yellow. Before this rose-cut gem of 137.27 carats reached Francis of Lorraine, who subsequently became the husband of Maria Theresa of Austria and head of the Holy Roman Empire, it was the subject of an astonishing tale. In 1477, when Charles the Bold, duke of Burgundy, was slain at the Battle of Nancy, he was wearing this diamond. It was found either by a soldier or by a peasant looking for goodies among the dead. Whoever spotted it is said to have considered it a pretty bit of glass and sold it to a merchant for a mere florin. It was sold many times thereafter and one of its owners is believed to have been Pope Julius II. Inevitably, this diamond became part of the Medici treasury and was seen by the relentless Tavernier in 1657, when he visited the duke of Tuscany in Florence. By this time, it had a double-rose cut and was somewhat more elaborate than the diamond that went into battle with Charles the Bold. It was probably recut by different owners. But Streeter thinks that the yellow diamond Tavernier saw was probably not the one worn to battle. Regardless, the man who was to become Francis I wanted the diamond. He held hostage the duchy of Lorraine. As part of the intricate machinations of the Holy Roman Empire early in the eighteenth century, he made a deal to swap Lorraine for Tuscany—plus the diamond. This was in 1737. The diamond, upon his coronation as head of the Holy Roman Empire in 1745, became part of the crown jewels. When the imperial family had to flee Austria after World War I, the Florentine went into exile with them. Thereafter, the travels of the diamond became obscure. One story is that it was stolen and turned up in South America in the 1920s; strayed to the United States where it was recut like so much Prohibition booze, and sold. In the words of a compilation of famous diamonds prepared by De Beers Consolidated Mines, Ltd., "it must be listed as missing."

The most famous golden diamond seems to be devoid of a fanciful history, but it is better known than many stones with more exciting stories. This is the Tiffany, a cushion-shaped brilliant of 128.51 carats and ninety facets. The De Beers catalogue of famous diamonds says it is believed to have been discovered in the Kimberley Mine of South Africa in 1878. The following year, it was owned by Tiffany & Co. as a rough of 287.42 carats and given its present form in Paris. The Tiffany has been shown at the Columbia Exposition of Chicago in 1893; the Century of Progress, also in Chicago, in 1933–34; and the New York World's Fair of 1939–40. It is on display at Tiffany's, New York. The diamond has been worn only once. This was in 1957, at the Tiffany Ball in Newport. The chairlady of the ball, Mrs. Sheldon Whitehouse, wore it in a necklace of white diamonds.

The House of Cartier, not to be outdone by Tiffany, sacrificed some 30 carats of very expensive diamond for perfection in a stone to be named after Louis Cartier. This diamond, after some two years of study and work, was thought to be perfect at 130 carats and was submitted to the New York Gemological Institute for certification. The institute refused after finding an almost imperceptible flaw. To get rid of this defect Cartier's craftsmen cut away some 30 carats and the final product was 107.07. It was the only diamond of more than 100 carats to be D flawless. It was insured for $5 million in 1976. It has been sold for a price and to a person the company does not wish to name.

Of all the strange tales of fabulous diamonds, the most fantastic is the one that has come to be known as The Affair of the Queen's Necklace. Not only is this the most incredible confidence game ever conceived in the diamond business, but its historical impact in France was also enormous. As the astonishing intrigue became public, the French statesman, Talleyrand, with his usual shrewdness, predicted: "Watch out for this diamond necklace business. It may well rock the throne of France." And Napoleon, as an emperor, with the fine vantage point of retrospect, said, "The Queen's [Marie Antoinette's] death must be dated from the Diamond Necklace Trial." Many years later, Thomas Carlyle became so fascinated with the ramifications of this case that, in 1837, some fifty years after the affair, he wrote an essay about it that was a starting point that led to his massive history of the French Revolution.

This crime had a cast of characters never equaled: Marie Antoinette; King Louis XVI; a French cardinal; Madame du Barry, the mistress of Louis XV; the Austrian Empress Maria Theresa; Cagliostro, the necromancer, alchemist, and adventurer; and a forger described by Carlyle as a "denizen of rascaldom." At the heart of the scheme was a young beauty known as the Countess Jeanne de St. Remy de Valois, who claimed descent from a bastard son of Henry

II; and her husband, a soi-disant count de Lamotte. Finally, there was the necklace, the most magnificent in history—a creation of 647 diamonds, weighing 2,800 carats.

In the mid-eighteenth century, two Parisian jewelers, Boehmer and Bassenger, became obsessed with the idea of creating an incomparable diamond necklace. They felt reasonably certain that, despite the cost, they could persuade Louis XV to buy it for Madame du Barry. They assembled the necklace, but before the king could buy it, he died. Suddenly, Madame du Barry had no powerful sponsor. The jewelers turned to Louis XVI and urged him to buy it for Marie Antoinette. Whether he refused or she declined is disputed. The necklace was offered in other countries without success. After the birth of the French dauphin, the jewelers renewed their campaign with Marie Antoinette. This time, though she did not agree, she seemed less reluctant; the jewelers got the impression that she might accept it if the money did not come from the royal treasury.

There was one person of considerable wealth, who might be interested if the necklace would restore him his former prestige. He was Cardinal Louis de Rohan, a prince of ancient family. He had blundered as the French ambassador to Vienna by babbling to Maria Theresa that her daughter was too flighty for a queen of France. The Austrian empress rebuked her daughter. Marie Antoinette became angry. The cardinal was recalled and pushed into oblivion.

Enter the beautiful countess de Valois, longing for money and the social recognition she was convinced she deserved. In 1784, after the cardinal had suffered ten years of obscurity, the countess told him how she could help him. She said she had the ear of the queen and was trying to win his restoration at court. At her instigation, he wrote letters to the queen and received answers, presumably from the queen. The queen's letters began with courtesy and warmed to considerable affection. The cardinal, encouraged by the countess, concluded that the queen loved him. The letters to the queen were handed to the countess, who assured him she would arrange their delivery. He received answers from the countess as well. The answers were written by a forger retained by the countess. The cardinal did not suspect forgery. He besought the countess to arrange a secret meeting between him and the queen. The countess agreed and a short time later told him the nocturnal meeting was to be held in a secluded section of the gardens at Versailles. On the specified summer night in 1784, the cardinal met with a woman he believed to be Marie Antoinette and gave her a rose. She whispered to him that his past faults would be forgiven. The countess, meanwhile, had been receiving substantial sums of money from the cardinal, earmarked for charities the queen favored. With the money, she became more prominent in society and was widely accepted as a confidante of the queen. She may, some aficianados of this affair believe, have been used by the queen to punish the cardinal.

Among those who believed in the influence of the countess, were the Parisian jewelers with the necklace. To them, she seemed the ideal broker in a deal to sell the necklace to the queen. For months the countess dangled the jewelers, telling them the queen was still not in the market for the necklace. On January 21,1785, the countess told the diamond men that the queen had finally decided she would like to have the necklace, but did not think it advisable to become involved directly in the purchase. The countess told the diamond men that the queen would entrust the negotiation to a most important personage. The countess's next step was to prevail upon the cardinal to act as intermediary in the necklace business. He agreed and the bargaining got under way. The cardinal was able to show to the gem dealers a note that seemed to be in the hand of the queen, authorizing him to purchase the necklace in installments. The necklace was turned over to him after the first payment. He took it to the countess's home, where he gave it to a man he believed he recognized as valet to the queen.

The joy of the jewelers was brief. The payments they received from the cardinal were far short. They finally decided to ask the queen directly for the money. She said she had never received the necklace and never asked for it.

On August 15, 1785, the king and queen were preparing to go to church for Assumption Day, where Cardinal Rohan was scheduled to officiate. That day the cardinal was arrested and taken to the Bastille. Three days later the countess was arrested. Her husband had fled the country and turned up in London. A man named Reteaux de Villatte was arrested and confessed to forging the queen's letters to the cardinal. Cagliostro was also arrested for having been involved as an adviser to the cardinal.

With the *Parlement* of Paris sitting in as judges, the sensational trial took place in 1786. The cardinal claimed to have destroyed the correspondence between himself and the queen. The public, particularly the embittered people of Paris, saw in this scandal a glaring example of royalty's indifference to the poverty of the people. The trial exonerated the cardinal, adjudging him a dupe. Cagliostro was also acquitted of serious complicity. The countess was condemned to be whipped, branded, and incarcerated. Her husband, in absentia, was condemned to the galleys for life. The forger was exiled.

The countess escaped and the angry public assumed that the French court had arranged it. She joined her husband in England.

The necklace had vanished.

Did the countess and her husband arrange the whole affair together, or was it, as the countess contended, that she was working blindly for her husband, and was as much a dupe as an accomplice? It is quite certain that Marie Antoinette never received the necklace and that the jewelers never got it back. The general belief among experts on this case is that the countess's husband took the necklace with him to England, broke it up, and sold the stones separately, some of them to important English families who may have known they were stolen.

Tell this story on Forty-seventh Street, and the response is a shrug and the comment: As usual, it is the diamond dealer who takes the beating.

13

HOW LONG IS FOREVER

"When the gap between the ideal and real becomes too wide," Barbara Tuchman wrote in her book, *A Distant Mirror*, "the system breaks down."

Is there such a danger on the horizon for the booming diamond business? The diamond people, the personification of pragmatism, think not. When economic systems wobble and inflation soars, the diamond becomes more precious than ever. When international economic and political turbulence subside the diamond still continues to make steady increases in value. On their side, the diamond people will tell you, they have the best of all possible worlds. Their product is among the most durable on earth and ample in supply. They have the benefits, exhilaration, and economic health of free competition—and are protected against price collapse by the shield of the Syndicate. They have, as allies, two of the most powerful human drives—vanity and greed. Nothing to worry about, they say. Just work hard and be smart.

They may be right. But important changes have occurred in their world that have already widened the gap between the ideal and the real. First, the Syndicate, though it is making bigger profits than ever, has become vulnerable. Africa and the Soviet Union are the sources of the rough diamonds that keep the Syndicate alive. African revolutions of recent years, have been leaning toward Marxism and the nationalization of their diamond mines. It has not yet happened in South Africa, the heart of the Syndicate, but it could. The possibility grows that a new syndicate could arise, formed by the Soviet Union, with the support of African nations, some of whom already withhold diamonds from the present Syndicate. To this, the diamond people respond: Any syndicate has one purpose—to make as much money as possible. For that, they will need us.

They point out that they and their ancestors have seen many political and economic upheavals; they have been expelled or fled from many countries since diamonds grew from royal playthings to a business. Always the diamond business has followed them. Remind them that cutting factories have opened in the world that do more work than the shops in New York, and in the entire United States, and they shrug. Many of these factories are working for dealers and even if they are out of the cutting business completely that is not significant. They will recount how, before Hitler, the Jews of the Low Countries had already graduated from most cutting work and had become dominant as dealers and manufacturers. Even on Forty-seventh Street, though the Hasidim are very active as cutters, the steady influx of Hispanics may make them far more numerous than Jews as mechanics. But the Jews are the diamond dealers, manufacturers, and brokers—more affluent than ever.

They are not worried that many Americans are buying diamonds for investment rather than for ornament. Shrewd Europeans were doing this generations ago and it did not hurt the business then. It helped. If the demand for diamonds is for investment, they will sell more loose diamonds to diamond investment firms or, better still, to investors, cutting out the middleman, giving the investor a better deal and themselves a bigger profit. Greed will work for them.

What about the threat of imitation diamonds, which have improved so much that few persons outside the diamond business can tell them apart from the real ones? The sale of imitation diamonds, no longer covert, has increased enormously. They are advertised widely and sold in attractive stores at huge suburban shopping malls, even on Forty-seventh Street. This does not perturb the diamond people either. Many hundreds of thousands and women, they will tell you, buy costume jewelry. That does not hurt diamonds either. When they want real jewelry, they buy diamonds. Never underestimate the power of vanity.

What of the deep fear of crime in New York's diamond center, the most important market in the world? This is serious, they admit. But if things get too bad, they can just pull out of all the office buildings altogether. They can follow the example of Israel. Put the whole business in one huge skyscraper far bigger than the Ramat Gan complex. Install absolute security, where they will be able to walk about carrying their diamonds without fear, putting them into vaults before they leave at the end of the day. They know that when Ramat Gan's skyscraper was first proposed for Israel's diamond industry it was called folly because the diamond business there was too small. New York City already has more than enough business for a much bigger skyscraper. With the rents skyrocketing in the buildings of mid-Manhattan, it may be that those who lost the argument in the Diamond Dealers Club for a skyscraper may win eventually.

Finally, there is the mazel und brucha code. Suppose, you ask them, that this code is undermined by the mores and changing business ethics of modern society. In every major industry in America, lawyers are rising into positions at the top. They live in a world of contracts and loopholes. They are not concerned with the tradition of the Old Testament, the Talmud, and Maimonides. Can the mazel und brucha withstand such force? So far, the diamond people will tell you, it has. They know they have bad people in the business. They say that they have probably always had some. Maybe not as many as now. But they think the mazel und brucha code has become even stronger as more Hasidim have entered the business and become dealers, manufacturers, and brokers. As long as the mazel und brucha code is strong, the diamond business will continue to flourish—but no longer than that, they say. That is their definition of forever.